Law, Ecology, and the Management of Complex Systems

This book addresses the role of law in the adaptive management of socio-ecological systems.

Recent years have witnessed a rise in discussion over the relation between adaptivity and law, as if after decades of insouciance, legal scholars have finally started to understand the impacts of the scientific paradigm called 'adaptive management' on the legal sphere. Even though the complicated relations between law and the adaptive management of socio-ecological systems have become more debated, a thorough examination of the scientific and theoretical fundamentals of such endeavours has yet to be presented. Using the illustrative example of European Union water governance and its path toward embracing adaptive management, this book emphasises the legal significance of properly understanding the manner in which scientific knowledge of the environment is produced. Though always pivotal, rigorously apprehending science is especially crucial when dealing with the management of complex ecosystems as the 'normative' is created gradually before law begins to examine the 'facts' of the matter. After examining the roots of adaptive management, this book argues that the legal needs to understand itself as an integral part of the process of the socio-ecological management of complex systems and not merely an external umpire resolving disputes.

As a whole, the book offers new insights into the EU regulator's approaches to scientific realities, making it an interesting read not only to academics and legal scholars but also to regulators striving to deepen their understanding or pondering which approach to adopt in the face of new regulatory challenges, and to scientists interested in the science and law aspects of their work.

Tiina Paloniitty is Postdoctoral Researcher at the Eric Castrén Institute of International Law and Human Rights, the Helsinki Institute of Sustainability Science and Faculty of Law, University of Helsinki, Finland.

Part of the Law, Science and Society series

Series editors

John Paterson
University of Aberdeen, UK

Julian Webb
University of Melbourne, Australia

For information about the series and details of previous and forthcoming titles, see https://www.routledge.com/law/series/CAV16

A GlassHouse book

Law, Ecology, and the Management of Complex Systems

The Case of Water Governance

Tiina Paloniitty

Routledge
Taylor & Francis Group
a GlassHouse Book

First published 2023
by Routledge
4 Park Square, Milton Park, Abingdon, Oxon OX14 4RN

and by Routledge
605 Third Avenue, New York, NY 10158

A GlassHouse book

Routledge is an imprint of the Taylor & Francis Group, an informa business

British Library Cataloguing-in-Publication Data
A catalogue record for this book is available from the British Library

Library of Congress Cataloging-in-Publication Data
A catalog record has been requested for this book

ISBN: 978-1-032-05499-5 (hbk)
ISBN: 978-1-032-05500-8 (pbk)
ISBN: 978-1-003-19782-9 (ebk)

DOI: 10.4324/9781003197829

Typeset in Bembo
by Deanta Global Publishing Services, Chennai, India

The Open Access version of this book was funded by University of Helsinki Library.

Contents

Acknowledgements

The most pleasant terrains are rolling, and the most intriguing paths are winding. The journey of this book has been such, and fortunately, the journey was taken in the company of good people. This book is based on the work originally conducted for a doctoral thesis. That work took place in three cities on three continents – Helsinki, Singapore, and Sydney – and was stimulated by the thoughts of and discussions with many friends and colleagues in innumerable seminars, conferences, and colloquia. You all constitute the academic family I have dearly missed in this pandemic while preparing this book for publication. This is a collective effort, stimulated by your input though written by me alone.

As a first-generation academic, I have Erkki J. Hollo to thank for everything, including arousing my interest in environmental law. As my supervisor, Ari Ekroos provided me with sage and level-headed advice and support on numerous occasions, and Anne Kumpula offered me not only mentorship but also countless cups of coffee, always encouraging me to pursue my own questions, as did Raimo Siltala and Kai Kokko. The colleagues in our perhaps old-fashioned reading circles debated law in ways I still admire, and the company of Emilia Korkea-aho and Panu Minkkinen has made the twists and turns of academic life easier to comprehend. My office in Helsinki has been at the premises of the Faculty of Theology for some time now. I would like to thank the theological community for having me and for making this 'in-house lawyer' feel at home.

Environmental problems may be global, but so is the academic family solving them. Thanks to Nicholas A. Robinson, I was introduced to Koh Kheng-Lian and Lye Lin Heng, resulting in the loveliest writing retreats at the Asia-Pacific Centre of Environmental Law, National University of Singapore. As the following pages reveal, this book relies on the thinking developed in New South Wales, Australia. Thank you, Donna Craig, Paul Martin, Miriam Verbeek, Brian J. Preston, and Amanda Kennedy for all the discussions and for your heartfelt hospitality while there. Back in Europe, Elizabeth Kirk and Helle Tegner Anker invested time and effort to improve this volume, for which thanks are due. Eventually, the good company of Emma Lees and Mariolina Eliantonio enlivened the isolated time spent finalising these pages.

This work would not have been realised without material and non-material support from the Kone Foundation, whose independence and curiosity have continued to be stimulating. Thanks are also due to two other foundations, Maa-ja vesitekniikan tuki ry and Olga ja Kaarle Oskari Laitisen Säätiö, who supported my work, as did the University of Helsinki Doctoral School in Humanities and Social Sciences, Faculty of Law, and later also the Helsinki Institute of Sustainability Science and Eric Castrén Institute of International Law and Human Rights. Mr Kenneth Quek diligently edited the language of this volume, and research assistants Ms Netta Karttunen, Ms Katariina Flinck, and Mr Tommi Kortelainen helped me with the final touches. In addition to them, I also wish to thank Colin Perrin and the editorial team at Routledge for their excellent collaboration and the reviewers for their insightful comments.

As with any scholarly input, this book has taken time, attention, and energy that could have been spent otherwise. Thanks are due to my partner, Mikko, for enduring by my side through all these years – and for staying at home with our Senni, so I have not needed to choose between academic life and motherhood. I dedicate this volume to my parents, Armo and Paula Korvela, who may well have pursued academic ambitions had they ever had the opportunities to do so. Of all the support and encouragement I have received, yours were the first.

Tiina Paloniitty
Helsinki

Chapter 1

Setting the Scene of Law, Ecology, and the Complexity of the Agricultural Runoff Dilemma

The (Also Epistemic) Dilemma of Regulating Agricultural Runoff

Some books are love stories; others are the records of prolonged anxiety management therapy.[1] This volume exemplifies the latter. The anxiety inducing this volume draws from the tension caused by two fundamental actualities. The regulation of agricultural runoff is a notorious and globally shared regulatory failure of complex systems. Agricultural runoff, or diffuse water pollution caused by agriculture, is a much-researched topic; its causalities have been well dissected, analysed, and brought to decision-makers' attention. The European Union (EU) is known as an ardent advocate of environmental concerns and, consequently, for its ambitious environmental regulation, but it nevertheless encloses a body of brackish water that is often referred to as the most polluted in the world, the Baltic Sea.[2] The poor condition of this sea – almost an inland sea of the EU – is heavily influenced by the runoff dilemma. That is why this volume draws its examples from the EU's regulatory action regarding agricultural runoff in that region, culminating in the instrument embracing adaptive management. This is the tension that provoked the anxiety inducing this book: how does the most zealous environmental regulator in the globe fail to such an extent that it encloses one of the most polluted seas in the world? To answer this question, this book presents the agricultural runoff (or land-based runoff) dilemma as an epistemic challenge to the law. Through the lens of strategic epistemology, it probes the role that science has had in the EU's regulatory actions and offers a critical analysis of the dynamics of power across the landscape that law, governance, and ecology create.

Consequently, much of the governance and regulation analysed in this volume originate from the EU and could be categorised as EU law. Concurring with the scholars who emphasise the contingency of environmental law, when

1 Emily Barritt, *The Foundations of the Aarhus Convention: Environmental Democracy, Rights and Stewardship* (Bloomsbury Publishing 2020) 1.

2 Matti Leppäranta and Kai Myrberg, *Physical Oceanography of the Baltic Sea* (Springer 2009) x, 336.

DOI: 10.4324/9781003197829-1

considerations of effective enforcement of EU law require it, the individual administrative-legal system of one Member State, Finland, is examined.[3] Finland's civil law system illustrates well the enforcement and efficacy dilemmas of EU regulation, and as can be seen later on in this book, some of its peculiarities serve the needs of this examination on the interface between science and law well.[4] Though four governance instruments are studied – the Nitrates Directive (ND), the Common Agricultural Policy (CAP), the EU Strategy for the Baltic Sea Region (SBSR), and the Water Framework Directive (WFD) – the focus is predominantly on the WFD.[5] Each instrument is studied from the viewpoint of considerations of normative agri-environmental governance,[6] and with keen interest in the understanding of, or reaction to, the science that the EU regulator manifests in its acts. Thus the book untangles the dynamics of science and law.

Even though each individual section has its own research questions, the overall questions for this study are as follows. First, how do the current governance and legal instruments fulfil the needs of agri-environmentality? Second, if adaptive management is taken as the scientific foundation of water governance – as the EU has done in its WFD – what dynamics are created by the paradigm embracing uncertainty and learning when it encounters the legal sphere? And third, can this regulatory challenge be resolved and a way forward crafted for a management system that satisfies the needs of both the scientific and legal realms?[7] Questions of scientific knowledge, the values embedded therein, and their presence and role in legal decision-making – of both the legislator and the adjudicator – are a recurring theme in the following pages. This volume uses a strategic epistemology of environmental law developed by Martin and Craig, belonging to the line of thinking that promulgates a disregard for strong science/doctrine dualism. Instead, they propose that 'a

3 Eloise Scotford, *Environmental Principles and the Evolution of Environmental Law* (Hart 2017) 272, 3, 11; Ole W. Pedersen, 'The Contingent Foundations of Environmental Law' (2018) JEL 30 <https://doi.org/10.1093/jel/eqy013>, 359, 363; also Michael Faure, 'Effectiveness of Environmental Law: What Does the Evidence Tell Us?' (2012) Wm & Mary Envtl L & Pol'y Rev 36(2) <https://dx.doi.org/10.2139/ssrn.2165715>, 295.

4 These peculiarities are presented in text to n 118–26 in this volume's ch 4.

5 The Council Directive 91/676/EEC concerning the protection of waters against pollution caused by nitrates from agricultural sources [1991] OJ L375; European Council, 'Presidency Conclusions of the Brussels European Council' (2009) 15265/1/09 REV 1; Commission, 'Communication from the Commission to the European Parliament, the Council, the European Economic and Social Committee and the Committee of the Regions Concerning the European Union Strategy for the Baltic Sea Region (the Strategy)' COM (2009) 248 final; Directive 2000/60/EC of 23 October 2000 establishing a framework for community action in the field of water policy [2000] OJ L327/1.

6 Viewpoint shared by e.g. Massimo Monteduro, 'Environmental Law and Agroecology. Transdisciplinary Approach to Public Ecosystem Services as a New Challenge for Environmental Legal Doctrine' (2013) EEELR 22(1) 2.

7 Admittedly, with these questions this volume promulgates an uncomfortably scientist worldview. This and the risks of technocracy it entails is returned to in the concluding Chapter 6.

constructive methodological path is to recognise that research on the effectiveness of environmental law is a strategic investigation rather than either a philosophic or a scientific one.' Consequently, an integrated approach is needed to ascertain real-world development. The integration is composed of objective facts, subjective beliefs, and dynamic systems, which result in analysis that consists of both objective and subjective elements (in other words, both deductive and inductive reasoning). The integrative approach is firmly rooted in the reality of environmental legislation and the common pitfalls of regulation where not all regulatory solutions work in every context. The emphasis is on finding the regulatory – or other – strategy that most effectively serves the objectives. These can be found within the scope of traditional legal research or elsewhere, in politics, economics, or even biophysical science.[8]

The approach is openly pragmatic, also in its analytical structure. In its agenda, the axiological considerations come first:

> 'In this *strategic epistemology*, matters of values and belief (axiology) inform choices of direction, inductive choices are made about likely futures, scientific deductions are used to better understand central facts, and pragmatic choices are made about resources and plans.'[9]

Thus strategic epistemology has three cornerstones: objectivity, subjectivity, and a keen interest in pragmatic solutions. As such, this epistemological approach exists in the continuum of scientific empiricism.[10] It can thus be taken to partly reflect the movement called post-empiricism, which is also rooted in philosophical pragmatism: post-empiricism is a group of viewpoints searching for a way out of positivism (understood as a methodology that emphasises the strict separation of facts and values) and rational choice theories in political research. Based on the belief that no such separation exists, post-empiricism seeks a greater variety of methodologies and/or the application of diverse methodologies in social sciences.[11] This objective is shared in the

8 Paul Martin and Donna Craig, 'Accelerating the evolution of environmental law through continuous learning from applied experience' in Paul Martin and Amanda Kennedy (eds), *Implementing Environmental Law* (The IUCN Academy of Environmental Law Series, Edward Elgar Publishing 2015) 27, 28–9.

9 Martin and Craig (n 8) 30 (emphasis here).

10 Martin and Craig (n 8) 34 with references to Thomas S Ulen, 'A Nobel Prize in Legal Science: Theory, Empirical Work, and the Scientific Method in the Study of Law' (2002) U Ill L Rev <https://dx.doi.org/10.2139/ssrn.419823>, 893.

11 Catarina Kinnvall, 'Not here, not now! The absence of a European perestroika movement' in Kristen Renwick Monroe (ed), *Perestroika! The Raucous Rebellion in Political Science* (Yale University Press 2005) 21.

strategic epistemology of environmental law research. Both find fault with the way that positivist approaches are blind to their dependency on value choices.[12]

The post-empiricists criticise positivist methodologies for the widespread application of rational choice methodology. Originally, rational choice methodology was seen as an escape from the blur of methodologies and the lack of 'scientificity' in social sciences – separating facts and values would bring objectivity and neutrality and make social or political sciences resemble other fields of science.[13] Ultimately this unbiased research would yield results independent of the researchers' preferences.[14] Post-empiricism claims that objectivity cannot be reached due to the socially constructed nature of all facts.[15] It is also claimed that rational choice methodologies are not only partisan or biased, but they have no means to verify the objectivity of their research or falsify the contrary.[16] The core of post-empiricist criticism deems that irrespective of their claims to neutrality, positivists hold to a rigid, albeit implicit, conception of society, presupposing that people are individuals conducting free, rational choices in pursuit of the maximisation of their self-interest.[17] In strategic epistemology, the critique of positivism has resulted in acknowledging the underpinning value choice of environmental law, that is, the inherent environmentalism justifying all environmental regulation. Environmental regulation itself represents a value choice that evades neutrality.

The pragmatic approach is concretised in solutions that are problem-oriented (concentrate on specific problems with proposed regulation), normative (recognise the conflicting values affecting decisions), discursive (include an open-ended evaluation of relevant options, relying on discussion and aiming at evaluating the values behind each option), and transparent (open and comprehensible to the public).[18] All four ought to be cherished in any juridical undertaking, legal scholarship included, and as the ensuing pages illustrate, this

12 The concept of 'normative' is not necessarily understood similarly in social sciences and legal research: in traditional legal positivism, the difference of perception is explained by the legal scholars' internal and social scientists' external point of view, see e.g. Aulis Aarnio, *The Rational as Reasonable: A Treatise on Legal Justification* (Reidel cop. 1987) XIX, 276 s, 12–13. On how pragmatists' value choices can be held relatively open, Sidney A Shapiro and Robert L Glicksman, *Risk Regulation at Risk: Restoring a Pragmatic Approach* (Robert L Glicksman ed, Stanford University Press 2003) 281, 21.

13 SA Shapiro and CH Schroeder, 'Beyond Cost-Benefit Analysis: A Pragmatic Reorientation' (2008) Harv Environ Law Rev 32(2) 433, 439–40.

14 Frank Fischer, *Reframing Public Policy: Discursive Politics and Deliberate Practices* (OUP 2003) 280, 118.

15 There are various perceptions within post-empiricism about what this constructivism means for the concept of truth or what relation holds between the chosen theory and the results gained. See Shapiro and Schroeder (n 13) 443.

16 Shapiro and Schroeder (n 13) 443.

17 Deborah A Stone, *Policy Paradox: The Art of Political Decision Making* (Rev. ed. edn, W.W. Norton cop. 2002), 9–11, 19–34.

18 Shapiro and Schroeder (n 13) 471–5.

volume attempts to abide by this request. Post-empiricists do not offer any perception of society to replace the positivist one; they argue that a viewpoint outside the debate is attainable, and that is pragmatism. Opting for alternatives that are for 'human betterment' is the answer to the axiological questions.[19] This again resonates with strategic epistemology – the self-image of environmentalism justifying environmental regulation is on the side of human betterment.

Acknowledging reality, as cumbersome as it is (instead of feigning coherence or clarity), the solution in both approaches lies in choosing a methodology that is both multidisciplinary and deliberative, and relies on practical reason.[20] Opting out of using broad and apparently homogenous terms – such as the precautionary principle, which in reality 'masks many competing objectives' – opens the door to the realisation that '[m]ethodology problems are not likely to be effectively solved by assuming away the messy realities, merely to create the pretence of tractable "scientific" research questions that fit available methodologies'.[21] Put otherwise, environmental law research includes not only questions examined with empirical tools but also axiological dilemmas, such as weighing and balancing of values or establishing predictions, all requiring judgement. Due to these characteristics – all fundamental and worthy of attention on their own – methods of environmental law research are inevitably pluralistic and pragmatic.[22] In this understanding, all research objectives in environmental law are based on firm axiological foundations. For example, the question of whether water pollution from agricultural sources is effectively regulated comes with a value-laden hypothesis that posing such a question is initially reasonable. Due to these axiological connections, environmental (law) research does not merely aim to acquire better knowledge, but also wishes to motivate societal change and affect policy-making. In the present case, regulating agricultural runoff more effectively might constitute that change. As rough as it might sound, the fundamental differences between admitted pragmatism and mere value-based suggestions are scientific standards of integrity and the structured form of the presentation.[23]

19 Shapiro and Schroeder (n 13) 443. For more on the origin of the thinking, see Douglas Torgenson, 'Contextual Orientation in Policy Analysis: The Contribution of Harold D. Lasswell' (1985) Policy Sciences 18(3) <https://doi.org/10.1007/BF00138911>, 241.

20 Shapiro and Schroeder (n 13) 444. The most recent step has been to turn to Lasswell's vision of political science as a contextual and normative field that is on a quest to build bridges between people and government; ibid 445; and Torgenson, 'Contextual Orientation in Policy Analysis' (ibid) 242–3.

21 Martin and Craig (n 8) 34–5.

22 Martin and Craig (n 8) 42, 44.

23 Components of scientific integrity are threefold and deal with transparency of data and the chosen methods, generalisability of conclusions, and peer review, Martin and Craig (n 8) 5, 48. In this reading, environmental law scholarship is akin to transdisciplinary research – both aim to solve societal

As its epistemological foundation, strategic epistemology is present throughout this volume. The work is both doctrinal and theoretical, representing the two mainstream fields of environmental law, but procedural questions are also strongly present, especially in Chapter 4. Chapter 2 consists of both doctrinal research and policy analysis. Chapter 3 describes adaptive natural resource management, explains the ways in which scientific knowledge relevant for water governance is produced, and the constraints these set for law if it wishes to exploit the acquired knowledge in its actions. Chapter 5 discusses the relation between facts, natural resource management, and judicial decision-making from a more jurisprudential perspective, and Chapter 6 concludes the results and discusses the possibility of thoroughly holistic, integrative, and adaptive regulation, titled a socio-eco-legal solution. The methodological tools have been chosen according to each chapter's needs, varying from policy analysis and doctrinal research to jurisprudence and also combining them if needed. Fitting all these into one volume might worry a purist mind, but this decision is made following a guideline expressed by Martin and Craig: 'The risk of elevating methodological purity over practical utility in coping with complexity ought not to be dismissed.'[24]

The EU Regulator's Four Faces in Agricultural Runoff Regulation

There are various ways to identify and analyse the path taken by the regulators. In environmental scholarship, the concept of 'first generation' is used to mark the difference between point source and diffuse pollution regulation: tackling point source pollution is the first generation of environmental regulation and addressing more diverse problems is the second generation. Following this logic, the approach in the WFD would constitute the third generation – and water law would again serve as a testing ground for environmental regulation.[25] This volume thus identifies the four faces of the EU regulator. The nicknames are derived from the research on the four instruments and, as is always the case with illustrative shorthand, a warning is in order: the reader ought not to read too much into them. They are simplifications of reality and as such, give only a partial view of the actions of the EU regulator in its various attempts to address the regulatory challenge. Having said that, the four faces are the erratic regulator (in the CAP), the naïve regulator (in the ND), the candid regulator (in

and scientific problems, Daniel J Lang and others, 'Transdisciplinary Research in Sustainability Science: Practice, Principles, and Challenges' (2012) Sustainability Science 7(1) 25, 26–7.

24 Martin and Craig (n 8) 39.

25 Sam Boyle, 'The Case for Regulation of Agricultural Water Pollution' (2014) Environmental Law Review 16(1) 4, 5; William Howarth, 'Accommodation without Resolution? Emission Controls and Environmental Quality Objectives in the Proposed EC Water Framework Directive' (1999) Environmental Law Review 1(1) <https://doi.org/10.1177/146145299900100103> 6–7.

the SBSR), and the ambitious regulator (in the WFD). The nickname 'erratic regulator' stems from the reality where the outcome of the instrument's revision rounds manages to surprise even the most careful observers. The naïve regulator is one who puts the complexity of the regulatory target to one side and decides to follow the straightforward logic of curtailing the entry of the pollutant into the environment. In the case of agricultural runoff, this means regulating farming practices. The candid regulator, on the contrary, takes societal complexities in particular seriously and strives to create regulatory instruments that also engage those actors who find other governance supplanting them. The final nickname, the 'ambitious regulator,' describes the regulator who is bold enough to embark on the journey of addressing the pivotal yet testing question of regulating adaptive management.

Another key concept introduced in this volume, the continuum of normativity (described in Chapter 4 in further detail), draws from the analysis of the ambitious regulator's venture.[26] In sum, no clear dividing line can be drawn between the different stages of decision-making activities in the regulation of adaptive management. Rather, a continuum of decision-making with normative influence can be rendered: establishing scientific knowledge by gathering, analysing, and assessing data, making management decisions, and evaluating the management through administrative or judicial processes. Due to this, fundamental problems linger at the roots of attempts to regulate adaptive natural resources management: when fact production and adjudication cannot be clearly distinguished from each other, the risk of either juristocracy – where the legal profession is left to decide on not only interpretation of the norms but also on facts and values – or bestowing excessive power on the experts – where scientific evaluation leaves no room for further decision-making – is tangible. Nonetheless, when the situation is made clear, administrative-legal systems can be amended to better accommodate the realities of this scientific paradigm.

Knowledge, Ecology, and Law – A Variety of Approaches

With the aforementioned commitments, this volume is one knot in the web of law, science, and technology studies, a vividly researched field with well-established roots that explain the diverse dynamics of science, scientific uncertainties, law, and governance.[27] Often these studies analyse the ways in which courts review science or scientific evidence, experts or expertise, the roles that scientific advisers have acquired in policy-making, or the particular challenges that certain scientific methods have posed to policy-makers – in sum, the

26 Text to n 203 ff in this volume's ch 4.

27 Sheila Jasanoff and others (eds), *Handbook of Science and Technology Studies* (Sage Publications 2001).

varied and various boundaries between science and law.[28] The work at hand contributes to this endeavour from the perspective that Lees, in particular, has presented: it discusses 'the judiciary as one actor within the decision-making process,' acts of whom are constrained by specific constitutional and procedural norms, differing from those of the first-instance authority or, as one proceeds to the other end of the continuum of normativity, the scientist who produces the knowledge for decision-making.[29] The role of the judiciary is examined in Chapter 4, but as the four faces construct suggests, the boundaries of science and law are in the limelight even before that, in the policy analysis of the chapters immediately following.[30] It is in the details of the analysis in Chapter 4 that the aforementioned necessity of detail is brought forth. In this regard, the book argues that legal remedies at the Member-State level must be included in the analysis if willing to accurately describe the dynamics between science and law the EU regulator has established, implied, or reinforced.

Then again, the approach chosen in this volume resembles Woolley's work on ecological governance – indeed, one could argue that what is presented below on the WFD offers a detailed example of the importance of the normativity of precaution, strategic policy-making, and the role of monitoring and measuring in securing the adaptivity of resilient ecosystem governance, whereas the study on the SBSR exemplifies the importance of collaborative action.[31] The holistic and system-sensitive viewpoint acquired here – on regulatory instruments on the one hand and watersheds as sources of land-based pollution on the other – also resembles the commitments of earth system governance, a research approach that lies on the nexus of governance theory and earth system analysis.[32] This emphasises the interlinkages of underlying problems and the importance of closer analysis of their features, adaptivity of governance, multi-actor governance, accountability, and legitimacy.[33] These aspects are part of this study as well

28 Sheila Jasanoff, 'World of Experts: Science and Global Environmental Constitutionalism' (2013) Environmental Affairs Law Review 40(2) 439; Gwen Ottinger, 'Changing Knowledge, Local Knowledge, and Knowledge Gaps: STS Insights into Procedural Justice' (2013) Science, Technology, & Human Values 38(2) <https://doi.org/10.1177/0162243912469669>, 250; Pasky Pascual, Wendy Wagner, and Elizabeth Fisher, 'Making Method Visible: Improving the Quality of Science-Based Regulation' (2012) Mich J Envtl Admin L 2 429; Thomas F Gieryn, 'Boundaries of science' in Sheila Jasanoff and others (eds), *Handbook of Science and Technology Studies* (Sage Publications 2001) 393.

29 Emma Lees, 'Allocation of Decision-Making Power Under the Habitats Directive' (2016) JEL 28(2) <https://doi.org/10.1093/jel/eqw002>, 191.

30 In this volume, text to n 186 ff in ch 4 and ch 2.

31 Olivia Woolley, *Ecological Governance: Reappraising Law's Role in Protecting Ecosystem Functionality* (CUP 2014), 8, 12–14 and 10–11.

32 Frank Biermann and others, 'Earth System Governance: A Research Framework' (2010) Int Environ Agreements 10(4) <https://doi.org/10.1007/s10784-010-9137-3>, 279.

33 Ibid 284–8. Development of the earth system governance has strong connections with the emergence of the Anthropocene discourse, referring to a new epoch into which humankind has thrusted

but in the more specific context of EU water law and governance. Alas, some of the critique can also apply: the study at hand is more on control and management and expert-driven central government than on power, authority, or subjectivity in adaptive water management.[34] The risks of falling into technocratism are acknowledged – one can only hope that sensitivity to questions of power is at least adequately covered in the following pages.

In the examination that follows, Chapter 2 presents three of the instruments – the ND, the CAP, and the SBSR – and Chapters 3 and 4 revolve around the third, the WFD and its scientific foundation. The division is done because the WFD is the only instrument of the four explicitly merging science and policy, thus offering a rich landscape to analyse. The other three need a more indirect approach as the regulator has not communicated the choices so openly, leaving the interpreter interested in the science and law interface with more opaque material to analyse. With specific question-setting and methodological diversity – in line with the strategic epistemology explained above – this issue can, however, be tackled. After these three chapters map the legal and scientific landscape, the penultimate Chapter 5 changes the viewpoint and methodology. With more jurisprudential analysis, it probes the combination of legal remedies and continuum of normativity, a crucial puzzle to solve if desiring to manage complex ecological systems by the best scientific and legal standards. Eventually, in Chapter 6, the concept of socio-eco-legal management is described as a normative summary of the previous chapters. Managing complexities in a legitimate manner is by far a simple task, and it is acknowledged that this socio-eco-legal management can never be enforceable or feasible. Imagination is, however, the first step in all action, regulatory and otherwise.[35]

Bibliography

Aarnio A, *The Rational as Reasonable: A Treatise on Legal Justification* (Reidel cop. 1987).

Barritt E, *The Foundations of the Aarhus Convention: Environmental Democracy, Rights and Stewardship* (Bloomsbury Publishing 2020).

Biermann F, *Earth System Governance: World Politics in the Anthropocene* (MIT Press 2014).

——— and others, 'Earth System Governance: A Research Framework' (2010) 10(4) Int Environ Agreements 277 <https://doi.org/10.1007/s10784-010-9137-3>.

Boyle S, 'The Case for Regulation of Agricultural Water Pollution' (2014) 16(1) Environmental Law Review 4.

the Earth; Frank Biermann, *Earth System Governance: World Politics in the Anthropocene* (MIT Press 2014) 4–8.

34 Eva Lövbrand, Johannes Stripple, and Bo Wiman, 'Earth System Governmentality: Reflections on Science in the Anthropocene' (2009) Global Environmental Change 19(1) <https://doi.org/10.1016/j.gloenvcha.2008.10.002>, 12.

35 Liz Fisher, 'EU Environmental Law and Legal Imagination' in Paul Craig and Gráinne De Búrca (eds) *The Evolution of EU Law* (OUP 2021) 847, 847.

Faure M, 'Effectiveness of Environmental Law: What Does the Evidence Tell Us?' (2012) 36(2) Wm & Mary Envtl L & Pol'y Rev 293 <https://doi.org/10.2139/ssrn.2165715>.

Fischer F, *Reframing Public Policy: Discursive Politics and Deliberate Practices* (OUP 2003).

Gieryn TF, 'Boundaries of Science' in Jasanoff S and others (eds), *Handbook of Science and Technology Studies* (Sage Publications 2001).

Howarth W, 'Accommodation without Resolution? Emission Controls and Environmental Quality Objectives in the Proposed EC Water Framework Directive' (1999) 1(1) Environmental Law Review 6 <https://doi.org/10.1177/146145299900100103>.

Jasanoff S, 'World of Experts: Science and Global Environmental Constitutionalism' (2013) 40(2) Environmental Affairs Law Review 439.

——— and others (eds), *Handbook of Science and Technology Studies* (Sage Publications 2001).

Kinnvall C, 'Not Here, Not Now! The Absence of a European Perestroika Movement' in Monroe KR (ed), *Perestroika! The Raucous Rebellion in Political Science* (Yale University Press 2005).

Lees E, 'Allocation of Decision-Making Power under the Habitats Directive' (2016) 28(2) JEL 191 <https://doi.org/10.1093/jel/eqw002>.

Leppäranta M and Myrberg K, *Physical Oceanography of the Baltic Sea* (Springer 2009).

Lövbrand E, Stripple J, and Wiman B, 'Earth System Governmentality: Reflections on Science in the Anthropocene' (2009) 19(1) Global Environmental Change 12 <https://doi.org/10.1016/j.gloenvcha.2008.10.002>.

Martin P and Craig D, 'Accelerating the Evolution of Environmental Law Through Continuous Learning from Applied Experience' in Martin P and Kennedy A (eds), *Implementing Environmental Law* (The IUCN Academy of Environmental Law Series, Edward Elgar Publishing 2015).

Monteduro M, 'Environmental Law and Agroecology. Transdisciplinary Approach to Public Ecosystem Services as a New Challenge for Environmental Legal Doctrine' (2013) 22(1) EEELR 2.

Ottinger G, 'Changing Knowledge, Local Knowledge, and Knowledge Gaps: STS Insights into Procedural Justice' (2013) 38(2) Science, Technology, & Human Values 250 <https://doi.org/10.1177/0162243912469669>.

Pascual P, Wendy W and Fisher E, 'Making Method Visible: Improving the Quality of Science-Based Regulation' (2012) 2 Mich J Envtl Admin L 429.

Pedersen OW, 'The Contingent Foundations of Environmental Law' (2018) 30 JEL 359 <https://doi.org/10.1093/jel/eqy013>.

Scotford E, *Environmental Principles and the Evolution of Environmental Law* (Hart 2017).

Shapiro SA and Glicksman RL, *Risk Regulation at Risk: Restoring a Pragmatic Approach* (Glicksman RL ed, Stanford University Press 2003).

Shapiro SA and Schroeder CH, 'Beyond Cost-Benefit Analysis: A Pragmatic Reorientation' (2008) 32(2) Harv Environ Law Rev 433.

Stone DA, *Policy Paradox: The Art of Political Decision Making* (Rev. ed. edn, W.W. Norton cop. 2002).

Torgenson D, 'Contextual Orientation in Policy Analysis: The Contribution of Harold D. Lasswell' (1985) 18(3) Policy Sciences 241 <https://doi.org/10.1007/BF00138911>.

Ulen TS, 'A Nobel Prize in Legal Science: Theory, Empirical Work, and the Scientific Method in the Study of Law' (2002) U Ill L Rev 875 <https://dx.doi.org/10.2139/ssrn.419823>.

Woolley O, *Ecological Governance: Reappraising Law's Role in Protecting Ecosystem Functionality* (CUP 2014).

Secondary EU Legislation

Directive 2000/60/EC of 23 October 2000 Establishing a Framework for Community Action in the Field of Water Policy [2000] OJ L327/1.

The Council Directive 91/676/EEC Concerning the Protection of Waters against Pollution Caused by Nitrates from Agricultural Sources [1991] OJ L375.

Communications, Reports, Decisions and Staff Working Documents

Commission, 'Communication from the Commission to the European Parliament, the Council, the European Economic and Social Committee and the Committee of the Regions Concerning the European Union Strategy for the Baltic Sea Region (the Strategy)' COM (2009) 248 final.

European Council

European Council, 'Presidency Conclusions of the Brussels European Council' (2009) 15265/1/09 REV 1.

Chapter 2

The First Three Faces: The Nitrates Directive, the Common Agricultural Policy, and the Strategy of the Baltic Sea Region

Introduction

This chapter probes three instruments the EU has used to address the issue of agricultural runoff: the Nitrates Directive (ND), the Common Agricultural Policy (CAP), and one of its macroregional strategies, the EU Strategy of the Baltic Sea Region (SBSR). First, the ND is examined, and the weak traces of adaptivity in the instrument targeting nutrient flows are described. Though a rather straightforward answer to the complex regulatory challenge, the ND is acknowledged as an important step of the EU regulator towards adaptivity. By then analysing the development of the CAP in reaching socio-ecological sustainability in the series of reforms – the MacSharry reform, Agenda 2000, the Fischler reform, the Fischler II reform, and the post-2013 reform – the chapter argues that the CAP has faced a constant yet unhurried movement towards accepting the ecological goals. From there, the chapter continues by analysing yet another governance instrument, the SBSR, and its role in the complex web of governance in the Baltic Sea region. The SBSR is credited for being the most inclusive of the tools, earning the EU regulator the nickname of 'candid regulator,' as it has managed to also include the farmers in the collaborative governance it embodies. When analysed together, these three instruments make a peculiar comparison; e.g. the CAP consumes a majority of the EU budget while the SBSR is known for its ban on allocating extra funds for governance. Together, the three form a diverse backdrop to the contemporary water governance analysed in the following chapter, partially explaining the EU regulator's desire for a more holistic approach. But before going there, first to the ND.

The Nitrates Directive – Straightforward Solutions to Complex Problems

The ND dates back to the 1990s, representing the first generation of environmental regulation with the logic of preventing polluting agents from entering the environment. Progress has been swift, partly since, in the EU, water has been a favourite object of environmental regulation when compared with

DOI: 10.4324/9781003197829-2

other environmental media, air or land.[1] In sum, the ND has served its place in the continuum of developing water law even if it was otherwise disappointing, since disappointment in the ND instigated the more recent rapid development of EU water law. Even though the reasons resulting in the Water Framework Directive (WFD) were manyfold, regarding the problem of agricultural runoff, the WFD was intended to repair the underachievements of the ND. In particular, the target orientation inherent in the WFD was meant to address the ND's non-fulfilment.[2]

The regulatory logic in the ND is straightforward and summarises the physical-realistic aspects of the nutrient runoff dilemma. The dates when manure can be spread on fields are set in the ND in order to balance the running of the nutrients to nearby waters with the needs of optimal growth (and the waste issues that livestock producers would otherwise face). The ND bestowed Member States with the right to declare parts of their areas as nitrate-vulnerable zones (NVZs) where stricter regulations apply; for example, Finland has confirmed the whole country as an NVZ.[3] Good agricultural practice is encouraged on a voluntary basis, the producers are obliged to gather and act on programmes (in the NVZs), and the Member States are obliged to monitor and report the implementation and its results.[4] At first glance, the system has every prospect of being sufficient. Surely restricting the use of the polluting medium solves the problem, and when the site-specific differences are also considered, the regulation should be adequate. What then are the reasons behind the lacklustre attitude around the ND and the regulatory approach it represents?

Unlike the more recent water regulation initiatives already mentioned, the ND represents a negative form of environmental regulation in its attempt to

1 William Howarth, 'Accommodation Without Resolution? Emission Controls and Environmental Quality Objectives in the Proposed EC Water Framework Directive' (1999) Environmental Law Review 1(1) <https://doi.org/10.1177/146145299900100103> 6.

2 Sam Boyle, 'The Case for Regulation of Agricultural Water Pollution' (2014) Environmental Law Review 16(1) 4, 7; William Howarth, 'Diffuse Water Pollution and Diffuse Environmental Laws' (2011) Journal of Environmental Law 23(1) <https://doi.org/10.1093/jel/eqq031>, 132–3. Officially or at least in the Commission's understanding the relation between the WFD and the ND is that the latter is to 'form an integral part of the WFD,' see EU Commission at <http://ec.europa.eu/environment/water/water-nitrates/index_en.html>.

3 Finland has implemented the ND with a so-called Nitrates Decree (The Nitrates Decree 1250/2014, Government Decree on Limiting Certain Emissions from Agriculture and Horticulture) legally non-binding English translation available at <http://www.finlex.fi/en/laki/kaannokset/2014/en20141250.pdf> (accessed 10 April 2021). For more on the Finnish implementation see text to n 22.

4 The Nitrates Directive, Art. 1, Art. 2 (k) and Art. 3–6 on the NVZs and good practices. The relationship between EU waste regulation and the ND was solved by the CJEU in 2005; spreading manure was not considered as discarding waste, Case C-416/02 *Commission v Spain* [2005] ECLI:EU:C:2005:511, paras 94–7; and Brian Jack, 'Member State Responsibilities Concerning Nitrate Pollution and Eutrophication: A Role for the Waste Framework Directive?' (2006) JEL 18(2) <https://doi.org/10.1093/jel/eql001>, 311.

curb the polluters instead of setting environmental objectives to be reached.[5] The overall aim of curbing the nutrient load to protect health and the environment, as established in Article 1 of the ND, has been deconstructed as consisting of four different aims: human health protection, animal health protection, preserving ecosystems, and safeguarding other water uses. One point of criticism is that these objectives are not prioritised nor balanced between each other, contradicting the concept of fitting measures for aims. For example, public health concerns necessitate a certain maximum amount of nitrate in drinking water prior to treatment, but the needs of a healthy and well-functioning ecosystem might be something else. The inability to prioritise or weigh and balance the aims is well illustrated by the establishment of the NVZs, where the zones declared vulnerable might or might not simultaneously be drinking water abstraction areas while the regulation remains the same.[6] Some Member States have applied a more nuanced approach. In Denmark, environmental permits are differentiated according to whether the area serves as a drinking water abstraction aquifer or not. As expected, this tailored approach has led to compensation for those farmers burdened with tighter regulation, construed as an insult to their property rights.[7] Also, the complexity of the agriculture runoff issue itself establishes reasons to criticise the approach: not all water bodies are as sensitive or require as much protection from the nutrient load as others. This natural variation between oligotrophic and eutrophic waters is not taken fully into account. Presumably because no clear resolution could be made of the proper balance or priority order of the competing aims, such a decision would require the challenging act of balancing complex values.[8] Also, the standards themselves were established in a 'generalised or obscure' manner rather than with diligent attention.[9]

5 For the positive version see ch 4 and ch 5 on the WFD. This strategic polarity has at times caused indecisiveness in the Commission, demonstrated by its regulatory endeavours; one example is the original Dangerous Substances Directive from the 1970s; Howarth (n 1) 7–8.

6 William Howarth, 'The Progression Towards Ecological Quality Standards' (2006) JEL 3 18(1) <https://doi.org/10.1093/jel/eqi049>, 14.

7 As a tell-tale sign, the compensation is called 'rule of reasonableness.' However, in the same country, regulation for livestock installations include no compensation clauses for farmers whose use of fertilisers or choice of cultivation practices is restricted in a new environmental permit given according to the Act on Environmental Permits on Livestock Installations. See Helle Tegner Anker, 'Agricultural Nitrate Pollution – Regulatory Approaches in the EU and Denmark' (2015) NMT 2 7, 18–19; Lasse Baaner and Helle Tegner Anker, *Danish Law on Controlling Emissions of Nutrients in the Baltic Sea Region* (Baltic Sea Centre 2013) <http://www.su.se/ostersjocentrum/english/beam/legal-aspects-of-the-ecosystem-approach/country-studies>, 57–9.

8 Howarth (n 1) 15–16, 35. It must be stated though that the ND, Annex I section (B), acknowledges how the nitrate compounds in the environment and differences in physical features of different waterbodies. The critique is thus on the insufficiency of these efforts.

9 Howarth (n 1) 17–18.

Interestingly, regarding the challenges of the WFD, this lack of diligence seems to originate from a limited understanding of the functions of ecosystems and their interactions, resulting in inadequate employment of environmental quality standards.[10] In its straightforward attempt to deal with the problem, the ND falls in the category of specification standards and process standards (instead of performance standards more familiar in contemporary water regulation).[11] In diffuse pollution in general, trajectories are difficult to establish, partly explaining the incompatibility between agricultural runoff regulation and more developed standards. As mentioned, the way in which nutrients compound in the environment also adds to the challenge, not to mention the realities of the continuous hydrological cycle.[12] The role of sediment in transferring nutrients is often underestimated: sediment, however, centrally governs the transfer of nutrients.[13]

All the features mentioned call for greater specificity in agricultural runoff regulation. Regarding the ND, this would mean combining its specification/process standards with site-specific measures.[14] Tailoring the required measures according to the needs of individual farms – and the surrounding bodies of water – represents a logical continuation of the ND's regulatory approach. Initiatives are called differentiation, tailoring, or site-specificity, depending on the source. Site-specificity is not uncommon in the implementation of the ND as it is. A rough example of the approach is the ability to establish NVZs, since they are concretised in a requirement of applying different measures to them than to other areas. This crude tailoring, combined with the fact that the ND obliges Member States to monitor and report, indicates weak traces of adaptivity in the ND.[15] The ND does not, however, properly represent adaptive water governance; its monitoring and reporting system is too restricted to fulfil the needs of the adaptive management paradigm.

Thus, the ND, to some extent, enables differentiation, but the chance is often diluted when the Member States, Finland included, declare all or most of

10 See also Tegner Anker (n 7) 10. Environmental quality standards refer to the set quality levels of certain environmental medium. This approach spurs the question of decisions upon baseline and naturalness, which are examined later when the WFD is studied – these same fundamental questions emerge in that context and have gained more thorough attention there; text to n 66 ff in ch 4.

11 Boyle (n 2) 6–8. The categorization originates from a landmark piece of writing in the field, Neil Gunningham and Darren Sinclair, 'Policy Instrument Choice and Diffuse Source Pollution' (2005) JEL 17(1) <https://doi.org/10.1093/envlaw/eqi003>, 51.

12 Boyle (n 2) 5; Howarth (n 2) 130.

13 AL Collins and DF McGonigle, 'Monitoring and Modelling Diffuse Pollution from Agriculture for Policy Support: UK and European Experience' (2008) Environ Sci & Policy 11(2) <https://doi.org/10.1016/j.envsci.2008.01.001>, 99.

14 The suggestion comes from Denmark where the farmers complain that the ND places an 'unnecessary' burden on them – referring to the situation in which all farms are treated the same, regardless of the composition or formation of their land, Tegner Anker (n 7) 9.

15 Tegner Anker (n 7) 14.

their area as NVZs.[16] Differentiation, if taken further, would match well with the individualised, waterbody-oriented approach of the WFD. This regulatory path has already been examined in at least the Netherlands and Denmark. Encouraging tailoring in the Dutch example begins with an interesting question: instead of adhering to the whole-territory solution, the Dutch considered loosening their nutrient regulations by opting out some regions as non-NVZ. This was a unique endeavour prompted by a long history of experimental nutrient regulation, the previous stages of which included the implementation of MINAS, an accounting system coupled with economic stimuli, assigned to establish a more target-oriented system within the ND. The Court of Justice of the European Union (CJEU), however, found the approach an infringement of the ND since it was considered not to properly secure the attainment of the ND's objectives.[17] The setback did not curb the Dutch creativity or will to address the problem of the overly strict interpretation of the ND, resulting in an excessive financial burden on the producers.[18]

Dutch investigation of a more flexible implementation of the ND continued with two policy choices: either to proceed with tailored manure dissemination policies or to further integrate the regimes of the ND and the WFD. Regarding the former, the level of differentiation was found to be decisive. One can tailor the regulation with the NVZs in the ordinary manner according to the soil types, at the level of individual farms and their production capacity, or differentiate the regulation between different river basin districts, as defined in the WFD.[19] It is noteworthy that, at least in the Dutch context, if tailoring is about choosing the measures for better environmental gains, monitoring at the farm level was not found to increase monitoring efforts or costs. The only cost increase is from the transition phase to the new administrative system, including confronting the resistance to change. Differentiation at the farm level based on farm performance would, however, increase monitoring efforts; the question of cost increase therein is too complex to be straightforwardly answered. Here the resistance to change would be minimal: target-oriented approaches are generally found acceptable and easier to digest. Thus, even though neither the EU regulations nor the European Commission (Commission) require

16 Nine of the twenty-seven Member States have stated the whole of their area to be NVZ; AM Keessen and others, 'The Need for Flexibility and Differentiation in the Protection of Vulnerable Areas in EU Environmental Law: The Implementation of the Nitrates Directive in the Netherlands' (2011) JEEPL 8(2) <https://doi.org/10.1163/187601011X576205>, 142.

17 C-322/00 *Commission v Netherlands* [2003] ECLI:EU:C:2003:532.

18 Keessen and others (n 16) 145–7.

19 The aim of these options is to balance the nitrogen needs of the cultivated plants and the added nitrogen (either in the form of manure or other fertilisers), both factors dependent on the soil type and quality; Keessen and others (n 16) 155.

reporting from the farm level, it could be beneficial given differences in soil types, land formations, and nearby water condition requirements.[20]

The lessons learned from the Danish example, first, teach that the already-mentioned private property rights concerns need to be attended to, and when doing so, the farm-level interference results in heterogenous regulation of producers. Second, since the ND only deals with manure dissemination and does not cover all fertiliser use, diversifying the regulatory framework would be needed to enhance its effectiveness. Third, the question of adequate information is fundamental: the ability to pinpoint exact emission sources and establish confirmed trajectories is the key difference between the concepts of diffuse and point-source pollution. As noted by Tegner Anker, the broader the span of differentiation extends, the more robust the scientific justifications required to legitimise the regulation.[21]

Implementation of the ND in Finland is a narrative filled with constitutionally fascinating details. As already mentioned, Finland implemented the ND with a Nitrates Decree. In the most recent amendment, the scope of the decree was extended: the current version, unlike its predecessor, also concerns ammonium nitrate discharge.[22] The whole country constitutes an NVZ. Given that the country has vast amounts of shallow surface water surrounded by agricultural land (and where that is less prominent, intensive forestry adds to the burden of water), the decision appears reasonable. No further differentiation was conducted, marking the implementation as sufficient but not ambitious. The ND was still implemented as a governmental decree, instead of an act of the parliament, a decision earning constitutional critique in a country where 'exercise of public powers shall be based on an Act' and where that principle has continually gained more weight.[23] A further reason to criticise the implementation level is that governmental or ministerial decrees are not accompanied by a governmental proposal, the main source of *travaux préparatoires*, elementary in the interpretation of regulations in a civil law context. A preparatory memorandum of 20 pages was made public alongside the amended Nitrates

20 Keessen and others (n 16) 156–8.

21 This is naturally the place where the 'political will' appears on the stage, currently in Denmark opposing any stricter differentiated regulation of the nutrient problem, Tegner Anker (n 7) 22.

22 The Nitrates Decree 1250/2014, Government Decree on Limiting Certain Emissions from Agriculture and Horticulture, legally non-binding English translation available at <http://www.finlex.fi/en/laki/kaannokset/2014/en20141250.pdf> (accessed 10 April 2021). The implementation of the Nitrates Decree in Finland has interesting connections with the lower-level environmental regulation, namely the one given at the communal level on manure spreading. These are discussed in Jussi Kauppila, *Vesienhoitosuunnitelman oikeudellisen vaikuttavuuden rakentuminen* [*The Legal Effectiveness of the River Basin Management Plan*] (University of Eastern Finland 2016), available at <http://urn.fi/URN:ISBN:978-952-61-2309-7>, 41–3 and ch 4.

23 Constitution of Finland (perustuslaki 731/1999) 2.3 §. The unofficial and legally non-binding English translation of the Constitution is available at <http://www.finlex.fi/en/laki/kaannokset/1999/en19990731.pdf> (accessed 10 April 2021).

Decree – but in its relatively limited extent, it hardly meets the standards of a governmental proposal.[24] In Finland, governmental or ministerial decrees can be issued only if a parliamentary act allows for one. This has created an interesting intersection in which the enactment of a decree on diffuse pollution is founded on point-source pollution legislation.[25] The newest version of the Nitrates Decree came into force for the spring growing season of 2015 and was substantially revised for the first time in the same autumn.[26]

The revision of 2015 was instigated partly by the Commission: even though Finland was not facing infringement proceedings, unlike ten other Member States, the practical enforcement challenges of the preceding implementing decree favoured re-examination.[27] In particular, the Commission's demands to further improve cultivation practices to minimise runoff were cited as reasons for the re-enactment. The Commission's requests were also duly followed when, for example, the time for distributing fertilisers to fields in autumn was shortened, and requirements for manure storage were tightened.[28] The more stringent regulation was, however, accompanied by an exception: given that conditions during the growing season allow, manure can also be distributed as late as November. In the hearings, the environmental non-governmental organisations (NGOs) found the consequences of this deviation harmful to surface waters due to climate change impacts, i.e. the rise of excessive autumnal rains and floods.[29] In the tradition of paid stewardship familiar from the CAP regime – where stricter regulation is accompanied by an increase in financial

24 The Nitrates Decree Memorandum, 18 December 2014 (Ministry of the Environment). Published with the Memorandum was an FAQ sheet of seven pages. Locating these questions and answers to the hierachy of legal sources is an interesting endeavour: they might or might not constitute official preparatory work. Since the FAQ memo includes mainly basic advice on the implementation of the Nitrates Decree, an inevitable – and unanswered – question is why this information was not simply provided in the Nitrates Decree Memorandum.

25 The first version of the Nitrates Decree (219/1998) was based on the Water Act (264/1961), then regulating both physical alterations and emissions into waters. The second version (931/2000, Government Decree on the Restriction of Discharge of Nitrates from Agriculture into Waters) was enacted under the Environmental Protection Act (implementing act of the Integrated Pollution Prevention and Control [IPPC] Directive), as is the current one also (EPA 9 and 10 §).

26 The first revisions were issued in the same spring, revision history consisting of Decrees n:o 1261/2015 (in force 15 October 2015), Decree n:o 435/2015 (in force 17 April 2015), and Decree n:o 220/2015 (in force 20 March 2015). Also in total, five corrections have been made to the official versions of the Decree or its October 2015 amendment.

27 Report from the Commission to the Council and the European Parliament on the Implementation of Council Directive 91/676/EEC Concerning the Protection of Waters Against Pollution Caused by Nitrates from Agricultural Sources Based on Member State Reports for the Period 2008–2011, 4 October 2013, COM(2013) 683 final, 10–11.

28 Respectively, the Nitrates Decree 10 § and 5 §. Manure storage needs to be spacious enough for manure collected during a year's cycle.

29 The opinion of the Finnish Association for Nature Conservation (30 September 2015). The opinion was given when the Decree was first amended in the year following its issuance.

compensation – Finland's Ministry of Agriculture and Forestry initiated plans for investment support for farmers burdened by the new regulation concurrently with the Finnish Ministry of Environment's re-enacted decree. The estimated costs in general and for a standard farmer were carefully calculated in the background memorandum made available with the Nitrates Decree, detailing the costs of the regulatory alternatives based on the existing capacity of manure storage space and the space required after the amendments.[30]

All in all, the Finnish implementation of the ND is rather straightforward. The scope of regulation was slightly widened when the ammonium runoff was also taken under regulation. Traces of tailoring are present when limits of nitrogen fertilisers distributed to the fields are differentiated according to the soil type, following the path of the Dutch example.[31] Addressing phosphorus runoff is a work in progress, even though during the legislative process, demands to incorporate the phosphorus regulation into the Nitrates Decree were firmly presented, to the extent of presenting dissenting opinions to the proposals of the law-drafting committee.[32] Either as an attempt to enhance the clarity of the Decree, or because of the influence of EU-style legal drafting, the key concepts are now defined at the beginning of the Decree.[33] Although there have been no deliberate attempts to wriggle out of the EU's demands, neither have there been ambitious domestic innovations to curb nutrient runoff. The Danish question of adequate knowledge exists primarily in the evaluation of numerical data over the number and capacity of manure storage facilities, but the fundamental question of regulating diffuse-sourced pollution is not examined in the (equivalent of) preparatory works. One could even claim the opposite since attempts at calculating the environmental consequences are absent, a fact that prompted criticism during the legislative process. The critique also concerned the relation between the Nitrates Decree and the obligations of the WFD, to no avail.[34] The amendments of 2015 left the environmentalists still waiting for, e.g. river-basin-sensitive nitrate regulation or nitrate regulation paying full attention to the programmes of measures listed according to the WFD. Site-specificity in runoff regulation should be possible, though, as well as incorporating the river-basin approach to nutrient flows. On a more general level, the WFD includes an obligation to secure the implementation of the ND. Article 10 of the WFD establishes the combined approach for point and diffuse sources, listing the ND as one of the legal instruments relevant to it. The combined approach also requires that the most stringent emission controls

30 The Nitrates Decree Memorandum, 2–6. Paid stewardship relates to the discourses with which the CAP is justified, which emerge at the confluence of the environmentalist and the food security approaches; see text to n 48 for closer examination.

31 The Nitrates Decree 11.2 §.

32 E.g. the opinion of the Finnish Association for Nature Conservation (3 June 2014).

33 The Nitrates Decree 3 §. The previous version omitted the definitions.

34 The opinion of the Finnish Association for Nature Conservation (30 September 2015).

must always be abided by – thus, if complying with the ND does not guarantee the achievement of the WFD's aims on water protection, the obligations of the latter bind the Member States nonetheless.[35] The combined approach has been accepted as the starting point of much scholarly work emphasising the substantial significance of the WFD, and this volume follows suit in studying the WFD in detail in Chapter 4.

Of the four instruments that are analysed in this volume, the ND was among the first to directly target the issue of agricultural water pollution. It was also the first step in the path the EU regulator has taken towards adopting an adaptive management approach in the WFD, for it entails traces of adaptivity. These may be weak, but they are there. In overall evaluation, however, the ND appears as too simple an answer to the complex dilemma of intense agriculture and eutrophication of the Baltic Sea – therefore, the regulator has earned the epithet of a naïve regulator in its actions with the ND. The site-specificity, specification standards, process standards, and NVZs or targeting are not adequate means to tackle the major problem at the food, water, and environment nexus. In what follows, we move on to the other instruments relevant to agricultural water governance. The CAP is scrutinised next. What will it reveal about the EU regulator's approaches to science?

The Erratic Regulator in the CAP Reforms

'Greening the CAP' or Blue-Greening the Sea?[36]

The CAP has been the EU's prime policy field for over half a century, especially in terms of its budget – over the years, the CAP has consumed as much as 70 per cent of the community budget. Here the policy behind the CAP is analysed from the agri-environmental point of view, with a keen interest in its effectiveness: what has the CAP's impact on agricultural runoff been? What has been the role of the environmental concerns in the CAP reform negotiations? Have the aims of 'greening the CAP' been fruitful – or can the fruit of this financial distribution tool be reasonably measured at all? When examining the CAP, it is worth remembering that even though the importance of agri-environmental aspects has steadily intensified therein, their formal status in EU agriculture policy has long been acknowledged: the aims of the environmental concerns already existed in the 1970s.[37] During its lengthy history in

35 WFD Article 10(2)–(3).

36 The title refers to blue-green algae (*cyanobacteria*), common in the Baltic Sea during summer – an excess of algae is a sign of eutrophication.

37 Isabelle Garzon, *Reforming the Common Agricultural Policy: History of a Paradigm Change* (Palgrave Macmillan 2006) 54. The primary concerns of the late 1960s and 1970s were overtly effective production increases that led to production surpluses in the dairy industry in particular, and the challenges of finding political solutions to the problem, David Harvey, 'What does the history of

EU policy-making, the CAP has undergone a number of revisions, although it remained intact for three decades before the era of structural reforms commenced.[38] The remodelling done in the late 1980s is known as the MacSharry reform (named after the EU Agriculture Commissioner of the era); later ones are the so-called Agenda 2000 and Fischler reforms. The second newest is referred to either as the 2013 reform or, rarely, as the Cioloş reform. While writing this, the reform dictating the instrument's future beyond 2020 has just been accepted; it is briefly glanced upon at the end of this section.

Methodologically speaking, analysing the first three reforms has proven to be challenging. Discourse analysis has not been considered adequate since, earlier on, the policy makers were not expected to justify their actions by the more modern standards.[39] As is common in governance research, the analysis with the most explanatory force combines multilevel, multifunctional, and multilateral approaches in order to grasp an overall picture of the policy change.[40] In the case of the CAP, the multilevel players of the field range from the Member States via EU organisations to the international level.[41] The multilateral aspect deals with the bargaining involved. Its suitability also describes the essence of the CAP reforms and negotiations concerning them: multilateral analysis is deemed most appropriate for examining non-co-operative negotiations involving various participants forming myriad coalitions.[42] Multifunctional alludes to the various issues at stake: budgetary and trade to begin with, with environment and regional development not to be forgotten. It is worth noting that as commonplace as it might be in contemporary governance research, multifunctional analysis may be construed as a paradigm shift in studies of agricultural regulation. That is since one aim of multifunctional analysis is to incorporate agriculture as a field of industry in the system of environmental law. The general objective of this endeavour would be to regulate the environmental impacts of agriculture similarly to the point-source

---

the Common Agricultural Policy tell us?' in Joseph A McMahon and Michael N Cardwell (eds), *Research Handbook on EU Agriculture Law* (Edward Elgar Publishing 2015) 3, 10–13.

38 Prior to that, a 'substantial status quo bias' influenced the decision-making process; Alessandro Olper, 'Constraints and causes of the 2003 EU Agricultural Policy Reforms' in Johan FM Swinnen (ed), *The Perfect Storm: The Political Economy of the Fischler Reforms of the Common Agricultural Policy* (Centre for European Policy Studies 2008) 83, 86.

39 Garzon (n 37) 170.

40 Garzon (n 37) 8–9.

41 This understanding originates from Putnam's theory of international negotiations as a 'two-level game,' accommodating demands at both domestic and international level; RD Putnam, 'Diplomacy and Domestic Politics: The Logic of Two-Level Games' (1988) International Organization 42(3) <https://doi.org/10.1017/S0020818300027697>, 427.

42 On modelling multilateral bargaining in non-co-operative policy negotiations in a game theory framework, see Gregory Adams, Gordon Rausser, and Leo Simon, 'Modelling Multilateral Negotiations: An Application to California Water Policy' (1996) Journal of Economic Behavior & Organization 30(1) <https://doi.org/10.1016/S0167-2681(96)00844-X>, 97.

activities causing environmental impacts, staging multifunctional analysis at the heart of the problem, and merging environmental law epistemology with that of agriculture.[43] Even when multifunctional analysis has other objectives than incorporating normativity into the agri-environmental regulation – the aims of the form of analysis are plural – it is noteworthy that the mere employment of multifunctional analysis may result in a change in how agricultural regulation is traditionally perceived.

Regarding the agri-environmental aspects of the reforms, a few points are worth mentioning. First, in the MacSharry reform from 1992, agri-environmentality was formally integrated into the CAP.[44] Environmental harm from intense agriculture had become more obvious from the 1970s on, leading to the diversification of agricultural policy.[45] Ostensibly due to these broadened horizons, the MacSharry reform has been described as 'the most important CAP reform until that time.'[46] The regulatory tool applied was of a rudimentary sort – command and control and establishment of firm baselines – chosen according to the significant issues the reform was planned to address. The 'holy trinity' of EU agricultural policy was at the negotiation table: excessive production levels, planned budget cuts, and international trade conflicts formed the three policy areas justifying the reform.[47] Nonetheless, those actors in the agricultural industry who wished to pursue even more ambitious objectives were encouraged with financial incentives. Even though the paid stewardship policy had already been initiated earlier, the MacSharry reform established it as part of EU policy.[48]

International trade negotiations of the time, regarding the Uruguay Round of the General Agreement on Tariffs and Trade (GATT), strongly influenced

43 Massimo Monteduro, 'Environmental Law and Agroecology. Transdisciplinary Approach to Public Ecosystem Services as a New Challenge for Environmental Legal Doctrine' (2013) European Energy and Environmental Law Review 22(1) 2, 5. Monteduro defines this aim of incorporation to be at least 30 years old.

44 Garzon (n 37) 51. Finding environmental causes as a novelty in the 1990s might be slightly surprising since the environmental concerns had already been public knowledge for a good 20 years. It is not meant to imply that environmental concerns had not influenced EU agriculture policy before the MacSharry reform, but it was formally incorporated to the CAP only then. Garzon (n 37) 53–4.

45 Uwe Latacz-Lohmann and Ian Hodge, 'European Agri-Environmental Policy for the 21st Century' (2003) Aust J Agric Resour Econ 47(1) <https://doi.org/10.1111/1467-8489.00206>, 124–5. These were, however, not the key factors behind the need for reform: the crumbling of the post-war monetary system and changes in macroeconomy were constituted as such, Tim Josling, 'External influences on CAP reforms: an historical perspective' in Johan FM Swinnen (ed), *The Perfect Storm: The Political Economy of the Fischler Reforms of the Common Agricultural Policy* (CEPS 2008) 57, 58–64.

46 Garzon (n 37) 54.

47 Arlindo Cunha and Alan Swinbank, *An Inside View of the CAP Reform Process: Explaining the MacSharry, Agenda 2000, and Fischler Reforms* (Oxford University Press 2011) 68–9.

48 Having been tested in the UK agriculture policy, 'paid stewardship' was taken to the EU level with Council Regulation (EEC) 797/85 on improving the efficiency of agricultural structures [1985] OJ L 93/1; Latacz-Lohmann and Hodge (n 45) 130.

the MacSharry reform. The main reason was the tensions that the underpinning challenge of surplus (dairy) production created between the EU and its trade partners.[49] The Uruguay Round was a complex set of negotiations with long-term effects on agriculture, primarily in developed countries. Conflicting assessments have been made of the negotiations. Some suggest that both main parties, the US and Europe, were able to acquiesce to each other's demands; others find that the negotiations included such elaborate measures that the end result defies logical analysis.[50] Negotiations were not particularly constructive and were about to deadlock at one point, creating external pressure for the EU to succeed in the CAP reform – which it did, enabling the finalisation of the GATT negotiations.[51] Keeping up with multilevel analysis, it has been suggested that the MacSharry reform accommodated these twists and turns in the international negotiations; the GATT negotiations were affected not only at their own level but also as a horizontally connected issue to the reform.[52] This coupling was so extensive that the MacSharry reform has been evaluated as a saviour not only of the CAP itself but also of the Uruguay Round.[53] The relation between the two processes is, however, a delicate matter, and there is a risk of over-emphasising the external impact.[54] Interestingly, the producers' interest groups were the only part of civil society influencing the discussions. Since the European Parliament was also absent from the negotiations at both the international and EU level, the reform was largely in the hands of the European Commission, influenced only by the farmers' organisations.[55] It must thus not come as a surprise that in the MacSharry reform, agri-environmentality was not a decisive matter.

49 Harvey (n 37) 16. On a more abstract level, this exemplifies a phenomenon called the status quo bias: 'policy reform requires a critical change in external conditions.' Jan Pokrivcak, Christophe Crombez, and Johan FW Swinnen, 'Impact of external changes and the European Commission on CAP reforms: insights from theory' in Johan FM Swinnen (ed), *The Perfect Storm: The Political Economy of the Fischler Reforms of the Common Agricultural Policy* (Centre for European Policy Studies 2008) 9, 16.

50 Respectively, Cunha and Swinbank (n 47) 71–2 and Harvey (n 37) 17–18.

51 Josling (n 45) 66; Garzon (n 37) 74. According to Josling, the negotiations resulted in recriminations rather than dialogue; ibid Josling 66.

52 Cunha and Swinbank (n 47) 72, 100; Garzon (n 37) 74. Moehler finds the relationship as 'interactive.' Rolf Moehler, 'The internal and external forces driving CAP reforms' in Johan FM Swinnen (ed), *The Perfect Storm: The Political Economy of the Fischler Reforms of the Common Agricultural Policy* (Centre for European Policy Studies 2008) 76, 81.

53 Josling (n 45) 61.

54 In the words of Moehler, 'reform of the CAP – was more the result of the domestic dynamics of the CAP and the internal reactions it triggered.' Moehler (n 52) 76. Intriguingly, MacSharry himself never admitted that the reforms of his era had any relation with the Uruguay negotiations; ibid 80.

55 Garzon (n 37) 75.

The weight and diversity of civil society present increased during the next reform, known as Agenda 2000.[56] Not only did the producers' organisations diversify, but environmental groups were also allowed to participate due to the new practice of assimilating environmental concerns into all EU policies.[57] Political interest was also secured since the burden of making ends meet had been shifted from consumers to taxpayers.[58] In this round, the agricultural ministers of the Member States played the leading role, even though the Parliament also became more active in the discussions. Eventually, however, the European Council heavily amended the conclusions reached.[59] Agenda 2000 was not as strongly influenced by the international negotiations as the previous reform. In some evaluations, the international level is found to have been nearly absent from the negotiations, but others have found the EU–US relationship to be significant.[60] The previous experiences were utilised: after the challenging Uruguay Round, the Commission wished to pursue more proactive and positive agendas to strengthen the EU's role in the negotiations, resulting in similarities between the EU and the US's strategies.[61]

Budgetary discipline was on the other hand rudimentary, as were considerations on cohesion, meaning issues emerging from the prospective enlargement of the EU.[62] Budgetary rigidity was handled in the negotiations with two options, co-financing and degressivity, the latter referring to progressive reduction from the producers, who would receive large sums in direct payments.[63] In this round, rural development was included in the CAP.[64] Even though the concept of rural development has remained ambiguous to date, in Agenda 2000, it referred to incorporating agri-environmental measures as the second pillar of the CAP.[65] In general, Agenda 2000 has been recalled as either a disappointment or a reform with a modest outcome – after all, environmental protection measures in the policy were still considered accompani-

56 Agenda 2000 was also seen as a package of measures preparing the EU for enlargement and other novelties the new century might bring, Cunha and Swinbank (n 47) 115; Josling (n 45) 69.

57 Garzon (n 37) 88–90. In order to justify its share of the EU budget, the CAP needed to meet the expectations of the public – this current became increasingly important in Agenda 2000; Moehler (n 52) 78.

58 Olper (n 38) 86.

59 Garzon (n 37) 91–2; Josling (n 45) 72.

60 Respectively, Garzon (n 37) 94; Robert Ackrill, *Common Agricultural Policy* (A&C Black 2000) 245, 116; Cunha and Swinbank (n 47) 105–6.

61 Josling (n 45) 68–9, 72.

62 Garzon (n 37) 93, 95. Not that the EU had not enlarged previously, but the previous rounds incorporated either net importers of agricultural products (UK) or countries wealthy enough (Austria, Finland, Sweden) to bear the burden budget-wise; the prospects of Eastern enlargement suggested a change; Moehler (n 52) 81–2.

63 Cunha and Swinbank (n 47) 112–3.

64 The addition affected even the title of the Directorate-General (DG) and the Commissioner, becoming officers for Agriculture and Rural Development; Moehler (n 52) 78.

65 Garzon (n 37) 54.

ments.[66] However, regarding agri-environmentality, there might be more to the story than mere disappointment: Agenda 2000 enlarged the participation of the environmental NGOs in the negotiation process. Though a procedural gain, this was a gain nonetheless, as the ensuing reforms prove.

The third of the reforms, the Fischler or Fischler II Reform, was negotiated shortly after Agenda 2000. The European Council initiated the reform, originally aspiring to a mid-term review and eventually receiving a full reform.[67] Some hitherto elementary issues, such as budgetary rigour, were not advanced in the Fischler round, whereas others, such as agri-environmentality, continued to improve their positions. The latter was due to civil society's growing significance after a severe food crisis and acknowledgement of the impact of EU agriculture on developing countries – as if the EU food policy began developing a conscience.[68] In the Fischler reform, new rules were presented to meet the environmental concerns, representing a change of dynamics between this and the prior reform.[69] The Fischler reform was led by the concept of decoupling, i.e. separating direct payments from production. Detaching production amounts, areas, or headages from payments was facilitated by having more diverse arguments at the table, justifying the decisions.[70] Since the idea of decoupling was, however, diluted by granting Member States different variants and options, the Fischler reform has been nicknamed the 'cafeteria CAP.'[71] In spite of the mockery, the diversification of the value base in the CAP negotiations was concretised in the Fischler reform: in this round, not only food security but also environmental security were fully considered. The broad choice of options given to the Member States might have diluted the result – but at least there was something to be diluted in the first place!

Even though international pressure was not necessary for the Fischler reform to commence, it eventually became a horizontally connected, significant issue of the overall reform.[72] The international aspects were a trigger, the forthcoming international negotiations serving as a driving force for the reform.[73] It is

66 Moehler (n 52) 79; Olper (n 38) 86.

67 Josling (n 45) 72. Fischler reforms began a mere day after Agenda 2000 was agreed upon; Olper (n 38) 86–7.

68 Olper (n 38) 86–7. Also, i.e. ethical issues started to gain significance; Cunha and Swinbank (n 47); Garzon (n 37) 99–100. The international dimension played a significant role in this reform: the Doha Agreement in 2001 caused external pressures, and at stake this time were the future prospects of agreements in agricultural policies between, e.g. the US and the EU; ibid Garzon, 100-1.

69 Garzon (n 37) 107.

70 Cunha and Swinbank (n 47) 131, 148. Even though the change was dramatic, its influence on the payment distribution remained low; Olper (n 38) 88.

71 Alan Greer, *Agricultural Policy in Europe* (Manchester University Press 2005), 208.

72 Garzon (n 37) 117.

73 Cunha and Swinbank (n 47) 147, A Swinbank and C Daugbjerg, 'The 2003 CAP Reform: Accommodating WTO Pressures' (2006) Comp Eur Polit 4(1) <https://doi.org/10.1057/palgrave.cep.6110069>, 47.

noteworthy that, ever since the MacSharry reform, external factors have been part of the CAP's structure, posing considerable challenges to evaluating their importance.[74] The Parliament's role has also been intensively debated. The Parliament's part in the growing emphasis on agri-environmental issues has been interpreted in multiple ways: in one estimation, it served as an arena for more diverse arguments to be heard and discussed, even to the extent that the Parliament went beyond its formal role.[75] Others have found the Parliament's role equivocal, while yet others identify the Parliament as an ally for the Commission to secure the negotiations.[76] The diversity of arguments was quite real, stemming from the fact that the Member States were less connected with producers' organisations.[77] The role of the Parliament was one variable in the equation, and its impact might be influenced by the changes in the Member States, funnelled to the EU decision-making most directly in the parliamentary work. This view finds support in the idea that the Fischler reform was mainly about securing the future of the CAP by justifying it to larger audiences.[78] However, Parliament's greater involvement might only have slowed down future reform processes.[79] The two features may result in the same outcome: seeking acceptability from broader audiences almost inevitably leads to lengthier processes.

In sum, the studies on the CAP's evolution have noted that the earlier reforms consist of three different discourses: productivist, neoliberal, and multifunctional.[80] The first emphasises the food security and farm income function of agriculture, the second is willing to admit more diverse functions to the industry, and the last focuses on the internal and external pressures this highly capitalised field faces, arising retrospectively from the EU budget negotiations and international trade negotiations.[81] Even though the earliest reforms elude discourse analysis, the latter reforms have moved solidly towards more neolib-

74 Available choices for the policy-makers have diminished from before, even to the extent of establishing a 'path dependency' pattern. Olper (n 38) 84 referring to M Iagatti and A Sorrentino, 'La path dependency nel processo di riforma della PAC' (2007) Agriregionieuropa 3(9) 50.

75 Garzon (n 37) 115, 119.

76 Respectively, Cunha and Swinbank (n 47) 145; Peter Nedergaard, 'The 2003 Reform of the Common Agricultural Policy: Against all Odds or Rational Explanations?' (2006) Journal of European Integration 28(3) <https://doi.org/10.1080/07036330600785749>, 217–18.

77 Garzon (n 37) 119.

78 Cunha and Swinbank (n 47) 149.

79 Cunha and Swinbank (n 47) 146.

80 The classification has also been expressed as that of neomercantilism, multifunctionality, and neoliberalism. Karmen Erjavec and Emil Erjavec, 'Changing EU Agricultural Policy Discourses? The Discourse Analysis of Commissioner's Speeches 2000–2007' (2009) Food Policy 34(2) <https://doi.org/10.1016/j.foodpol.2008.10.009>, 224.

81 Karmen Erjavec and Emil Erjavec, '"Greening the CAP" – Just a Fashionable Justification? A Discourse Analysis of the 2014–2020 CAP Reform Documents' (2015) Food Policy 51 <https://doi.org/10.1016/j.foodpol.2014.12.006>, 55.

eral justifications of the CAP.[82] Where does this leave the environment and its concerns, and how are these reflected in the 2013 reform and the newest reform that was finally adopted in December 2021?

From the Green Light for the 2013 Reform to a Green Deal CAP

The Fischler reform(s) were completed during the health check conducted at the CAP in 2007 before the newest full and completed reform.[83] The Lisbon Treaty of 2007 had greatly altered the negotiation procedure for the CAP post-2013: the power of the Member States' agricultural ministers diminished in favour of a co-decision process including the Parliament, the Council, and the Commission as the initiator and facilitator.[84] The Commission started the negotiations with a document entitled 'Greening the CAP' – but how environmentally friendly did the reform eventually come to be, and how did the environmental concerns weather the neomercantilist tides?

Even though the reform was envisaged as a profound transformation, eventually productivist discourse was favoured in the reform that moulded the CAP for 2014–2020.[85] The triumph of productivism can be explained by the economic crisis of 2008 and the preferences of the EU Commissioner.[86] The negotiated result is a compromise in which the basic payment component of the new direct payments scheme amounts to an income support mechanism for farmers – but this interpretation also has fierce opponents.[87] Among other things, direct payments include a mandatory 'greening' component, resulting in farming mechanisms such as crop diversification, maintenance of permanent grassland, and ecological focus areas. 'Mandatory' means that a Member State cannot opt-out of implementing the component: its allocation is 30 per cent of each Member State's national ceiling for direct payments. This end result, even though an improvement from before, is not what the Commission instigated: it sought more stringent environmental protection by placing the green payments inside Pillar I of the CAP's payments, but the Parliament was not willing

82 Erjavec and Erjavec (n 80) 224.

83 European Commission (2007), 'Preparing for the "Health Check" of the CAP reform,' Communication from the Commission to the Council and the European Parliament, COM(2007) 722, 20 November; Giovanni Anania and Maria Rosaria Pupo D'Andrea, 'The 2013 Reform of the Common Agricultural Policy' in Johan Swinnen (ed), *The Political Economy of the 2014–2020 Common Agricultural Policy: An Imperfect Storm* (Centre for European Policy Studies 2015) 33, 35.

84 Anania and D'Andrea (ibid) 39.

85 Erjavec and Erjavec (n 81) 55.

86 Cordula Rutz, Janet Dwyer, and Jörg Schramek, 'More New Wine in the Same Old Bottles? The Evolving Nature of the CAP Reform Debate in Europe, and Prospects for the Future' (2014) Sociologia Ruralis 54(3) <https://doi.org/10.1111/soru.12033>, 266.

87 Anania and D'Andrea (n 83) 52, cf. Harvey (n 37) 3, 33–5.

to green the CAP to the extent the Commission desired.[88] The Member States were, however, given an opportunity to shift resources between the two pillars, a chance most of them opted for. Flexibility and a multitude of voluntary measures by and large characterise the post-2013 CAP – even to the extent of generating discussion of whether it still lives up to its name, 'Common.'[89]

As it had been during the previous decades, the international realm is relevant as one curb on the EU's ability to finance its agricultural industry. Internal pressures, with externals playing a lesser role, have mostly influenced the latest completed CAP reform. The 'bruising experience' of the Uruguay Round is credited for the development that the 2013 reform resulted in the Doha Agricultural Modalities having only a limited role in the negotiations. The boundaries of international trade were naturally taken into account in the reform, even to the extent that the CAP in its current form should not face pressure to change from the World Trade Organization (WTO).[90] The calming of the previously turbulent relationship is partly due to global uncertainty on what 21st-century agriculture trade policies should be. The definition of food security – is it equivalent to farmer security, and what is the role of further liberalisation of trade and food sovereignty or self-sufficiency – the role of the right to food, and the role of environmental protection on the whole, are all questions that need answering. The EU's focus has also shifted from multilateral negotiations to bilateral or plurilateral ones, a tendency that further explains the WTO's diminished role.[91]

By combining critical discourse analysis with policy instrument analysis, one can examine whether and how the discourses held during the negotiations

88 Bernard O'Connor, 'The impact of the Doha Round on the European Union's Common Agricultural Policy' in Joseph A McMahon and Michael N Cardwell (eds), *Research Handbook on EU Agriculture Law* (Edward Elgar Publishing Ltd. 2015) 417; Anania and D'Andrea (n 83) 52–3, 57; A Matthews, 'Greening Agricultural Payments in the EU's Common Agricultural Policy' (2013) Bio-based and Applied Economics 2(1) <https://doi.org/10.22004/ag.econ.149214>, 4, 16–19, 22.; ibid Anania and D'Andrea 71. For a summary of other parts of the Commission's original plan that did not materialise, see Jean-Christophe Bureau and Louis-Pascal Mahé, 'Was the CAP reform a success?' in Johan FM Swinnen (ed), *The Political Economy of the 2014–2020 Common Agricultural Policy: An Imperfect Storm* (Centre for European Policy Studies 2015) 87, 96.

89 Anania and D'Andrea (n 83) 81.

90 O'Connor (n 88) 388–9. This is merely the general outline: compliance issues may emerge in details of the CAP and Doha Modalities. Ibid 404.

91 O'Connor (n 88) 404–5, 410; Christian Häberli, 'The story of Community preference for food security' in Joseph A McMahon and Michael N Cardwell (eds), *Research Handbook on EU Agriculture Law* (Edward Elgar Publishing Ltd. 2015) 437, 440. Evaluation given with the assumption that political changes can be predicted at all in the fast-changing world of today. On the concept of right to food see ibid O'Connor, 410 fn 110 and 111. There have, however, been views that the WTO might have influenced the CAP process in the background, Alan Swinbank, 'The WTO: No longer relevant for CAP reform?' in Johan FM Swinnen (ed), *The Political Economy of the 2014–2020 Common Agricultural Policy: An Imperfect Storm* (Centre for European Policy Studies 2015) 193.

were transformed into policy processes and instruments.[92] Multifunctional discourse, highlighting the environmental aspects, justified the new direct payment scheme. The same combination of arguments was also present in the later negotiations on CAP reform. Discourses on the basic payment scheme were rather 'blank,' consisting mainly of bureaucratic formulations or figures with little to debate around. However, traces of productivist discourse were deciphered from the data.[93] Thus it can be concluded that greening becomes relevant only after the basic level of production and income are secured. The fact that greening discourse was more prominent in the early stages of the policy drafting might have had a grim outcome: the prospect of a greener CAP might have saved the policy from budget cuts, even when the end result was not as green as anticipated.[94] Significant levels of productivist discourse were found in the sum of the preparatory and negotiation documents: support measures for young farmers, coupled payments, and flexibility options for direct payment systems were all justified with mainly productivist arguments.[95] In other words, even when food security concerns were again in the limelight, the productivist discourse seems to have been reintroduced with a slightly new tone: food produced ought to be 'safe and high quality nutritious food.'[96]

The same conclusion is reached if the policy analysis also considers the distribution of funds. After assigning measures to certain discourses and comparing their share of the total CAP budget, it was found that productivist discourse repatriated 60 per cent of the total budget. The multifunctional discourse earned 30 per cent of the total, while the neo-liberalist discourse faced near extinction. While the greening of the CAP was the key element in the multifunctional discourse, its share of the result is greater than in the earlier versions of the CAP. A danger of oversimplification still exists: earlier CAP reforms already coupled greening elements with payments.[97] Also, after all the drafting and negotiating, the productivist discourse was again underlined at

92 Erjavec and Erjavec (n 81) 54, 56. Since CAP is a redistributive instrument and the research was conducted while the implementation was still a work in progress, analysing the efficacy of the transformation is dependent on the implementation at the Member-State level. Ibid 57. For a gradual analysis of the negotiation process see Emil Erjavec, Marko Lovec, and Karmen Erjavec, 'From "greening" to "greenwash": drivers and discourses of the CAP 2020 "Reform"' in Johan FM Swinnen (ed), *The Political Economy of the 2014–2020 Common Agricultural Policy: An Imperfect Storm* (Centre for European Policy Studies 2015) 215.

93 Erjavec and Erjavec (n 81) 57.

94 Kaley Hart, 'The fate of green direct payments in the CAP reform negotiations' in Johan FM Swinnen (ed), *The Political Economy of the 2014–2020 Common Agricultural Policy: An Imperfect Storm* (Centre for European Political Studies 2015) 245, 262.

95 Other discourse types were hybrids of productivist discourse and the multifunctional discourse. Erjavec and Erjavec (n 81) 58–9.

96 O'Connor (n 88) 387, 401.

97 E.g. the cross compliance mechanism introduced in the Fischler reform is already an element of 'greening.'

the decision-making stage.[98] The bleak fact is that the language in the policy documents does not necessarily result in equivalent measures and budget distributions, and even less so in the case of the post-2013 CAP.[99]

In general, the 2013 reform was deemed a disappointment, a missed opportunity to fundamentally refocus the policy. The procedure was, once again, lengthier than before, and some commentators have found an inverse correlation between the length of the drafting process and the impetus of reform it carries.[100] The greening element was partially to blame for the tardiness: the stances of Parliament and the Council differed so greatly from the Commission's intentions that they should be held responsible for any lack of environmentalism in the CAP.[101] A noteworthy new player in the field was the Committee on Agriculture and Rural Development (COMAGRI), a parliamentary committee, participants of which are and were notoriously biased towards the productivist or neoliberal discourse. COMAGRI held a central role as a responsible committee in the legislative process, and much influence was vested in the committee, in which only a minority shared the Commission's visions for developing the CAP – all this irrespective of the fact that diverse interest groups lobbied the committee during the legislative process.[102] This is not to imply that the work of COMAGRI would have occurred without controversy. The reality was very different: the committee was mired in various conflicts of interests, the Parliament's political groups struggled to find common ground between themselves, and as a result, the vote on the amendments had to be taken by an open show of hands.[103]

Unlike in the Fischler reforms, this time, the factors influencing the reform did not catalyse a successful change but rather obstructed development.[104]

98 Erjavec and Erjavec (n 81) 60.

99 Erjavec and Erjavec (n 81) 61. Certain types of argumentation may also be absent since the concerns in question have been taken into the structure of the CAP. O'Connor (n 88) 403.

100 Bureau and Mahé (n 88) 128, 87.

101 The Commission, then again, could have reasoned its case more thoroughly, Hart (n 94) 261, 269. In its internal proceedings the Parliament opted for Rule 70a which on its part slowed down the work. Christilla Roederer-Rynning, 'COMAGRI and the "CAP after 2013" reform: in search of a collective sense of purpose' in Johan FM Swinnen (ed), *The Political Economy of the 2014–2020 Common Agricultural Policy: An Imperfect Storm* (Centre for European Policy Studies 2015) 331, 334, 347.

102 In the legislature that drafted the CAP still in force, 31 per cent of the COMAGRI's members were estimated to have 'special interest' and 24 per cent 'special expertise' in agriculture. However, it is debatable how long the agriculture sector will keep its hold on the committee. Roederer-Rynning (n 101) 338–40, 346 and Fig. 13.2. In the process towards the 2013 reform other parliamentary committees with more multifunctional attitudes were able to balance out COMAGRI's bias. Hart (n 94) 271.

103 Roederer-Rynning (n 101) 349–50.

104 An opposite situation would have created a 'perfect storm,' whereas the 2013 reform became an imperfect one, Johan FM Swinnen, 'The political economy of the 2014–2020 Common Agricultural Policy: introduction and key conclusions' in Johan FM Swinnen (ed), *The Political*

Flexibility between the two pillars and a vast amount of voluntary measures resulted in a CAP that is more challenging to decipher or co-ordinate than it was before 2013.[105] Having a mandatory component of greening in the direct payments is often presented as a success of the 2013 reform, but the flexibility accepted in it and elsewhere in the policy makes assessing the outcome difficult. Flexibility can work towards pro-environmentalist objectives, but one should not read too much into the 'mandatoriness' of the component.[106] The Fischler and 2013 CAP reforms, with ten years between them, make for an odd comparison. The Fischler reform of 2003 was not meant to be much of a transformation but turned into a significant one, whereas the 2013 reform, a thoroughly prepared initiative that intended to include a paradigm shift, eventually failed to meet expectations.[107] When combined with the unpredictable weight of the environmentalist objectives, the epithet 'erratic regulator' appears incontrovertible.

Having said that, the conclusion that 'greening the CAP' is nothing but greenwashing might be an exaggeration. It was only in the 1990s that the multifunctional discourse began to gain momentum. The CAP has been and is composed of three aspects – trade, food supply and security, and environmental causes – each bringing their own interests to the negotiations. Bearing that in mind, the progress of environmental concerns seems clear and determined, even when the 2013 reform was a disappointment to the environmentalist. Another question is whether the money, however labelled, is effectively spent. The efficacy of the financial distribution in relation to the environmental quality of the Baltic Sea can be examined with economic tools; such studies were also conducted in Finland before the 2013 reform. In counterfactual analysis, the focal point is a linkage between the money spent on agri-environmental programmes and the environmental benefits gained through measures funded. The results of the 'social cost–benefit analysis' were rather discouraging: environmental gains of reduced nutrient runoff were considerably less than the money spent.[108] The result is less surprising when we note that during the years Finland has had its agri-environmental programme, the amount of nitrate runoff has increased, not decreased, contradicting the programme's aims.[109] As noted above, there are justified reasons to oppose cost–benefit analysis in

Economy of the 2014–2020 Common Agricultural Policy: An Imperfect Storm (Centre for European Policy Studies 2015) 1, 2.

105 Bureau and Mahé (n 88) 102–3.

106 Bureau and Mahé (n 88) 106–9.

107 Bureau and Mahé (n 88) 131.

108 Jussi Lankoski and Markku Ollikainen, 'Counterfactual Approach for Assessing Agri-Environmental Policy: Theory with an Application to Finnish Water Protection Policy' (2011) University of Helsinki, Department of Economics and Management Discussion Papers (56).

109 Amounts of soil phosphorus have even increased in some parts of the country, also proving the inefficacy of the program, Lankoski and Ollikainen (ibid) 5.

policy research.[110] For analysing benefit distribution, however, cost–benefit analysis is an apt choice.

The complexity of the theme renders easy solutions difficult to establish. Natural reality adds to the challenge: since nutrients in water ecosystems compound, eutrophication is caused not only by current or recent emissions but also by emissions from years back that have settled on the seabed. This natural phenomenon hampers evaluations of the efficacy of the measures meant to address the dilemma, in economic analysis or otherwise.[111] Some lines of thought from the process leading to the post-2013 CAP are worth remembering. First, pursuing change by amending Pillar I is difficult, almost inevitably leading to adverse responses and diluted results. A more regional or even local focus might be more efficient, aiming for tailored solutions in the regions involved and paying full attention to their priorities and needs. These tendencies resulted in a more flexible CAP. Also, in the parliamentary process, especially in the COMAGRI, the CAP was 'decoupled' from the WFD and its ambitious objectives for the water environment.[112] Currently, all these features counteract the CAP's environmentality – and the ability of the WFD to achieve its aims – and rethinking their relations might be worthwhile.[113]

At the time of writing, the reform taking the CAP into the post-2020 era has just been adopted. The Commission presented its proposal in June 2018, only to find the negotiations between the Parliament and the Council going on for three and a half years, until December 2021. The rules in force in the previous regulation have been extended. The internal pressures have heavily influenced this episode of the CAP reforms, with the Commission's desire to couple the policy with the European Green Deal, a policy aimed at seeking sustainable biodiversity with the help of a circular economy. In the earlier reforms, the three main interests present were trade, food supply and security, and the environment. In the 2021 reform, each one of these was present too,

110 Text to n 43ff.

111 In the bleakest simulations, the post-2013 CAP is bound to fail. Jordan Hristov and others, 'Impacts of the EU's Common Agricultural Policy "Greening" Reform on Agricultural Development, Biodiversity, and Ecosystem Services' (2020) Applied Economic Perspectives and Policy 42(4) <https://doi.org/10.1002/aepp.13037>, 716.

112 Hart (n 94) 272–3, in line with Matthews (n 88) 22–3. The detachment was enacted by removing binding references from the CAP to the WFD (and the Pesticides Directive, soil and groundwater protection, to name but a few); Roederer-Rynning (n 101) 350.

113 Given that 'reform fatigue' allows for a major and ambitious CAP reform, that is. For analysis of the terrain during the CAP 2021 reform negotiations see Allan Buckwell, 'Where should the CAP go post-2020?' in Johan FM Swinnen (ed), *The Political Economy of the 2014–2020 Common Agricultural Policy: An Imperfect Storm* (Centre for European Policy Studies 2015) 509; Alan Matthews, 'Reflections on the CAP post-2014' in Johan FM Swinnen (ed), *The Political Economy of the 2014–2020 Common Agricultural Policy: An Imperfect Storm* (Centre for European Policy Studies 2015) 493. Discussion on the WFD and the CAP is continued in the concluding Chapter 6.

this time as separate strategies the reform ought to contribute to: the European Green Deal, the Farm to Fork strategy, and the biodiversity strategy. The outcome, CAP for 2023–27, leaves room for manoeuvre for the Member States, significantly risking the dilution of the sustainability aims amid growing pressure from climate change and biodiversity loss.[114] Unfortunately, it appears the policy may have fallen short of the high ambitions of the era.[115] The CAP is an instrument that has weathered storms of multitudinous internal and external pressures before, and as already mentioned, the move towards greening the instrument has been steady yet slow. The future will tell how the Member States use the leeway granted to them. In the multilevel governance that the EU and its Member States create, the pressing environmental concerns of this era are now at the hands of the nations constituting the EU.

The SBSR: The Candid Regulator of a Macroregional Entity

From the CAP, and the strategic choices in preparation therein, we move to a regulatory instrument colloquially known as the SBSR. In 2009, the Council approved a strategic road map, followed by the Commission's communication on the matter.[116] With the rich governance history of the Baltic region, the SBSR was not sown on unprepared soil; fast-forwarding from the times of the Hanseatic League, the immediately preceding step was the EU Programme for the Baltic Sea region from 2007. Along the lines set in the beginning, this subsection focuses on the position of agricultural runoff – and the science calling for action on it – in the latest SBSR. What role does it play in the SBSR? Which type of reaction or attitude to the scientific consensus (on the role of agriculture in the condition of the sea) does the SBSR convey?

114 Guy Pe'er and others, 'Action Needed for the EU Common Agricultural Policy to Address Sustainability Challenges' (2020) People and Nature 2(2) <https://doi.org/10.1002/pan3.10080>, 305. The number of the 'others' is remarkable here: the statement of the scientific community's concerns had 3,600 signatories.

115 Katharine Heyl and others, 'The Common Agricultural Policy Beyond 2020: A Critical Review in Light of Global Environmental Goals' (2021) *RECIEL* 30(1) <https://doi.org/10.1111/reel.12351>, 95.

116 European Council 'Presidency Conclusions of the Brussels European Council' (2009) 15265/1/09 REV 1; Commission, 'Communication from the Commission to the European Parliament, the Council, the European Economic and Social Committee and the Committee of the Regions Concerning the European Union Strategy for the Baltic Sea Region (the Strategy)' COM (2009) 248 final.

Territorial Cohesion with a Ratio Moderatio *of Its Own*

Attempting to balance its enlargement and mind its external relations, the EU developed an approach focusing on regions.[117] The work is rooted in a current treaty provision, Article 174 of the Treaty on the Functioning of the European Union (TFEU), which places the EU's focus on strengthening economic, social, and territorial development. The SBSR was initiated as a part of work aiming to promote a territorial cohesion approach, an attempt to decentralise territorial development in the EU and increase stakeholder co-operation in the regions.[118] Previous steps in the development included the White Paper on European Governance (2001) and Territorial State and Perspectives of the European Union (2005).[119] The Commission published a green paper on territorial cohesion in 2008 with the hope of deepening the understanding of the concept via more active discussion.[120] The work was concluded five years later when the cornerstones of macroregional strategies were set in the Common Provisions Regulation: a mature macroregional strategy ought to be an integrated one, aimed at tackling shared problems, including the Member States and third parties of the region, whose reinforced co-operation (on three fields mentioned in Article 174 of the TFEU) should benefit the strategy.[121] The exact meaning of 'integration' in this context is contested, but there is an often-shared understanding that regional drivers of growth are distinctly

117 Kristine Kern, 'Governance for Sustainable Development in the Baltic Sea Region' (2011) Journal of Baltic Studies 42(1) <https://doi.org/10.1080/01629778.2011.538517>, 22, 29.

118 Also this is part of a continuum: for a long time the EU integration and development has required turning to the regions and balancing the economic and social discrepancies between them. Frank Othengrafen and Andreas P Cornett, 'A Critical Assessment of the Added Value of Territorial Cohesion' (2013) European Journal of Spatial Development <https://doi.org/10.15488/1851>.

119 Territorial Agenda of the European Union (2007) Agreed on the Occasion of the Informal Ministerial Meeting on Urban Development and Territorial Cohesion in Leipzig on 24–25 May 2007; Commission, 'Communication from the Commission to the Council, the European Parliament, the Committee of the Regions and the European Economic and Social Committee Green Paper on Territorial Cohesion Turning Territorial Diversity into Strength' COM (2008) 616 final, 7, 12; Alexandre Dubois and others, *EU Macro-Regions and Macro-Regional Strategies – A SCOPING STUDY* (Nordregio 2009) 43, 21–2.

120 Ibid Commission (2008) 616 final. For a critical stance on the territorialism in general, see Andreas Faludi, 'Multi-Level (Territorial) Governance: Three Criticisms' (2012) Planning Theory & Practice 13(2) <https://doi.org/10.1080/14649357.2012.677578>, 198.

121 Some commentators have found these features as merely symbolic. James Scott, 'Cross-Border Governance in the Baltic Sea Region' (2002) Regional & Federal Studies 12(4) <https://doi.org/10.1080/714004777>, 142. Regulation 1303/2013 laying down common provisions on the European Regional Development Fund, the European Social Fund, the Cohesion Fund, the European Agricultural Fund for Rural Development and the European Maritime and Fisheries Fund and laying down general provisions on the European Regional Development Fund, the European Social Fund, the Cohesion Fund and the European Maritime and Fisheries Fund and repealing Council Regulation (EC) No 1083/2006 [2013] OJ L 347/320.

interdependent.[122] The Commission presented the SBSR in 2009 after a joint drafting process with the stakeholders and the Member States. Rather surprisingly, the results of the collaborative process were quite congruent, with all parties favouring an integrated and multisectoral approach.[123]

The Baltic region was a natural choice for a territorial cohesion project: its nature as a geographical space between international and national levels is such that well-established analytical concepts such as 'meso,' or 'macroregion,' or a definition of peripheral subregion describe it well. A macroregion, the most established of these concepts, refers to 'a meso-level bringing together a group of units that are at the same time part of (or related to) a more comprehensive political entity.'[124] Irrespective of the label used, the Baltic Sea is undisputedly the most established area for co-operation in Europe, with the longest tradition in the field.[125] That is not to say that the Baltic Sea region is a homogenous area; on the contrary: the region contains a great deal of variety in socio-economic factors. The key common feature is the highly polluted sea shared by the littoral states.[126] This apparently grim reality adds to the Baltic Sea region's suitability for the macroregional governance approach, necessitating a shared purpose. Macroregional governance exemplifies functional governance, a development from governance based merely on territories. In the SBSR, the functional aspect is especially about the agricultural runoff and the sea – addressing the issue in an integrated manner across the whole region is one of the SBSR's justifications.[127] Since macroregional governance entails at least one shared problem justifying the governance apparatus, this key problem could be called *ratio moderatio* (as an analogy to *ratio legis*). The condition of the Baltic Sea would then be the *ratio moderatio* of the SBSR.[128]

122 For a summary of the discussion see Tamás Kaiser, 'The Added Value of The Integrated Approach: The Case of Hungary' (Conference on the EU Strategy for the Danube Region: Challenges and Chances 2014–2020 2015) 100, 102.

123 The Strategy COM (2009) 248 final, 1, 4.

124 Stefan Gänzle and Kristine Kern, 'Macro-Region, "Macro-Regionalization" and Macro-Regional Strategies in the European Union: Towards a New Form of European Governance?' in Stefan Gänzle and Kristine Kern (eds), *A 'Macro-Regional' Europe in the Making: Theoretical Approaches and Empirical Evidence* (Palgrave Macmillan 2016) 3, 5. The concept 'transnational regionalism' is also employed, Scott (n 121) 136.

125 Stefan Gänzle, 'Introduction: Transnational Governance and Policy-Making in the Baltic Sea Region' (2011) Journal of Baltic Studies 42(1) <https://doi.org/10.1080/01629778.2011.538509>, 1, 4.

126 Dubois and others (n 119) 25–9.

127 Gänzle and Kern (n 124) 3.

128 *Ratio legis* refers to the 'reason of the law,' the policy reason for a specific norm or act of legislation. Here the notion of *ratio moderatio* would thus refer to the reasons underlying the functional governance instrument. The term was first introduced in Tiina Paloniitty, 'Does It Take Three to Tango? The Practitioner's Viewpoint to Three EU Governance Instruments Addressing the Agricultural Runoff Dilemma' in Erkki J Hollo (ed) *Water Resource Management and the Law* (EE 2017). Tynkkynen and others find that the Baltic Sea governance system lacks a 'primus

Apart from being macroregional in essence, the SBSR exemplifies transnational governance, in which public and private actors have an influence on the political and/or legal spheres at both the international and regional levels. The partners in transnational governance ought to be somewhat equal and share a level of cultural affinity, but the region should still be heterogeneous in its character.[129] As noted above, the SBSR is not the first attempt to regionalise the governance of the Baltic region. Where does the SBSR lay in the web of governance in the region, and what is the novelty value it yields?

Laboratory of Environmental Governance

The SBSR is thus a prime example of macroregional governance due to its preceding characteristics, such as institutions, interdependence, and cultural resemblance.[130] It aimed to augment the functionality of the region's extensive co-operation. For example, the European Council highlighted themes that created the need for closer regional co-operation. The Council promoted the initiative partly because of environmental concerns but also due to a lack of co-ordination and out of fear of inconsistency in the development of the riparian states.[131] It was crucial to protect the highly vulnerable ecosystem of the Baltic Sea. Later in the drafting process, the Parliament and the Commission held different, even opposing views on the nature of the SBSR; the views of the former were more ambitious and concerned the institutional development and funding funnelled to the strategy and region.[132]

Irrespective of these disparities, the environmental aspects remained a key feature, originally establishing the first of four pillars. The SBSR is presented as four pillars for structural purposes only; their order or arrangement does not convey any independent meaning – on the contrary, the Commission encourages seeing the four pillars as entwined, emphasising the integrated and holistic nature of the SBSR.[133] Within these environmental concerns, the question of

---

motor,' an actor or institution that could cover all of the area in a joint attempt to mitigate the eutrophication issue. Nina Tynkkynen and others, 'The Governance of the Mitigation of the Baltic Sea Eutrophication: Exploring the Challenges of the Formal Governing System' (2014) AMBIO – A Journal of the Human Environment 43(1) <https://doi.org/10.1007/s13280-013-0481-8>, 108.

129 As defined by EO Eriksen and JE Fossum, 'Europe at a Crossroads – Government or Transnational Governance?' (2002) ARENA Working Papers 02/35 (University of Oslo, ARENA); Gänzle (n 125) 4.

130 The region has been characterised as being of 'hybrid nature,' so dense and variegated are the preceding governance initiatives in the area – even a rough listing of the apparatuses takes more than a page; Scott (n 121) 138–9.

131 Rikard Bengtsson, 'An EU Strategy for the Baltic Sea Region: Good Intentions Meet Complex Challenges' (2009) European Policy Analysis 9 1, 1–2. European Council 2007.

132 Gänzle (n 125) 1, 3.

133 The Strategy COM (2009) 248 final, 6.

nutrient runoff was the first; others deal with biodiversity protection, hazardous substances, clean shipping, and climate change mitigation and adaption.[134] The SBSR is accompanied by a list of priority areas. Of seventeen groups in total, two concern agriculture: the first regarding sustainable agriculture in general and the eleventh nutrient runoff to the sea.[135] Even though the order of the pillars is not decisive and the priority list is flexible and reviewed on a regular basis, the structure supports the claims that the position of agri-environmental causes in the SBSR is strong.[136] The SBSR has kept developing further when the Commission initiated distilling the SBSR's objectives into three in 2012: enhancing environmental quality, connectivity, and economic prosperity. To secure the progress mechanism, observation was introduced in the form of indicators and specified targets.[137] In other words, the already holistic SBSR was strengthened with a feedback loop enabling monitoring and learning from experience, showing glimpses of adaptivity.[138] The SBSR's Action Plan was also re-enacted, consisting now of thirteen policy areas and four horizontal actions in which the SBSR is to be fulfilled.[139] Even though the Commission still holds the pivotal role in the execution of the SBSR, Member States are given responsibility as co-ordinators of the policy areas and horizontal actions.[140] Of the three main objectives, the environmental 'Saving the Sea' is regarded as a prerequisite for achieving the other two. Thus tackling eutrophication is still in among the priorities of the SBSR: clearing the seawater is the first sub-objective of the environmental goals.[141]

134 The other three being economic prosperity, accessibility and attractiveness, and safety and security. Jonathan Metzger and Peter Schmitt, 'When Soft Spaces Harden: The EU Strategy for the Baltic Sea Region' (2012) Environment and Planning A 44(2) <https://doi.org/10.1068/a44188>, 272.

135 The Strategy COM (2009) 248 final, 3, 6–7 and the SBSR priority areas, 1, <http://ec.europa.eu/regional_policy/sources/cooperate/baltic/doc/priority_areas.pdf>.

136 Bengtsson (n 131) 3–4.

137 Commission, 'Communication from the Commission to the European Parliament, the Council, the European Economic and Social Committee and the Committee of the Regions Concerning the European Union Strategy for the Baltic Sea Region' COM (2012) 128 final, 3.

138 More closely examined in ch 3.

139 Commission, 'Commission Staff Working Document European Union Strategy For The Baltic Sea Region ACTION PLAN (The SBSR Action Plan)' SWD (2015) 177 final, 8. The previous action plans are from 2013 and 2009, respectively SEC (2009) 712/2 and SEC (2009) 712. All three go by the same title, being staff working documents to the original Commission communication of the SBSR. The broad range of areas of interest can also form an obstacle for the Strategy's efficient implementation, especially in the era of scarcer resources. Commission, 'Commission Staff Working Document Accompanying the Document Report from the Commission to the European Parliament, the Council, the European Economic and Social Committee and the Committee of the Regions on the Implementation of EU Macro-Regional Strategies (Staff Working Document [SWD] on the Implementation)' SWD (2016) 443 final, 16.

140 Responsibilities are listed in the SBSR Action Plan COM (2009) 248, 10–15. Apart from Member States other actors can also be coordinators. Ibid 8.

141 The SBSR Action Plan SWD (2015) 177 final, 35, 37, 41.

Close collaboration with the Helsinki Commission (HELCOM) is one of the mechanisms for achieving the environmental objectives.[142] The Helsinki Convention, with HELCOM as its secretariat, has sought to improve the ecosystem of the Baltic Sea from the 1970s, giving more than 200 recommendations to the riparian states. It has become an intergovernmental steering body on co-operation in environmental issues.[143] HELCOM's main objective is environmental: to protect, restore, and enhance the marine ecosystem that is notoriously fragile and polluted.[144] Even though the absence of sanctions in cases of non-conformity has resulted in debates over the efficacy of HELCOM's work, its significance as a regional network is generally accepted.[145] Regarding its scope and time, the merits of HELCOM are unquestionable: the Helsinki Convention was the first regional sea convention and, as such, set an example for others to follow. HELCOM represents intergovernmental tradition, partly due to its age: HELCOM was initiated during the strong East–West divide. It was a laboratory of environmental co-operation at a time when collaborative actions in the environmental field were not as common as they are nowadays and, perhaps, more importantly, co-operation in a region where attitudes towards environmental pollution have varied strongly, to the extent of forming two distinct groups. Eagerness to become a member of the EU facilitated the change toward a more coherent understanding, though differences can still be traced. Even after the enlargement of the EU, HELCOM's scope is its asset since it includes the region in its totality, including even Russia.[146]

Even though attitudes change more slowly than societal systems collapse, transnational governance and collaborative actions were better off after the end of the East–West divide, especially in the environmental and/or economic sectors. HELCOM's leading role in intergovernmental activities has more recently been enhanced by other environmental initiatives wishing to include private and non-governmental actors in the governance processes, to the extent that

142 The SBSR Action Plan SWD (2015) 177 final, 37.

143 Gänzle (n 125) 2. Even though they are non-binding, the recommendations are HELCOM's main policy tool. Accepted only unanimously, their range is broad, from scientific questions to regulatory ones. Stacy D Van Deveer, 'Networked Baltic Environmental Cooperation' (2011) Journal of Baltic Studies 42(1) <https://doi.org/10.1080/01629778.2011.538516>, 40, which also serves as a short summary of HELCOM, its working practice, and its place in the network of operators.

144 Kern (n 117) 26–7.

145 Tynkkynen and others (n 128) 109; Gänzle (n 125) 4–5.

146 Kern (n 117) 23, 25, 30. As with the others, the Baltic States and Poland were obliged to embrace *acquis communautaire* prior to their acceptance to the EU; adhering to regional planning and values it entails were part of it, Scott (n 121) 137. Being a major agriculture producer, Poland's admission to the EU was also regarded as an opportunity for the EU to improve its efforts with the eutrophication issue, scenarios varying according to the direction that Poland's agriculture would take after entering the EU. Markus Larsson and Artur Granstedt, 'Sustainable Governance of the Agriculture and the Baltic Sea — Agricultural Reforms, Food Production and Curbed Eutrophication' (2010) Ecol Econ 69(10) <https://doi.org/10.1016/j.ecolecon.2010.05.003>, 1945.

the Baltic region could be labelled as a laboratory for environmental governance.[147] The environmental collaboration appears in networks defined by theme, resulting in overlapping participation – one organisation can be and often is a member of multiple networks, each having its own distinct political influence. In the case of eutrophication, organisations aiming to tackle the issue do not form one single (regional or environmental) network but many. The aim of these organisations might be the same, but the way in which they interact in the development of normative or scientific data varies. This flux of influence and dense networks makes measuring their impact difficult. Even if development at the level of concrete matter occurs, attributing the development to the actions of particular organisations or networks is nearly impossible. This challenge has not gone unnoticed, and the role of implementation and efficacy has gained weight among the goals of the actors, as is also seen in the focus on monitoring and assessment in the renewed SBSR Action Plan.[148] As already noted, eutrophication is challenging to curb since nutrients compound on the seabed, and current measures might not have a visible impact for decades to come, making trajectories difficult to establish. To further complicate the matter, in the Baltic Sea region, the same applies to the institutional structure. Actors are so numerous that establishing causalities is a challenge – but perhaps there is no desire for such crediting either.

Adding Value Without Adding Input?

The multitude of actors and initiatives and the difficulty of establishing patterns of causality have prompted questions about the SBSR's rationale, especially due to its focus on agri-environmentality.[149] Being built on the three 'no's has sparked evaluations of whether the SBSR can bring any added value to the region. The three 'no's sum up the stance of the Commission, which accepted no new institutions, legislation, or instruments while initiating or implementing the SBSR.[150] The reasoning justifying the decision was the very networked nature of the Baltic region – a point acknowledged in the SBSR but with a comment that further co-ordination between sectoral policies is needed.[151] However, the EU lacks the competence to enhance co-operation. Since other goals might be better pursued in the works of HELCOM and other established

147 Coalition Clean Baltic, Union of the Baltic Cities, and Baltic Sea Action Group being some of them. Gänzle (n 125) 4–5; Kern (n 117) 23–4. An extensive even though still partial list of environmental initiatives in the area is in Table 1 of Van Deveer (n 143) 37.

148 Van Deveer (n 143) 38–9; The SBSR Action Plan COM (2009) 248, 3.

149 Bengtsson (n 131) 6.

150 Metzger and Schmitt (n 134) 272–3.

151 The Strategy COM (2009) 248 final, 6. The stance on the benefits of coordination and synergy is reconfirmed in the most recent evaluations of the Strategy, SWD on the Implementation SWD (2016) 443 final, 6.

players in the field, the added value from the SBSR is sometimes said to be limited.[152] This critique did not go unnoticed by the Commission, which in 2013 acknowledged the challenge of measuring the effectiveness of strategies and their implementation and, as noted, took efficacy under even closer scrutiny in the renewed SBSR Action Plan.[153] Thus, from the EU's perspective, due to the three 'no's, all value from the strategies – in the Baltic Sea region and elsewhere – is added value since no additional input is required. Successful parts of strategies could be replicated in other areas, and the existing strategies could be developed based on the lessons learned, an iterative process that the Commission has also diligently pursued.[154]

In its role as a facilitator, the SBSR's relation and benefit to other existing regional networks are of interest. HELCOM, the most relevant network eutrophication-wise, was considered not successful enough in finding support from all relevant sectors. This is due to HELCOM's notoriously environmentalist approach, which has caused the agriculture sector to shy away from its work. In the Commission's view, the SBSR has thrived better in this regard: the SBSR's cross-sectoral approach has proved successful and as such, the SBSR has added value to regional development.[155] In having the assessment of cross-border externalities better co-ordinated, the SBSR has brought about tactical benefits relating to agricultural runoff. The reasons for this are two-fold. First, not all riparian states are EU members and thus obliged to implement other EU legislation or policies. Second, due to the sensitivity of the issue, some riparian countries might want to proceed further than the EU legislation requires, action that the SBSR can facilitate.[156] However, there seems to be a slight discrepancy in the evaluations: some find HELCOM to be the actor better equipped for collaboration beyond the EU's borders in the Baltic region; others find that the SBSR is equally suitable for the task.

The question of added value does not stop with the questions of the differences and similarities between the different governance networks. From a broader view, value is added only if the SBSR can increase and empower existing actors and trigger them into better performance in their macroregional

152 Bengtsson (n 131) 6.

153 Commission, 'Report from the Commission to the European Parliament, the Council, the European Economic and Social Committee and the Committee of the Regions Concerning the Added Value of Macro-regional Strategies' COM (2013) 468 final. The Commission's reaction was an answer to the Council's reply in General Affairs Council Conclusions of 13 April 2011, point 20.

154 Between the years 2012–16 the Commission issued eight reports, communications, or related staff working documents on the SBSR, along with a vast amount of other publications.

155 Other strategic benefits were the ability to tackle issues shared in certain regions but not across the whole EU. Á Kelemen, 'Assessing the added value of macro-regional strategies – Environment Discussion paper,' 46, as is directly quoted by the Commission in COM (2013) 468 final, 6.

156 Kelemen (ibid) 45.

network(s).[157] Viewed from this definition, the Commission's evaluation of added value has been criticised for being overly positive and omitting issues relevant to the stakeholders. The Commission's reports on macroregional governance can reasonably be criticised as biased, assessments that ought to be categorised as internal evaluations; such a position is naturally deficient in objectivity.[158] In evaluating the success of the strategies, the Commission takes at least three roles: that of the contractor, the evaluator, and the one whose work is being evaluated. Even though the merging of roles to this extent might sound alarming, neither objectivity nor results are automatically endangered, as the report clarifies the concept of macroregional strategies and considers the stakeholders' perspectives. This is as far as the Commission's final report is concerned. The survey delivering background information to the reports had more fundamental flaws. The main question in it was normative to the extent that it enquired after the added value the strategies had contributed. The question setting was thus leading in its encouragement of affirmative answers and positive feedback. [159]

Even though the evaluation absolved the Commission's reports, the criticism brings up important questions about the SBSR.[160] The macroregional strategies ought to represent collaborative governance. Criticising such an endeavour of not considering the stakeholders' views or attempting to pose leading questions when being heard are findings from the scale's rough end. The collaborative multilevel governance of a macroregion with water quality as *ratio moderatio* is not the most straightforward version of collaborative governance in the first place: it can be 'messy, elaborate, cumbersome, ad hoc and defiantly unconventional,' with various challenges ranging from institutional to participatory and beyond.[161] The problems encountered in the SBSR and its assessments are far from unique: fine-tuning the collaborative process to better answer the stakeholders' needs is also a challenge in similar projects. At worst, the concept 'stakeholder' has been evaluated as tentatively conceiving and enabling system abuse, when in the worst-case scenario, the collaborative

157 As defined in Stefan Gänzle and Kristine Kern, '"Macro-regional cooperation" as a New Form of European Governance: The European Union's Strategies for the Baltic Sea and the Danube Region' (Conference on the EU Strategy for the Danube Region: Challenges and Chances 2014–2020 2015) 13, 18.

158 Commission, 'Report from the Commission to the European Parliament, to the Council, the European Economic and Social Committee and the Committee of the Regions Concerning the Governance of Macro-Regional Strategies' COM (2014) 284 final.

159 Katja Vonhoff and Franziska Sielk, 'The European Commission's evaluation of macro-regional strategies: An academic assessment' (Conference on the EU Strategy for the Danube Region: Challenges and Chances 2014–2020 2015) 39, 39–40, 43, 46.

160 Vonhoff and Sielk (ibid) 46.

161 Bradley C Karkkainen, 'Collaborative Ecosystem Governance: Scale, Complexity, and Dynamism' (2002) Virginia Environmental Law Journal 21 189, 234–5.

process consists of superficially listening to all possible interest groups and then proceeding with already-decided plans.[162]

Fortunately, in the case of the SBSR, awareness had risen and critique apparently been heard when in the most recent action plan, the SBSR's governance was moulded anew. In discussions over the concept of added value, the Council had emphasised that honest stakeholder participation serves as a prerequisite for the SBSR's success, prompting the revision.[163] During the revision process, the desire was to increase the stakeholders' ownership of the SBSR by granting leadership positions to the Member States and other participants.[164] The political leadership ought to be in the hands of the Member States, and the Commission ought to handle only the strategic co-ordination and monitoring of the SBSR.[165] The governance structure also includes national co-ordinators, who form a group whose leadership rotates biannually.[166] Structural changes ought to fortify the SBSR in meeting the expectations laid down for it: according to strong views, the added value of the SBSR should not only be apparent, but it should have already been delivered. Especially when remembering the temporal realities of addressing eutrophication, the expectations are, if not excessive, at least hasty, and having a better-justified governance structure enables the achievement of the SBSR's long-term goals.[167] The Commission, as the main co-ordinator, also acknowledges the need to relocate focus from processes to substance. Instead of streamlining the governance structure, attention will be paid to achieving the substantive objectives of the SBSR, a policy line that ought to eventually amplify the SBSR's value.[168]

162 Karkkainen (ibid) 237–43.

163 Council, 'Council conclusions on added value of macro-regional strategies. GENERAL AFFAIRS Council meeting Luxembourg' 22 October 2013, 3.

164 SWD on the Implementation SWD (2016) 443 final, 10, and Commission, 'Report from the Commission to the European Parliament, the Council, the European Economic and Social Committee and the Committee of the Regions on the Implementation of EU Macro-Regional Strategies (Commission on the Implementation)' COM (2016) 805 final, 6.

165 EUSBSR National Contact Points: Non paper on EUSBSR governance FINAL-2014-2-12, Guiding Principles.

166 Also each policy area and horizontal action has its own co-ordinators, the SBSR Action Plan SWD (2015) 177 final, 12–14 and EUSBSR National Contact Points: Non paper on EUSBSR governance FINAL-2014-2-12, Elements of Governance.

167 SWD on the Implementation SWD (2016) 443 final, 10.

168 Commission on the Implementation COM (2016) 805 final, 6; SWD on the Implementation SWD (2016) 443 final, 18. This is not to say that governance structure would not be further developed, Commission on the Implementation COM (2016) 805 final, 11; Andreas Faludi, 'Beyond Lisbon: Soft European Spatial Planning' (2010) disP – The Planning Review 46(182) <https://doi.org/10.1080/02513625.2010.10557098>, 14.

Spongy Governance, Centralised Power?

The SBSR exemplifies the EU's attempt to regionalise strategic planning.[169] The SBSR ought to bring results effectively and add value, but spatial planning is a sovereign right of Member States. What role does the SBSR play in this, and how is national spatial planning comprehended in the SBSR? During the drafting process, the SBSR was also discussed in a meeting of the spatial planning and regional development ministers in 2007, resulting in the Leipzig Agenda. The Agenda lingered over questions of polycentralised governance more than agri-environmental issues (that later dominated the SBSR), even though general notes on sustainable management and urban–rural collaboration were also presented.[170] Even though the SBSR evolved into something more, the spatial planning aspects were not discarded in the development.

In the case of the SBSR, defining the outcome is difficult when the activity itself defies definition. Instead of regional or national spatial planning, the SBSR exemplifies so-called 'soft spaces' of spatial planning in its flexibility and collaborativity. In the SBSR, multiple actors from various levels of governance are gathered into 'a quasi-formalized and territorially fuzzy transnational policy setting.'[171] 'Soft' planning refers to spatial governance taking place elsewhere from or alongside formal and more structured planning; in the case of the EU, planning done in nation-states constitutes the formal aspect. Fuzziness can be a deliberate tactic, but it can also come about due to a lack of natural, geographic, or territorial boundaries, such as water catchment areas, as is the case in the SBSR.[172] Fuzziness and flexibility have not gone unrecognised in this region, where developments after the collapse of the Soviet Union divide have been rapid and numerous, to the extent that there was a leadership deficit for decades.[173] The Baltic Sea region also demonstrates the growing interest in

169 Rasmus Kløcker Larsen and Neil Powell, 'Making Sense of Accountability in Baltic Agro-Environmental Governance: The Case of Denmark's Green Growth Strategy' (2013) Social and Environmental Accountability Journal 33(2) <http://dx.doi.org/10.1080/0969160X.2012.743276>, 72.

170 Territorial Agenda of the European Union (2007) fn 138, points 3, 5.

171 Phil Allmendinger and Graham Haughton, 'Soft Spaces, Fuzzy Boundaries, and Metagovernance: The New Spatial Planning in the Thames Gateway' (2009) Environment and Planning A 41(3) <https://doi.org/10.1068/a40208>, 621–2; Metzger and Schmitt (n 134) 275. The latter work is rooted on the ideas of multilevel governance and multilevel metagovernance as presented by Jessop in 'Multi-level governance and multi-level meta-governance', in I Bache and M Flinders (eds), *Multi-Level Governance* (OUP 2004) 49–74.

172 Graham Haughton, Phil Allmendinger, and Stijn Oosterlynck, 'Spaces of Neoliberal Experimentation: Soft Spaces, Postpolitics, and Neoliberal Governmentality' (2013) Environment and Planning A 45(1) <https://doi.org/10.1068/a45121>, 218. The authors see 'soft' spatial planning as a form of neoliberal governance in which the quasi-state apparatuses and emphasis on self-management of actors have institutionalised the neoliberal paradigm and made *politic proper* in the Rancièrian sense impossible. Ibid 231–2.

173 Metzger and Schmitt (n 134) 263, 270, 275.

region-building processes crossing existing borders, beginning with abstract plans and concretising on the way to political or governmental action – all this at the same time that 'region' itself remains a vague concept adapted to serve the needs of diverse projects of diverse scales and diverse political aims.[174] Due to the lack of leadership, fuzziness is not a deliberate tactic but rather a state of affairs caused by the natural boundaries of the region and the political reality in the littoral states. The fuzziness makes it impossible to measure outcomes: 'establishing a counterfactual scenario' is a challenge when the SBSR is as flexible and blurry as it is.[175] Originally, demands for democracy and regionalised decision-making justified territorial cohesion policy.[176]

Pleading fuzziness has not hindered the presentation of stern assessments, nor claims that the policy has only strengthened the Commission's role in the Baltic Sea region and it has not *de facto* redistributed power to the regions. This interpretation draws on the understanding, in itself correct, that since previous collaborations in the area were soft and adjustable, 'regionalisation' inevitably forges this spongy reality into a more robust and better-organised one, a process in which some actors strengthen their positions. In these critical remarks, it is posited that this reinforced actor is the Commission.[177] This reading of the situation is based on the idea that previous developments in the region were 'distinctly multiple and fuzzy in the numerous – sometimes overlapping, sometimes conflicting – strategies, visions, programmes, and projects of the plethora of groupings and actors engaged in articulating a Baltic Sea Region.'[178] Even though the SBSR and its drafting aimed to be as inclusive and discursive as possible, the attempt was futile since power never left the Commission's headquarters. The Commission holds the metagovernor's role in its obligation to govern the governance while filling the gaps created when the three 'no's commanded absence of new institutions at the dawn of the SBSR. The Commission is seen as having taken this role even while initiating the SBSR, positing itself as convenor and legitimate spokesperson.[179] If the analysis is correct and the Commission's role in the Baltic region overtly emphasised, the development has not been found excessive or intimidating in the non-member

174 Martin Jones and Anssi Paasi, 'Guest Editorial: Regional World(s): Advancing the Geography of Regions' (2013) Reg Stud 47(1) <http://dx.doi.org/10.1080/00343404.2013.746437>, 2.

175 Kelemen (n 155) 46.

176 This has remained intact: macroregional strategies are still regarded as elementary in forging the EU's future. Commission on the Implementation COM (2016) 805 final, 11.

177 Metzger and Schmitt (n 134) 269–70. The concept of a 'territorial spokesperson' comes from actor-network theory's father Bruno Latour, *Reassembling the Social: An Introduction to Actor-Network-Theory* (OUP 2005).

178 Metzger and Schmitt (n 134) 271.

179 Metzger and Schmitt (n 134) 272, 274–5.

parts of the region; these features have not caused the non-member littoral states to object.[180]

However, this analysis also has its shortcomings, partially admitted by the authors: multi-actor and multifunctional regional collaboration is work in constant flux that cannot be dismantled entirely. The development might seem to go in one direction, but the movement is not fixed or determined and thus is a challenge to evaluate or predict.[181] Also, the critique relies on the fact that the Commission initiated the SBSR in the first place.[182] Bearing in mind the Commission's role as the executive of the EU, established in the treaties, the Commission employing its powers hardly constitutes an abuse of power. The criticism may be well justified from other points of view, but the justification the constitutional aspects deliver remains intact. In other words, deciphering counterfactual scenarios is a tedious undertaking – the EU is bound to its treaties and the process order detailed in them. Critique can, however, be heard, which to some extent was done when the governance structure of the SBSR was amended. The Member States and also other stakeholders hold more political and co-ordinating power, and even though employed in close co-operation with the Commission, steps towards regionalised leadership and co-ordination have at least been taken.[183]

Benefits of the Interactionist Perspective

Even when the SBSR does not allow for new institutions or legislation, it is nonetheless new governance, and as such, questions of accountability are justified. As noted above, multilevel and multifunctional governance is at risk of being vague or equivocal, but even then, accountability can be established as a 'master value' securing the legitimacy of the governance actions taken.[184] The macroregional sphere only requires a redefinition of accountability: due to the vast number of parties involved, accountability is seen as more of a work in progress, a continuous process between different actors, existing in their discussions and exchanges and being itself also subject to constant change. Accountability is comprehended as part of this unending process of various actors and acts, not as a dipstick used to evaluate the process.[185] Such accountability comes in

180 This is unlike the reaction to the EU's efforts to strengthen its influence in the Arctic region – a reality presumably explained by the Baltic Sea's position as the EU's internal sea. Diana Wallis and Stewart Arnold, 'Governing Common Seas: From a Baltic Strategy to an Arctic Policy' (2011) Journal of Baltic Studies 42(1) <https://doi.org/10.1080/01629778.2011.538514>, 106.
181 Metzger and Schmitt (n 134) 277.
182 Metzger and Schmitt (n 134) 275.
183 The SBSR Action Plan SWD (2015) 177 final, 12, point 5.
184 Larsen and Powell (n 169) 72, 75.
185 This understanding of accountability differs from a strictly legal understanding of accountability or normative responsibility, readily admitted by the authors, Larsen and Powell (n 169) 75–6.

three forms when agricultural runoff and the Baltic Sea are considered. The model created with the WFD, examined in the following chapters, exemplifies a reductionist perspective in which ecological problems are isolated from socio-economic ones and regulated by focusing on the ecological or biological characteristics of the matter.[186] HELCOM's Baltic Sea Action Plans fit in with the holistic and expert systems' perspective that emphasises intersectoral collaboration in which previously distant parts of the whole are brought to the same table – or in the case of HELCOM, to the same governance device. Developing from this, the SBSR is representative of an *interactionist* perspective: it is acknowledged that in the agricultural runoff dilemma, multiple and contradictory interests are at stake, and the SBSR is a balancing tool amongst them. The SBSR is about co-operation between different actors and their values, not merely about enhancing scientific knowledge (which, as noted, can lead to the knowledge gained having an unnecessarily adverse impact on certain stakeholders).[187]

The SBSR has proven its value in the laboratory of governance called the Baltic Sea region. It suffers from the same faults of being cumbersome and muddy as most collaborative water governance initiatives, but it also has indisputable benefits on its side. For the questions posed in this volume, the most interesting aspect of the SBSR is how the EU has conjured a governance instrument that, for all its fuzziness, circumvents the pitfall of excluding some stakeholders. With more than one nucleus, the SBSR has managed to accommodate the needs of various sets of stakeholders. By doing so, the EU regulator deserves the epithet 'candid regulator.' In the next chapters, further steps towards governance are taken when adaptive management and regulation embracing it in the EU come into view. Could its implementation in the EU bring benefits to areas that are not in the scope of the SBSR and govern the complexities of agricultural runoff so that effectiveness is secured as well? In what follows, in Chapter 3, an approach called adaptive management is first deconstructed and described, revolving around the components that are of interest to law and regulation. Thereafter, in Chapter 4, this rather scientific analysis, drawing heavily on the findings of natural resource management studies, is continued with a legal doctrinal examination of EU water governance and its possibilities to accommodate adaptivity in general or some of its components in particular. These considerations are then reflected in a jurisprudential

186 This is regardless of what the underpinning scientific theory of the WFD would prefer; see ch 3.

187 Larsen and Powell (n 169) 77–9; on how not all stakeholders readily embrace HELCOM's work, see text at n 174. Interestingly, in Denmark, a joined strategy was initiated to meet the water quality obligations under the WFD, the Nitrates Directive, and the Baltic Sea Action Plans. The rationale was to combine all plans of curbing nutrient run-off from fields to waters into one instrument. The governance model adapted in the Strategy ended up on the losing side in the negotiations; the focus on scientific knowledge triumphed in its collaborative approach. Ibid Larsen and Powell 73, 84, 87.

setting in the penultimate Chapter 5, and in the concluding Chapter 6, I return to the instruments discussed thus far – the ND, the CAP, and the SBSR – for a hopefully comprehensive analysis.

Bibliography

Adams G, Rausser G and Simon L, 'Modelling Multilateral Negotiations: An Application to California Water Policy' (1996) 30(1) Journal of Economic Behavior & Organization 97 <https://doi.org/10.1016/S0167-2681(96)00844-X>.

Allmendinger P and Haughton G, 'Soft Spaces, Fuzzy Boundaries, and Metagovernance: The New Spatial Planning in the Thames Gateway' (2009) 41(3) Environment and Planning A 617 <https://doi.org/10.1068/a40208>.

Baaner L and Tegner Anker H, *Danish Law on Controlling Emissions of Nutrients in the Baltic Sea Region* (Baltic Sea Centre 2013) <http://www.su.se/ostersjocentrum/english/beam/legal-aspects-of-the-ecosystem-approach/country-studies>.

Bengtsson R, 'An EU Strategy for the Baltic Sea Region: Good Intentions Meet Complex Challenges' (2009) 9 European Policy Analysis 1, 1–2. European Council 2007.

Boyle S, 'The Case for Regulation of Agricultural Water Pollution' (2014) 16(1) Environmental Law Review 4.

Buckwell A, 'Where Should the CAP Go Post-2020?' in Swinnen J (ed), *The Political Economy of the 2014–2020 Common Agricultural Policy: An Imperfect Storm* (Centre for European Policy Studies 2015).

Bureau J-C and Mahé L-P, 'Was the CAP Reform a Success?' in Swinnen JFM (ed), *The Political Economy of the 2014–2020 Common Agricultural Policy: An Imperfect Storm* (Centre for European Policy Studies 2015).

Collins AL and McGonigle DF, 'Monitoring and Modelling Diffuse Pollution from Agriculture for Policy Support: UK and European Experience' (2008) 11(2) Environ Sci & Policy 97 <https://doi.org/10.1016/j.envsci.2008.01.001>.

Cunha A and Alan Swinbank A, *An Inside View of the CAP Reform Process: Explaining the MacSharry, Agenda 2000, and Fischler Reforms* (Oxford University Press 2011).

Dubois A and others, *EU Macro-Regions and Macro-Regional Strategies – A Scoping Study* (Nordregio 2009).

Eriksen EO and Fossum JE, 'Europe at a Crossroads – Government or Transnational Governance?' (2002) ARENA Working Papers 02/35 (University of Oslo, ARENA).

Erjavec K and Erjavec E, 'Changing EU Agricultural Policy Discourses? The Discourse Analysis of Commissioner's Speeches 2000–2007' (2009) 34(2) Food Policy 218 <https://doi.org/10.1016/j.foodpol.2008.10.009>.

Erjavec K and Erjavec E, "Greening the CAP' – Just a Fashionable Justification? A Discourse Analysis of the 2014–2020 CAP Reform Documents' (2015) 51 Food Policy 53 <https://doi.org/10.1016/j.foodpol.2014.12.006>.

Erjavec E, Lovec M and Erjavec K, 'From 'Greening' to 'Greenwash': Drivers and Discourses of the CAP 2020 'Reform'' in Swinnen J (ed), *The Political Economy of the 2014–2020 Common Agricultural Policy: An Imperfect Storm* (Centre for European Policy Studies 2015).

Faludi A, 'Beyond Lisbon: Soft European Spatial Planning' (2010) 46(182) disP – The Planning Review 14 <https://doi.org/10.1080/02513625.2010.10557098>.

——— 'Multi-Level (Territorial) Governance: Three Criticisms' (2012) 13(2) Planning Theory & Practice 197 <https://doi.org/10.1080/14649357.2012.677578>.

Gänzle S, 'Introduction: Transnational Governance and Policy-Making in the Baltic Sea Region' (2011) 42(1) Journal of Baltic Studies 1 <https://doi.org/10.1080/01629778.2011.538509>.

——— and Kern K, "Macro-Regional Cooperation' as a New Form of European Governance: The European Union's Strategies for the Baltic Sea and the Danube Region' (Conference on the EU Strategy for the Danube Region: Challenges and Chances 2014–2020 2015).

——— and Kern K, 'Macro-Region, 'Macro-regionalization' and Macro-Regional Strategies in the European Union: Towards a New Form of European Governance?' in Gänzle S and Kern K (eds), *A 'Macro-Regional' Europe in the Making: Theoretical Approaches and Empirical Evidence* (Palgrave Macmillan 2016).

Garzon I, *Reforming the Common Agricultural Policy: History of a Paradigm Change* (Palgrave Studies in European Union Politics, Palgrave Macmillan 2006).

Giovanni Anania G and D'andrea MRP, 'The 2013 Reform of the Common Agricultural Policy' in Swinnen J (ed), *The Political Economy of the 2014–2020 Common Agricultural Policy: An Imperfect Storm* (Centre for European Policy Studies 2015).

Greer A, *Agricultural Policy in Europe* (Manchester University Press 2005).

Gunningham N and Sinclair D, 'Policy Instrument Choice and Diffuse Source Pollution' (2005) 17(1) JEL 51 <https://doi.org/10.1093/envlaw/eqi003>.

Häberli C, 'The Story of Community Preference for Food Security' in McMahon JA and Cardwell MN (eds), *Research Handbook on EU Agriculture Law* (1st edn, Edward Elgar Publishing Ltd. 2015).

Hart K, 'The Fate of Green Direct Payments in the CAP Reform Negotiations' in Swinnen J (ed), *The Political Economy of the 2014–2020 Common Agricultural Policy: An Imperfect Storm* (Centre for European Political Studies 2015).

Harvey D, 'What does the History of the Common Agricultural Policy tell us?' in McMahon JA and Cardwell MN (eds), *Research Handbook on EU Agriculture Law* (1st edn, Edward Elgar Publishing 2015).

Haughton G, Allmendinger P and Oosterlynck S, 'Spaces of Neoliberal Experimentation: Soft Spaces, Postpolitics, and Neoliberal Governmentality' (2013) 45(1) Environment and Planning A 217 <https://doi.org/10.1068/a45121>.

Heyl K and others, 'The Common Agricultural Policy Beyond 2020: A Critical Review in Light of Global Environmental Goals' (2021) 30(1) RECIEL 95 <https://doi.org/10.1111/reel.12351>.

Howarth W, 'Accommodation without Resolution? Emission Controls and Environmental Quality Objectives in the Proposed EC Water Framework Directive' (1999) 1(1) Environmental Law Review 6 <https://doi.org/10.1177/146145299900100103>.

——— 'The Progression Towards Ecological Quality Standards' (2006) 18(1) JEL 3 <https://doi.org/10.1093/jel/eqi049>.

——— 'Diffuse Water Pollution and Diffuse Environmental Laws' (2011) 23(1) Journal of Environmental Law 129 <https://doi.org/10.1093/jel/eqq031>.

Hristov J and others, 'Impacts of the EU's Common Agricultural Policy "Greening" Reform on Agricultural Development, Biodiversity, and Ecosystem Services' (2020) 42(4) Applied Economic Perspectives and Policy 716 <https://doi.org/10.1002/aepp.13037>.

Iagatti M and Sorrentino A, 'La path dependency nel processo di riforma della PAC' (2007) 3(9) Agriregionieuropa 50.

Jack B, 'Member State Responsibilities Concerning Nitrate Pollution and Eutrophication: A Role for the Waste Framework Directive?' (2006) 18(2) JEL 301 <https://doi.org/10.1093/jel/eql001>.

Jessop B, 'Multi-Level Governance and Multi-Level Meta-Governance', in Bache I and Flinders M (eds), *Multi-Level Governance* (OUP 2004).

Jones M and Paasi A, 'Guest Editorial: Regional World(s): Advancing the Geography of Regions' (2013) 47(1) Reg Stud 1 <http://doi.org/10.1080/00343404.2013.746437>.

Josling T, 'External Influences on CAP Reforms: An Historical Perspective' in Swinnen JFM (ed), *The Perfect Storm: The Political Economy of the Fischler Reforms of the Common Agricultural Policy* (CEPS 2008).

Kaiser T, 'The Added Value of the Integrated Approach: The Case of Hungary' (Conference on the EU Strategy for the Danube Region: Challenges and Chances 2014–2020 2015).

Karkkainen BC, 'Collaborative Ecosystem Governance: Scale, Complexity, and Dynamism' (2002) 21 Virginia Environmental Law Journal 189.

Kauppila J, *Vesienhoitosuunnitelman oikeudellisen vaikuttavuuden rakentuminen* [*The Legal Effectiveness of the River Basin Management Plan*] (University of Eastern Finland 2016) <http://urn.fi/URN:ISBN:978-952-61-2309-7>.

Keessen AM and others, 'The Need for Flexibility and Differentiation in the Protection of Vulnerable Areas in EU Environmental Law: The Implementation of the Nitrates Directive in the Netherlands' (2011) 8(2) JEEPL 141 <https://doi.org/10.1163/187601011X576205>.

Kelemen Á, 'Assessing the Added Value of Macro-Regional Strategies – Environment Discussion paper', 46, as is directly quoted by Commission in COM (2013) 468 final, 6.

Kern K, 'Governance for Sustainable Development in the Baltic Sea Region' (2011) 42(1) Journal of Baltic Studies 21 <https://doi.org/10.1080/01629778.2011.538517>.

Lankoski J and Ollikainen M, 'Counterfactual Approach for Assessing Agri-Environmental Policy: Theory with an Application to Finnish Water Protection Policy' (2011) (56) University of Helsinki, Department of Economics and Management Discussion Papers.

Larsen RK and Powell N, 'Making Sense of Accountability in Baltic Agro-Environmental Governance: The Case of Denmark's Green Growth Strategy' (2013) 33(2) Social and Environmental Accountability Journal 71, 72, <http://doi.org/10.1080/0969160X.2012.743276>.

Larsson M and Granstedt A, 'Sustainable Governance of the Agriculture and the Baltic Sea — Agricultural Reforms, Food Production and Curbed Eutrophication' (2010) 69(10) Ecol Econ 1943 <https://doi.org/10.1016/j.ecolecon.2010.05.003>.

Latacz-Lohmann U and Hodge I, 'European Agri-Environmental Policy for the 21st Century' (2003) 47(1) Aust J Agric Resour Econ 123 <https://doi.org/10.1111/1467-8489.00206>.

Latour B, *Reassembling the Social: An Introduction to Actor-Network-Theory* (OUP 2005).

Matthews A, 'Greening Agricultural Payments in the EU's Common Agricultural Policy' (2013) 2(1) Bio-Based and Applied Economics 1 <https://doi.org/10.22004/ag.econ.149214>.

——— 'Reflections on the CAP Post-2014' in Swinnen J (ed), *The Political Economy of the 2014–2020 Common Agricultural Policy: An Imperfect Storm* (Centre for European Policy Studies 2015).

Metzger J and Schmitt P, 'When Soft Spaces Harden: The EU Strategy for the Baltic Sea Region' (2012) 44(2) Environment and Planning A 263 <https://doi.org/10.1068/a44188>.

Moehler R, 'The Internal and External Forces Driving Cap Reforms' in Swinnen JFM (ed), *The Perfect Storm: The Political Economy of the Fischler Reforms of the Common Agricultural Policy* (Centre for European Policy Studies 2008).

Monteduro M, 'Environmental Law and Agroecology. Transdisciplinary Approach to Public Ecosystem Services as a New Challenge for Environmental Legal Doctrine' (2013) 22(1) European Energy and Environmental Law Review 2.

Nedergaard P, 'The 2003 Reform of the Common Agricultural Policy: Against all Odds or Rational Explanations?' (2006) 28(3) Journal of European Integration 203 <https://doi.org/10.1080/07036330600785749>.

O'Connor B, 'The Impact of the Doha Round on the European Union's Common Agricultural Policy' in McMahon JA and Cardwell MN (eds), *Research Handbook on EU Agriculture Law* (1st edn, Edward Elgar Publishing Ltd. 2015).

Olper A, 'Constraints and Causes of the 2003 EU Agricultural Policy Reforms' in Swinnen JFM (ed), *The Perfect Storm: The Political Economy of the Fischler Reforms of the Common Agricultural Policy* (Centre for European Policy Studies 2008).

Othengrafen F and Cornett AP, 'A Critical Assessment of the Added Value of Territorial Cohesion' (2013) European Journal of Spatial Development <https://doi.org/10.15488/1851>.

Pe'er G and others, 'Action Needed for the EU Common Agricultural Policy to Address Sustainability Challenges' (2020) 2(2) People and Nature 305 <https://doi.org/10.1002/pan3.10080>.

Pokrivcak J, Crombez C and Swinnen JFW, 'Impact of External Changes and the European Commission on Cap Reforms: Insights from Theory' in Swinnen JFM (ed), *The Perfect Storm: The Political Economy of the Fischler Reforms of the Common Agricultural Policy* (Centre for European Policy Studies 2008).

Putnam RD, 'Diplomacy and Domestic Politics: The Logic of Two-Level Games' (1988) 42(3) International Organization 427 <https://doi.org/10.1017/S0020818300027697>.

Roederer-Rynning C, 'COMAGRI and the 'CAP after 2013' Reform: In Search of a Collective Sense of Purpose' in Swinnen J (ed), *The Political Economy of the 2014–2020 Common Agricultural Policy: An Imperfect Storm* (Centre for European Policy Studies 2015).

Rutz C, Dwyer J and Schramek J, 'More New Wine in the Same Old Bottles? The Evolving Nature of the CAP Reform Debate in Europe, and Prospects for the Future' (2014) 54(3) Sociologia Ruralis 266 <https://doi.org/10.1111/soru.12033>.

Scott J, 'Cross-Border Governance in the Baltic Sea Region' (2002) 12(4) Regional & Federal Studies 135 <https://doi.org/10.1080/714004777>.

Swinbank A, 'The WTO: No Longer Relevant for CAP Reform?' in Swinnen J (ed), *The Political Economy of the 2014–2020 Common Agricultural Policy: An Imperfect Storm* (Centre for European Policy Studies 2015).

Swinbank A and Daugbjerg C, 'The 2003 CAP Reform: Accommodating WTO Pressures' (2006) 4(1) Comp Eur Polit 47 <https://doi.org/10.1057/palgrave.cep.6110069>.

Swinnen J, 'The Political Economy of the 2014–2020 Common Agricultural Policy: Introduction and Key Conclusions' in Swinnen J (ed), *The Political Economy of the 2014–2020 Common Agricultural Policy: An Imperfect Storm* (Centre for European Policy Studies 2015).

Tegner Anker H, 'Agricultural Nitrate Pollution – Regulatory Approaches in the EU and Denmark' (2015) 2 NMT 7.

Tynkkynen N and others, 'The Governance of the Mitigation of the Baltic Sea Eutrophication: Exploring the Challenges of the Formal Governing System' (2014) 43(1) AMBIO - A Journal of the Human Environment 105 <https://doi.org/10.1007/s13280-013-0481-8>.

VanDeveer SD, 'Networked Baltic Environmental Cooperation' (2011) 42(1) Journal of Baltic Studies 37 <https://doi.org/10.1080/01629778.2011.538516>.
Vonhoff K and Sielk F, 'The European Commission's Evaluation of Macro-Regional Strategies: An Academic Assessment' (Conference on the EU Strategy for the Danube Region: Challenges and Chances 2014–2020 2015).
Wallis D and Arnold S, 'Governing Common Seas: From a Baltic Strategy to an Arctic Policy' (2011) 42(1) Journal of Baltic Studies 103 <https://doi.org/10.1080/01629778.2011.538514>.

ECJ Case Law

Case C-416/02 *Commission v Spain* [2005] ECLI:EU:C:2005:511.
Case C-322/00 *Commission v Netherlands* [2003] ECLI:EU:C:2003:532.

Secondary EU Legislation

Regulation 1303/2013 Laying Down Common Provisions on the European Regional Development Fund, the European Social Fund, the Cohesion Fund, the European Agricultural Fund for Rural Development and the European Maritime and Fisheries Fund and Laying Down General Provisions on the European Regional Development Fund, the European Social Fund, the Cohesion Fund and the European Maritime and Fisheries Fund and repealing Council Regulation (EC) No 1083/2006 [2013] OJ L 347/320.
Directive 2000/60/EC of 23 October 2000 Establishing a Framework for Community Action in the Field of Water Policy [2000] OJ L327/1.
The Council Directive 91/676/EEC Concerning the Protection of Waters against Pollution Caused by Nitrates from Agricultural Sources [1991] OJ L375.
Council Regulation (EEC) 797/85 on Improving the Efficiency of Agricultural Structures [1985] OJ L 93/1.

European Council

Council, 'Council Conclusions on Added Value of Macro-Regional Strategies GENERAL AFFAIRS Council Meeting Luxembourg' (22 October 2013).
European Council 'Presidency Conclusions of the Brussels European Council' (2009) 15265/1/09 REV 1.

Communications, Reports, Decisions and Staff Working Documents

Commission, 'Report from the Commission to the European Parliament, the Council, the European Economic and Social Committee and the Committee of the Regions on the Implementation of EU Macro-regional Strategies (Commission on the Implementation)' COM (2016) 805 final.
Commission, 'Commission Staff Working Document Accompanying the Document Report from the Commission to the European Parliament, the Council, the

European Economic and Social Committee and the Committee of the Regions on the Implementation of EU Macro-regional Strategies (SWD on the Implementation)' SWD (2016) 443 final.

Commission, 'Commission Staff Working Document European Union Strategy for the Baltic Sea Region ACTION PLAN (The SBSR Action Plan)' SWD (2015) 177 final.

Commission, 'Report from the Commission to the European Parliament, to the Council, the European Economic and Social Committee and the Committee of the Regions Concerning the Governance of Macro-regional Strategies' COM (2014) 284 final.

Commission, 'Report from the Commission to the European Parliament, the Council, the European Economic and Social Committee and the Committee of the Regions Concerning the Added Value of Macro-regional Strategies' COM (2013) 468 final.

Commission, 'Communication from the Commission to the European Parliament, the Council, the European Economic and Social Committee and the Committee of the Regions Concerning the European Union Strategy for the Baltic Sea Region' COM (2012) 128 final.

Commission, 'Commission Staff Working Document European Union Strategy for the Baltic Sea Region ACTION PLAN' SEC (2009) 712/2.

Commission, 'Communication from the Commission to the European Parliament, the Council, the European Economic and Social Committee and the Committee of the Regions Concerning the European Union Strategy for the Baltic Sea Region (the Strategy)' COM (2009) 248 final.

Commission, 'Communication from the Commission to the Council, the European Parliament, the Committee of the Regions and the European Economic and Social Committee Green Paper on Territorial Cohesion Turning Territorial Diversity into Strength' COM (2008) 616 final.

Commission, 'Communication from the Commission to the European Parliament and the Council – Preparing for the 'Health Check' of the CAP Reform' COM(2007) 722.

Other EU Sources

EU Commission, 'The Nitrates Directive' <http://ec.europa.eu/environment/water/water-nitrates/index_en.html>.

EUSBSR National Contact Points: Non Paper on EUSBSR Governance FINAL-2014-2-12, Guiding Principles.

EUSBSR National Contact Points: Non Paper on EUSBSR Governance FINAL-2014-2-12, Elements of Governance.

Territorial Agenda of the European Union (2007) Agreed on the occasion of the Informal Ministerial Meeting on Urban Development and Territorial Cohesion in Leipzig on 24–25 May 2007.

Finnish Legislation

Constitution of Finland (perustuslaki) 731/1999, Legally Non-Binding English translation <http://www.finlex.fi/en/laki/kaannokset/1999/en19990731.pdf>.

Environmental Protection Act (ympäristönsuojelulaki) 1096/1996, Since 2011 not Updated and Legally Non-Binding English translation <http://www.finlex.fi/fi/laki/kaannokset/1996/en19961096>.

Water Act (vesilaki) 264/1961, Legally Non-Binding English translation <https://www.fi/en/laki/kaannokset/2011/en20110587>.

Nitrates Decree (Valtioneuvoston päätös maataloudesta peräisin olevien nitraattien vesiin pääsyn rajoittamisesta) 219/1998.

Government Decree on Limiting Certain Emissions from Agriculture and Horticulture 1250/2014 (Valtioneuvoston asetus eräiden maa- ja puutarhataloudesta peräisin olevien päästöjen rajoittamisesta), legally non-binding English translation <http://www.finlex.fi/en/laki/kaannokset/2014/en20141250.pdf>.

Government Decree on the Restriction of Discharge of Nitrates from Agriculture into Waters (Valtioneuvoston asetus maataloudesta peräisin olevien nitraattien vesiin pääsyn rajoittamisesta) 931/2000.

Preparatory Documents

The Nitrates Decree Memorandum, 18 December 2014 (Ministry of the Environment).

Other Sources

The Opinion of the Finnish Association for Nature Conservation (30 September 2015).

The Opinion of the Finnish Association for Nature Conservation (3 June 2014).

Chapter 3

Adapting (to) the Management

Introduction

From the point of view of the regulation under examination, the complexity of ecological and social systems might appear paralysing. In the actions of the European Union regulator, the complexity of the agricultural runoff dilemma has inspired various reactions. In the Nitrates Directive, the regulator opted for a straightforward solution; in the Common Agricultural Policy, it has been slow to act on the ecological realities; and in the EU Strategy for the Baltic Sea (SBSR), it has managed to address the exclusion-spurring consequences of those governance instruments that are more heedful of science. However, none of the instruments thus far have brought complexity to the fore. This brave action was reserved for the Water Framework Directive (WFD), the focus of this chapter and the following. The object of enquiry in this chapter is the adaptive management of natural resources, and my discussion of it is both descriptive and normative: descriptive in the sense that I aim to guide the reader with no prior knowledge through the closer content of this paradigm, decisive in any natural resources management, waters included. But the examination is also normative: I presuppose that the legal sphere should abide by this scientific paradigm. The risks of technocracy and scientism entailed by this presumption are apparent. The continuum of normativity concluding this chapter addresses these questions on a practical level; the jurisprudential consequences are discussed in Chapter 5.

'ECO': Taking Ecological Systems Seriously

Adaptive management grew out of frustration. During the 1970s, a group of conservationists and scientists became displeased with the then-standard procedures of natural resources management and started to dream of something better. Even though they did not reach a flawless end result – as noted in one seminal piece, 'prediction is never perfect' – their work became highly

DOI: 10.4324/9781003197829-3

influential in their field.[1] In the early days, adaptive management was understood not as a novel way to solve problems but as an approach including a set of issues, concepts, and techniques with which to address pragmatic challenges.[2] In retrospect, this call for amendment marks, however, the beginning of an era or a paradigm shift.

The developers of adaptive management found multiple faults in the environmental management of their time: back then, research desired stability, designed fixed sets of measures, and allowed economic or social goals to triumph over ecological ones. Each individual management project was understood as novel when there was a willingness to include all variables in the management. One illustration of these myths was the management area drawn according to physical boundaries, e.g. watersheds (river basins) – since environmental impacts have no boundaries, watersheds as management area borders result in consequences as poor as those that managing in line with political boundaries would.[3] No wonder scientific studies often failed to contribute to regulation hinging on generalisations to function.[4] On a broader scale, the development that started at this very early stage has much later developed into constantly more fine-grained understandings of cause and effect in environment, complexity thinking, and complex systems research.[5]

Even in its early forms, adaptive management valued ecological information highly. Due to the inherent challenges of ecological knowledge, using ongoing projects as examples of the alterations caused to the environment was

1 The quote is a chapter title from CS Holling (ed), *Adaptive Environmental Assessment and Management* (Wiley-Interscience 1978) 133. The book has had immense influence in the field. Lucy Rist, Bruce M Campbell, and Peter Frost, 'Adaptive Management: Where Are We Now?' (2013) Environmental Conservation 40(1) <https://doi.org/10.1017/S0376892912000240>, 5.

2 Holling (n 1) 2. The examination here begins with partially historical aspects, and deliberately so. Even though the era of 'new ecology' seeks to portray itself as a source of new ideas and concepts, they were essentially present in the early writings. Lowell Pritchard and Steven E Sanderson, 'The Dynamics of Political Discourse in Seeking Sustainability' in Lance Gunderson and CS Holling (eds), *Panarchy: Understanding Transformations in Human and Natural Systems* (Island Press 2002) 147, 149.

3 Holling (n 1) 2–4. The authors have named the presuppositions present in the environmental management of their era as myths. Even though physical boundaries are mentioned in the title line of myth #10, they are no longer mentioned in the comment below that covers only political jurisdictions. Later, river basin oriented management has been considered as development from the politically chosen areas, as in the case of the WFD.

4 Lena Wahlberg, *Legal Questions and Scientific Answers: Ontological Differences and Epistemic Gaps in the Assessment of Causal Relations* (Lund University 2010) 230.

5 Most of these are not discussed in this volume – dynamics between 'adaptive management' and them would take another volume to explore (and make a fascinating read). However, in what follows, the part 'socio' touches upon work on complex adaptive systems thinking, especially regarding Ruhl's contributions to the matter; text to n 53.

suggested. It cannot be emphasised enough how much this suggestion differs from a simple 'learning-by-doing,' 'trial-and-error,' or 'test-and-trial' approach – these confusions have been persistent later on, springing up sporadically even in contemporary discussions.[6] When experimentality is adhered to, clear questions become elementary: they establish a connection between the experiment and the adaptive management approach. Without clear questions, the experiment is at risk of proceeding to business as usual, at the worst, using adaptive management as a mere smokescreen. Adaptive management and trial and error may be derived from the same well of learning, but adaptive management was coined as a development of trial and error, not as its replacement.[7]

Having said that, a concession is admitted: confusing adaptive management with trial and error is understandable. Learning by doing was the only answer that early ecology was able to produce. It was thought that any counterproductive management would soon be detected and corrected; in the case of smaller systems causing only minor errors, this assumption might even have been realistic. When ignorance caused no significant harm and the benefits were evident, the desired production increase from various natural resources was enabled. The situation changed even in the 1970s when management started to have more drastic consequences.[8] These early steps are best described as blissful ignorance analogically with the first step of the rise of environmental awareness.[9] The complexity of ecological knowledge relates to uncertainty, and the particulars of the interactions between uncertainty, adaptive management, and ecological knowledge have caused a constant debate. With regard to regulation, uncertainty in adaptive management is of utmost interest irrespective of its origins or closer components.[10]

6 'The inherent challenges with ecological knowledge' refer to the complexity, even the 'debilitating' realisation that ecosystems are too complex to be fully understood and consequently their managers cannot present a full record of their actions' scientific reasons. See e.g. Bradley C Karkkainen, 'Panarchy and Adaptive Change: Around the Loop and Back Again' (2005) Minn JL Sci & Tech 7 59, 65.

7 Holling (n 1) 8–9, 137.

8 CS Holling and William C Clark, 'Notes towards a science of ecological management' in WH van Dobben and RH Lowe-McConnell (eds), *Unifying Concepts in Ecology* (Dr. W. Junk B. V. Publ. 1975) 247, 248. Nuclear power plants were given as an example of management with more detrimental effects; the example is interesting since power plants and other point-source pollution sources are not the most obvious examples of ecosystem complexity that adaptive management strived to correct.

9 Nicholas A Robinson, 'Legal Systems, Decisionmaking, and the Science of Earth's Systems: Procedural Missing Links' (2000–1) Ecology L Q 27 <https://www.jstor.org/stable/24114052>, 1100 ff.

10 In what follows, adaptive management is not target-specified but examples are drawn from all areas of adaptive management.

Embracing Uncertainty

The natural resource management paradigms employed prior to adaptive management have been described with the apt names of nature benign (ecosystems as capable of recovering from any disturbance caused whatsoever), nature ephemeral (ecosystems deemed so unstable and fragile that only small-scale approaches are applicable), or nature the practical joker (the ways of nature are utterly unpredictable). The gap that adaptive management covered was that none of the approaches addressed variability properly.[11] Also, its stance on uncertainty distinguishes adaptive management from these earlier paradigms: instead of searching for or presupposing certainty, uncertainty is accepted, even cherished, and that shift in attitudes began to acknowledge the resilient essence of nature – that, however, has its limits, as we unfortunately witness in the world today.[12] Adaptive management first developed in a world already familiar with environmental impact assessments (EIAs), and the key difference between these two is illustrative: in EIAs, one presumes that a goal exists and that it can be reached, whereas in adaptive management, the process is an ongoing investigation of the development.[13] In adaptive management, the attempt is not to envisage the whole project beforehand but to take for granted that information will be acquired during the process. Even though prediction is risky, 'postdiction' might be more fruitful. It is allowed that decisions made today affect the decisions available in the future, resulting in the learning of the system being managed.[14] Thus, inevitably, critique and prejudices about adaptive management revolve around uncertainty – its approach to uncertainty is why lawyers tend(ed) to dislike adaptive management and the regulations founded on it.[15]

Attempts to analyse and categorise uncertainty have existed from the beginning of the paradigm shift. In the least worrying form of uncertainty, events can be predefined, as can their direct effects and even the probabilities that the effects will take place. In the second variation, events can still be predefined, but their effects and consequently also their probability are unknown. In the roughest category of uncertainty, neither the events nor, logically, their

11 As Holling (n 1) 9–11 categorises and evaluates.

12 Holling (n 1) 7, 10. Later, at text to n 49 ff, I discuss the limits of this resilience, the possibility of nature losing the feature.

13 Positing that the combination of an EIA and an environmental permit are so straightforward would be an oversimplification when the process continues in revisions and surveillance. It is, however, postulated that a difference exists between the understanding of uncertainty in command-and-control approaches and the adaptive management approaches.

14 Holling (n 1) 133, 135, 138.

15 As Karkkainen put it, '[l]awyers like rules. We like enforceable rules. We want our rules to be optimal, tidy, and timeless' in Bradley C Karkkainen, 'Collaborative Ecosystem Governance: Scale, Complexity, and Dynamism' (2002b) Virginia Environmental Law Journal 21 <https://www.jstor.org/stable/24785995>, 234–5.

effects can be established in advance.[16] Adaptive management's uncertainty was already divided in two even in the early days: things known but excluded and things unknown and thus omitted, referred to as *residual uncertainty*. It is noteworthy that residual uncertainty can have a significant influence in a managed situation even when it remains unknown.[17] As a result, 'some amount of' uncertainty is accepted as a part of the approach, as expressed in axiomatic terms: 'There exists a serious trade-off between designs aimed at preventing failure and designs that respond and survive when that failure does occur.'[18]

Categorisation of uncertainty comes in various forms, even though the conclusions drawn might be alike. One seminal piece differentiates between descriptive uncertainty, which is uncertainty relating to the limited ecological knowledge of the ecosystems in question. Then there is prescriptive uncertainty of the often hidden societal aims set for the management. These uncertainties are manageable, mainly via system analysis. The stakes are higher in the next category, which focuses on the unpredictable changes affecting both of these groups, descriptive and prescriptive uncertainty. These ignorances affect the basic structures of the managed system, fundamentally altering its patterns of behaviour. This is where the concept of resilience has its origin: the disturbances that a system can take before it moves to this new balance.[19] The more resilient the managed system is, the more it can tolerate *ad hoc* and trial-and-error management, unexpected new species, or uninvited economic or political changes. The equilibrium can be so strong that even the strongest exogenous disturbances do not cause qualitative behaviour to change. Regrettably, cumulative detrimental decisions of the past act alike, as the eutrophication issue illustrates: much of today's problems are due to compounded emissions on the seabed that have been allowed for decades before.[20]

This context is not a stranger to natural variation, and some scholars have emphasised uncertainty more than others. Even though the different lines of thought share the same view on the preferred type of resilience – ecosystem over equilibrium – some are more rooted in applied mathematics and applied resource ecology, implementing inductive theory formation instead of deductive. Walters' work is an illustrative example of this.[21] Walters was even ready to embrace uncertainty, stating that at the end of the day, managing natural resources is nothing more than a gamble. The degrading connotation of

16 Holling (n 1) 133–4.

17 As Holling and others put it, '[t]he unexpected is to be expected'; Holling (n 1) 134.

18 Holling (n 1) 138 referring to an earlier work; Holling and Clark (n 8) 247, 250.

19 Holling and Clark (n 8) 249.

20 Holling and Clark (n 8) 249–50.

21 Later this line of thought was described as best suited for small-scale adaptive management projects, see CS Holling and Gary K Meffe, 'Command and Control and the Pathology of Natural Resource Management' (1996) Conserv Biol 10(2) <https://doi.org/10.1046/j.1523-1739.1996.10020328.x>, 333.

gambling is noted but nonetheless seen as more reasonable than the inaction required for prolonged studies.[22] With gambling as a starting point, the logical consequence was to refer to statistical decision-making theories. The first step in the chosen pattern included identifying those possible effects that might occur, assigning the probability of each effect, and then using those odds to make decisions. It should be noted that placing odds is different from setting confidence limits – not least in being more difficult. Placing the odds might happen by use of mere imagination or, more formally, with a matrix to compare the expected values of the various possible effects.[23]

The end results of implementing decision theory to natural resource management are trifurcated, hinging on the management experiences at disposal. Even though distinguishing one stage from another does not come effortlessly, the first, pre-adaptive phase, is based on earlier management experiences from systems sufficiently like the one in question – that means no information from the system in question is yet available. The second, adaptive phase, can exploit some data from the field while categorising the initial hypotheses, and the third (presumably unachievable) stage, called the certainty-equivalent phase, is where almost all uncertainty is abolished and the most suitable management option can be attained. The importance of sheer luck is duly noted, existing throughout the process.[24] It is admitted that management as a game includes more assumptions than would be acceptable in pure statistical sciences, but that is taken as a consequence of reality: natural resource management is not meant to be the same in every situation. This decision theory leads to the axiom that '*any* inference from data to decision must be based somehow on prior beliefs, likelihoods, and models.' The question of setting expected values on perfect information is also present – after all, decision theory is exploited since the parameter of 'waiting until the system is thoroughly known' is currently unavailable.[25] For the same reason, it must be accepted that the numbers treated as parameters for the statistics are more indices or estimates than exact figures. An extra challenge for setting the expected value on perfect information comes from the notion that, while setting it, managers are not aware of how future decision-makers will choose to value the knowledge they have. Due to this, questions on sufficient information slide towards trial and error.[26]

These differences put aside, at least accepting uncertainty, forms the founding stone of adaptive management. That is not to say that uncertainty would be the terminus – on the contrary, it is followed by an eager desire to learn from

22 Carl J Walters, *Adaptive Management of Renewable Resources* (Macmillan 1986) 374, 159.

23 Walters (ibid) 160.

24 An act of balancing prevails between the questions answered and the ones still open. Establishing possible effects and their proportions is a sensible matter and hence all suggestions of representing a 'test-and-trial' approach are firmly denied; Walters (n 22) 163–4.

25 Walters (n 22) 185, 194–5.

26 Walters (n 22) 200, 202, 212.

the management process; the firm denial of trial and error points in the same direction. What are the components of this learning?

To Learn Is to Manage – or to Manage Is to Learn?

Uncertainty and attitudes towards it are pertinent to the adaptive management approaches of today too. For the needs of law drafting or adjudicating, an extra twist is introduced in the everyday reality where science and policy do not share the understanding of compelling questions and a reasonable level of proof. Disparity in setting the goal underpins their different approaches to uncertainty. In science, avoiding mistakes is crucial since any mistake made will accumulate in future research. Policy-making, on the other hand, aims to address societal challenges where avoiding mistakes is not as fundamental: policy-makers are expected to be prompt and proceed even with insufficient information. The perception of risk differs, and thus the standards of proof employed also differ. These differences are epistemological in essence and lead to certain prevalent problems, communication challenges, and a lack of policy-relevant research included.[27] Due to their understanding of uncertainty, scientists might find it challenging to express the amount of uncertainty present in their results. The difficulties in discussion are only bound to worsen if no assessment of probability is included. And then again, discussing probabilities as if deciding upon them was part of the scientists' repertoire – as if the decisions were objective and neutral – may lead to hiding value choices from public view.[28]

For a long time, learning, as a fundamental part of the adaptive management paradigm, created a slightly paradoxical situation: the importance of learning was acknowledged, but the aspects of learning were not further detailed. Learning was taken as a normative goal of the adaptive process, but persistent uncertainty prevailed on details over the 'who, what, when' trichotomy. It might be that familiarity with the concept has veiled it from the more analytical examination. From time to time, learning might even have been superficial, making only a small contribution to the management process.[29] It is not that learning could not be deconstructed. Learning is a concept, and as such, it is

27 More extensively in text to n 1 in ch 5.

28 The trade-offs embedded into solutions of environmental problems give an illustrative example: the value choice in them is inherent and prevails regardless of whether the choice is made by a policy-maker, a scientist, or a layman. Ann Kinzig and David Starrett, 'Coping with Uncertainty: A Call for a New Science-Policy Forum' (2003) Ambio 32(5) <http://www.jstor.org/stable/4315393>, 330–1. The issue is ever more present when mathematical modelling is used to assess environmental change; text to n 204 in ch 4.

29 Derek Armitage, Melissa Marschke, and Ryan Plummer, 'Adaptive Co-Management and the Paradox of Learning' (2008) Global Environ Change 18(1) <https://doi.org/10.1016/j.gloenvcha.2007.07.002>, 87, 97.

defined in a certain manner – the concept has a typology of its own. These variations have evolved into a trichotomy of experimental, transformative, and social learning, all present in different adaptive management practices and major studies on them.[30]

Learning consists of objectives and evaluation and the different collaborators in the process have different motivations. As noted later, acknowledging this variety is crucial to the success of a management project.[31] The question of objectives brings us to the question of subjects, the learners. This aspect is especially relevant in co-management, where various groups, some of them marginal or otherwise underprivileged, take part in the management process. Since learning is a normative goal, mitigation is inevitable among the various groups and their various objectives, leading to tentatively challenging trade-offs.[32] Last but not least, there is always the methodology of learning or the pedagogical aspect of learning. Since learning has been used to mean many things and is conducted by a diverse group of collaborators, it comes as no surprise that the best learning methodologies are diverse ones: the greater the variety of mechanisms used, the better.[33] Distinguishing the features of learning serves the theoretical foundation but does not necessarily enhance the actual management results. In adaptive management of natural resources, risk concretises at the lowest level in the lives and the livelihoods of individuals or groups affected.[34] In terms of short- and long-term costs, the question boils down to smaller communities struggling to meet the short-term costs. Often, vulnerable and dependent communities are (understandably) unwilling to take risks if their burden is front-heavy and the benefits are expected over a longer time span. Ethical aspects of management are certainly not straightforward when the benefits of learning in management can accumulate in time so that the learners themselves do not gain the results.[35]

Twisted Circle Decreasing Uncertainty

As learning, the contents of inherent uncertainty can also be further deconstructed, and some of the frameworks have already been presented above.[36]

30 Interestingly the first two are mainly modelled on individual learners, only the last one has originated from groups' learning. The concept has multiple roots, extending from organisational development or business management to adult education; Armitage, Marschke, and Plummer (n 29) 87–8.

31 Armitage, Marschke, and Plummer (n 29) 89. Whether setting objectives is even possible in the reality of diverse political ambitions is discussed at text to n 88 ff.

32 Armitage, Marschke, and Plummer (n 29) 93–4. More on the trade-offs see text to n 63 ff.

33 Armitage, Marschke, and Plummer (n 29) 98.

34 Armitage, Marschke, and Plummer (n 29) 95.

35 Armitage, Marschke, and Plummer (n 29) 96. Some ethical questions are elaborated elsewhere when trade-offs and value choices in the management are scrutinised. See text to n 63–87.

36 See text to n 15 ff.

One way of dichotomising the concept is to differentiate between the uncertainty of the desired objectives and the uncertainty of the structures and mechanisms with which the objectives are to be reached, a dichotomy also present in the legal argumentation of the WFD's objectives.[37] Often the counterparts are dealt with separately, but attempts have been made to include them in the same framework, enabling a holistic description of the adaptive management process that applies to both the substantial and procedural sides of the practice.[38] If the paradigm were understood correctly, evaluating outcomes might be easier, and maybe, the theory itself would face fairer, less polarised treatment.[39] In order to better understand how management and value decisions are coupled, one mechanism for reducing uncertainty is explained.

Familiar to someone with a background in law, the differentiation between substance and process also applies in this context. A two-fold stochastic structure first includes only the procedural uncertainty and later also encompasses uncertainty of objectives. The first base is grounded on a Markovian decision framework in which decision-making is linked with time. Management actions are specific in their location and time, but with Bayes' theorem, the accumulation of knowledge over time can be incorporated into the scheme, explaining why learning is continuously enhanced. However, even more is promised when it is stated that 'learning occurs through management itself, with what is learned being used to guide future management actions,' illustrating an iterative process of learning or life-long learning pattern. In the second phase, a stochastic link is presupposed, which moulds management into a pattern in which stakeholders' commitment to the shared aim is combined with said subjects' belief that the chosen model is a correct representation of the dynamics of the managed resources.[40] The uncertainties of the objectives are understood as value functions, resulting in values correlating with the chosen management policy option and depending on the state of the managed resource at a given time.[41] Eventually, then, learning of both objectives and models of it occur concurrently. The management measures are considered hypotheses that are studied with collected monitoring data; the objectives are similarly seen as hypotheses, supported by data or not. When the objectives are value functions, the model itself – inclusive of the objectives and the process – develops in relation to the evolution of the value-bound objectives.[42] Given that the underlying values are considered decisive stochastic structures, this appears to be a highly interesting model for adaptive management.

37 Text to n 16 in ch 4.

38 On attending to the parts separately, i.e. setting the objectives see text to n 88.

39 For a detailed explanation see text to n 170 ff.

40 Byron K Williams, 'Reducing Uncertainty About Objective Functions in Adaptive Management' (2012) Ecological Modelling 225 <https://doi.org/10.1016/j.ecolmodel.2011.11.009>, 61–2.

41 Williams (ibid) 63.

42 Williams (n 40) 63–4.

The social and technical aspects of learning are enhanced when adaptive management practice is seen to consist of movement between deliberative and iterative phases. The purpose of the deliberative phase is to find, define, and develop the essential features of the management project in question: e.g. defining and involving the stakeholders, establishing the objectives and searching for alternatives, and deciding upon modelling and monitoring patterns.[43] In the iterative phase, the aspects are placed into an iterative cycle also consisting of multiple features: decision-making, follow-up monitoring, assessment, and, most importantly, learning. The aspects ought to form an ongoing cycle, replicating over the management timespan and eventually enabling learning.[44] The iterative cycle produces institutional or social learning increasing knowledge of institutional arrangements and other societal aspects, and thus forms a bridge between the ever-changing value factors and management practice. The changing values affect, for example, stakeholders' positions, which via an iterative process, affect the management. This mechanism is titled 'double-loop learning.'[45] The ultimate goal is to reduce the amount of uncertainty. However, proving that learning *de facto* also happens has been challenging since incorporating learning in the management practice would need readjustment of, e.g. decision-making patterns and institutional structures. The latter often ought to become more flexible and inclusive – a task that might seem smaller than it actually is. Changes needed in decision-making patterns wait to be documented. Regarding uncertainty and learning, the theory is well developed, but the practical mechanisms are less advanced.[46] As such, learning, as long as management is inclusive enough, ought to result in less bureaucracy and lead toward 'pluralistic democracy,' in which natural resources management varies almost automatically according to the chances in the value base.[47]

The Panarchy Thesis ∞

Learning in adaptive management is thus double-looped: single would refer to learning from the resource only but double includes learning from the regulation of management. In the standard model of the adaptive cycle, early-stage growth turns into a conservation phase, predestined to damnation as overly

43 Byron K Williams and Eleanor D Brown, 'Adaptive Management: From More Talk to Real Action' (2014) Environ Manage 53(2) <https://doi.org/10.1007/s00267-013-0205-7>, 467.

44 The dichotomies continue, though, since placing the aspects in the iterative cycle vary as a function of time and space: in a sequential option, the interventions take place one at a time, in a parallel option, multiple interventions occur simultaneously in different places; Williams and Brown (n 43) 468.

45 Williams and Brown (n 43) 468.

46 Williams and Brown (n 43) 474–5. As a consequence, successful examples of adaptive management practices are few.

47 Pritchard and Sanderson (n 2) 164.

stable and non-resilient. Relief is offered by an uncontrollable chaos phase, followed in due course by an era of reorganisation. When the growth and conservation phases form a forward loop of the cycle and the uncontrollable chaos and reorganisation phases form the back loop, the adaptive cycle can be illustrated with the symbol of eternity, ∞. One must not be tempted to assume that this adaptive cycle would be stable: the development can direct itself to whichever course it pleases. The factor of scale is relevant – in practice, resource management developments can occur on various scales – but the creation is never fully anarchistic. It is instead convened as a *panarchy*, hence the label, the panarchy thesis.[48]

The panarchy thesis marks the second stage in the development of adaptive management theory. In panarchy, the forward loop can be described with positive concepts such as innovation, growth, and predictability and the back loop with the less favourable counterparts of release, instability, and even collapse.[49] The phases of the ongoing cycle are named exploitation, conservation, release, and reorganisation.[50] This structure is supposed to incorporate both natural and social learning. However, the pattern in which panarchy enables social and scientific learning has been described as 'vexingly complex,' so ambitious claims have been promulgated under its name – one being that learned outcomes can jump from one place and scale to another (slightly resembling whooping cough). Also, human societies, it is claimed, have experienced these shifts in their development, a point worth noting when attempting to regulate adaptive management processes.[51] Regarding this ongoing change and learning, it is also elementary to note that the cycle and its features do not incline to an equilibrium but move hither and yon in a 'basin of attraction' of three elements: latitude, resistance, and precariousness.[52] Socio-ecological systems adapt within these basins. There might be many of them, all existing and bordering other basins in a 'stability landscape' consisting of various basins and their borders. When a subsystem moves around in its basin of attraction, it can change its place but also move from one basin to a neighbouring one, redrawing the

48 Lance Gunderson, CS Holling, and Donald Ludwig, 'In Quest of a Theory of Adaptive Change' in Lance Gunderson and CS Holling (eds), *Panarchy: Understanding Transformations in Human and Natural Systems* (Island Press 2002) 3, 5; Brian Walker and others, 'Resilience, Adaptability and Transformability in Social–Ecological Systems' (2004) Ecology and Society 9(2) <https://www.jstor.org/stable/26267673>, 5.

49 CS Holling and Lance Gunderson, 'Resilience and Adaptive Cycles' in Lance Gunderson and CS Holling (eds), *Panarchy: Understanding Transformations in Human and Natural Systems* (Island Press 2002) 25, 33–40, 47–9; Karkkainen (n 6) 62.

50 Holling and Gunderson (ibid) 34.

51 Karkkainen (n 6) 62–3.

52 'Latitude' refers to the width of the basin of attractors, the three aspects of change: number of basins of attractors, their position regarding the state space (variables that constitute the whole system), and their borders with each other, Walker and others (n 48).

borders between the two. Due to the fact that adaptive socio-ecological systems exist on multiple scales, systems below and above them affect the system.

An illustrative example from eutrophication caused by agricultural runoff concretises this. At first, a larger basin of attraction of clear water co-exists in the same stability landscape with a smaller basin of attraction of murky waters. After agricultural runoff has diminished the quality of the water in the water body in question, the latter basin of the attractor has grown bigger and the former smaller. Change occurs in two ways: either the system crosses a border (called the threshold), or the border moves across the system. What is interesting to note is that sometimes loss of resilience is desired: when a larger-scale system aspires to change, the amount of resilience in the smaller-scale systems ought to decline to enable the change.[53]

Even when socio-ecological systems adapt in the described manner, they can also find themselves in a basin of attraction so wide or so deep that no way out exists (imagine a rabbit hole). In these cases, adapting via learning is no longer tenable, and transformation takes place – exemplified by exploiting vast grasslands for agricultural needs and, after overconsuming the resource, finding livelihood in ecotourism. The demands for adaptive governance begin to accumulate. Governance is needed to facilitate these changes, the adaptability and transformability – but simultaneously extensive flexibility is needed to enable the double-loop system, especially the back loop, to work as adjustably as is needed.[54] As summarised by Ruhl: '[t]o take advantage of their inherently adaptive qualities, however, these regulatory instruments must themselves be managed adaptively.'[55]

The panarchy thesis has not gone without criticism. The eternal double-loop learning may imply determinism: since the double-loop is in an eternal process of folding and unfolding, it could as well be described as a 'mad ecologist's vision of a *Huis Clos*.' The pattern is positioned as inescapable without explaining or reasoning why this would be the case – and even though uncertainty persists, variables are multiple and combinations of them almost unending; the pattern itself, its phases, are fixed. The deterministic attitude appears an odd presence in an otherwise adaptable and flexible paradigm. Why could societies not develop an *Ausfahrt*, or exit, from the double-loop, their predestined highway to nowhere? The deterministic aura of the panarchy thesis has even been claimed to contradict the adaptive management research itself since adaptive management ought to deal with terms such as uncertainty, unpredictability, and non-linearity. Was it the case, how could the archetype of said

53 Walker and others (n 48).
54 Walker and others (n 48).
55 JB Ruhl, 'Regulation by Adaptive Management—Is It Possible?' (2005) Minn JL Sci & Tech 7 <http://hdl.handle.net/1803/6643>, 21, 27.

behaviour form a fixed pattern of any kind?[56] The reply to the deterministic critique claims that the panarchy thesis is not actually a model but a metaphor: it should not be read literally but as a more abstract description of how adaptive management proceeds and evolves.[57] This reply unfortunately creates more questions than it gives answers. If the panarchy thesis is a mere metaphor, an illustrative description of reality, and not an ecological or socio-ecological model, why should regulators feel obliged to use it as the foundation of their work? Poor implementation of adaptive management, or poor regulation of adaptive management, only adds to the problem.[58]

Another aspect of the criticism regards the human factor. The panarchy thesis presupposes human influence but deals with societal aspects with lesser scrutiny than ecological ones. In particular, the (alleged) possibilities of human societies – or human behaviour within a socio-ecological system – are described in a rather superficial and vague manner, leading to the alarming possibility that panarchy thesis draws an excessively pessimistic picture of its highly complex research topic. As put by Karkkainen,

> Presumably, then, our understanding of the dynamics of system change itself has the potential to change the way we act within the system, thereby altering the trajectory of system change – though perhaps, given complexity, nonlinearity, and inherent stochasticity, in ways we cannot entirely predict or control.[59]

This aspect of the panarchy thesis is a con: the thesis is not as positive and encouraging as the original adaptive management pattern was and it does not bring clarity to the same extent.[60] Then again, those of us who do not find themselves in the ranks of evolutionary optimists might be delighted with the development: at least the hypothesis does not overestimate the impact of the positive tendencies.

Irrespective of one's worldview, some interesting developments can be drafted. Holling and others' first version of adaptive management might have encouraged ecologists and those employing their results to 'epistemic humility'

56 Karkkainen (n 6) 64–5, referring to Sartre's play *Huis Clos* or 'No Exit'. Legal scholarship is not in the position to make claims about the function of ecosystems. However, this question is also left unanswered when addressed at ecosystems alone.

57 Holling and Gunderson (n 49) 51; Karkkainen (n 6) 63.

58 To certain extent, the WFD has been regarded as one; see text to n 7 in ch 4.

59 Karkkainen (n 6) 64. The pessimistic nature most likely stems from the manner in which positive feedback loops are regarded as dangerous due to the 'risk spirals' that management can create – managing lesser risk results in larger losses elsewhere; John A Dearing and others, 'Group report: integrating socioenvironmental interactions over centennial timescales' in Robert Costanza, Lisa J Graumlich, and Will Steffen (eds), *Sustainability or Collapse? An Integrated History and Future of People on Earth* (MIT Press 2007) 244, 266.

60 Karkkainen (n 6) 64–5.

before the unpredictable natural cycles: instead of asking after fixed answers, regulators were encouraged to cherish uncertainty, not be halted by it. The forecast that the panarchy thesis offers is of socio-ecological systems' inevitable collapse, albeit the collapse brings along further development.[61] But why would any regulator in their right mind utilise a disaster-predicting metaphor? That brings us to the third criticism of the panarchy thesis. The earliest developments of adaptive management theory may, and the latest certainly do, produce delicate models rather than answers. Their explicit endeavour is to fabricate metaphors (in the most extreme version) or models and patterns (in the more conventional version). Regulators and other actors of the legal sphere are, however, traditionally used to input facts (or intelligent guesses at the minimum) in order to produce rules or decisions. In that context, with an input of metaphor, the output is at risk of becoming mere guesswork.[62] Thus the investigation must continue. First, I probe whether further structures could aid in circumventing this worst-case scenario.

Ordnung muß sein! Structures and Trade-Offs

Cherishing uncertainty has not meant that structuring chaos has not been attempted. Let us place some of these attempts under closer scrutiny in order to better understand how, within adaptive management, decision-making behaves and power relations are mended in highly uncertain situations.

As mentioned, the adaptive management paradigm seeks to draw a clear line between itself and learning-by-doing management. Attempts at clearing this doctrinal divide have resulted in deepening our understanding of the decision-making process in adaptive management.[63] Combining adaptive management with *multi-criteria decision analysis (MCDA)* helps to develop the structure or rationality of decision-making: by applying MCDA within adaptive management, the managers get a more comprehensive overview of the trade-offs required when deciding between various management options.[64] Even though the objective of adaptive management has always been to incorporate

61 Karkkainen (n 6) 66.

62 When studying complex adaptive systems explanatory power does not necessarily result in successful predictions – the outcome is rather to develop understanding in order to create a desired future; Robert Costanza, Lisa J Graumlich, and Will Steffen, 'Sustainability or collapse: lessons from integrating the history of humans and the rest of the nature' in Robert Costanza, Lisa J Graumlich, and Will Steffen (eds), *Sustainability or Collapse? An Integrated History and Future of People on Earth* (MIT Press 2007) 3, 14–15.

63 Derek R Armitage and others, 'Adaptive Co-Management for Social-Ecological Complexity' (2009) Frontiers in Ecology and the Environment 7(2) <http://www.jstor.org/stable/25595062>, 95–6.

64 Armitage and others (ibid) 97–8; Igor Linkov and others, 'From Comparative Risk Assessment to Multi-Criteria Decision Analysis and Adaptive Management: Recent Developments and Applications' (2006) Environ Int 32(8) <https://doi.org/10.1016/j.envint.2006.06.013>, 1090.

environmental, economic, socio-political, technical, ecological, and other factors in management, quite often only some of these aspects are included.[65] The unstructured manner in which adaptive management decisions are made may explain this: when no framework exists to integrate and organise all the relevant aspects, some are more easily left in the margins than others. Incorporating MCDA essentially adds feedback loops to the various stages of adaptive management decision-making – cunningly, in MCDA, adaptive management is applied to the decision-making within the management itself.[66] The aim of MCDA is to ascertain that the worldviews, problem-solving techniques, and societal responsibilities of different participating groups of people are taken into account as extensively as possible, noting also that their involvement varies over different stages of the process. The MCDA's gains recall greatly those of Alexy's work on balancing in legal decision-making and reaping similar benefits to those obtained through a detailed balancing scheme.[67] Thus the MCDA is an iterative process that can and is supposed to be repeated as many times as the subtle development of the management process requires, remembering that new details can emerge and necessitate further negotiations.[68]

While EU water governance is examined in Chapter 4, the approach to implementing an *analytical hierarchy process* in the decision-making is of interest here.[69] It was developed for the needs of forestry management that were considered not transparent or comprehensible enough, thus aggravating the disputes between parties instead of mending them.[70] The suggested solution focused on project-level forest management, in which forest-level management goals are concretised with site-specific measures. In order to incorporate structure into the management, a formal hierarchy of management goals was suggested. The goal hierarchy would cover the values of all parties involved and provide an in-depth understanding of the context (although competing goal hierarchies might well exist).[71] It was found that even though deciding upon

65 Armitage and others (n 63) 99.

66 Armitage and others (n 63) 99–100.

67 Robert Alexy, 'On Balancing and Subsumption. A Structural Comparison' (2003) Ratio Juris 16(4) 433–49. Linkov and others (n 64) 1072, 1087. The need for weighing and balancing in judicial decision-making is discussed further at text to n 76 in ch 5.

68 Linkov and others (n 64) 1088–90; Carl Folke and others, 'Adaptive Governance of Social-Ecological Systems' (2005) Annual Review of Environment & Resources 30(1) <https://doi.org/10.1146/annurev.energy.30.050504.144511>, 441, 457.

69 Per Olsson, Carl Folke, and Fikret Berkes, 'Adaptive Comanagement for Building Resilience in Social–Ecological Systems' (2004) Environ Manage 34(1) <https://doi.org/10.1007/s00267-003-0101-7>, 75, 76–7.

70 Even accusations of halting the management projects were presented; H Michael Rauscher and others, 'A Practical Decision-Analysis Process for Forest Ecosystem Management' (2000) Comput Electron Agric 27(1–3) <https://doi.org/10.1016/S0168-1699(00)00108-3>, 195, 196.

71 Rauscher and others (ibid) 195–6.

goals is a value choice, the goal-setting in the lower ranks is not. The lowest level of goals, called desired future conditions, is regarded as factual knowledge. There can be a set of them due to the inherent uncertainty, but any such set consists of pure factual knowledge, hence value choice is no longer present or required.[72] The development of goal hierarchies for complex problems is seen to be 'more art than science': guidelines for formulating it can be given, but a more detailed method is not available. Due to the desired future conditions existing in groups, the next step is to distinguish the most suitable one among the alternatives. This selection entails a prescription component, referring to the action–location–time nexus in which the chosen option will be executed. The prescription component is an iterative process coupling decision science expertise with hands-on resource management.[73] There are various methods for choosing between the alternatives. As noted, the desired future goals consist of pure factual knowledge and '[e]ach desired future condition is defined by an observable component that can be compared to the value produced by any alternative.'[74] Thus even if one part of the equation consisted of so-called pure facts, the other does not: the value that alternatives earn is a value choice per se. Application of the equation might benefit the managers in giving them a detailed and logically consistent pattern to follow, but it does not solve the underlying dilemma of, at the end of the day, choosing between different or contrasting values.

Generally, in any society, and specifically in adaptively managed projects, if resilience is desired, then trade-offs between often-incompatible, short-term gains and long-term objectives linger.[75] In combinations of analytical hierarchy process and adaptive management, Keeney's value-making theory is elementary for both establishing the hierarchical set of goals and the evaluation of the whole suggestion, but the theory also illustrates generally how recognising value trade-offs can be executed. As Keeney states, '[v]alues are more fundamental to a decision problem than are alternatives.'[76] Value-focused thinking is a complement of alternatives-focused thinking (often the most intuitive choice), and since certain value choices limit the available alternatives, it is also a preceding step if the two are considered together.[77] It is proactive and, importantly, value-neutral since the emphasis is put on the values with which a decision is made, not on the available alternatives.[78] As if adjudging with

72 Rauscher and others (n 70) 200.

73 Rauscher and others (n 70) 201; Ralph L Keeney, *Value-Focused Thinking: A Path to Creative Decision Making* (Harvard University Press 1992) 416, 99.

74 In the field of forestry, a series of programmes have tried to address the problem of choosing between alternatives. The programmes are described in brief by Rauscher and others (n 70) 202–4.

75 Costanza, Raumlich, and Steffen (n 62) 14.

76 Keeney (n 73) 3.

77 Keeney (n 73) 31–3, 47 ff.

78 This is why the method is used when deciding on management goals; Keeney (n 73) 4, 6, 47, 52.

no strings attached, value-focused thinking benefits the goal-setting part of management praxis. While enhancing communication, it also aids in building awareness of the subconscious values that might be relevant to decision-making.[79] Keeney's theory includes a detailed pattern on how goals can be structured and differentiates between fundamental objectives and means objectives and whether a question being addressed concerns a certain objective or a relationship between objectives.[80] It consists of activities in which one tries 'to define listed objectives more clearly, to relate them to another, and to relate them to objectives not yet defined.'[81] Structuring is fundamental since the aim is to use quantitative modelling based on the structure so elucidated. By quantifying objectives with value models, managers can identify hidden objectives and clarify their meanings.[82] Recognising and solving value trade-offs is at the core of the theory. Since not all objectives can be reached with the same measures, but some measures can be even counterproductive to some objectives, value trade-offs are one way to make this inherent trading visible – in other words, value trade-offs tackle the question of balancing the desired objectives.[83]

Trade-offs between time and financial means have been found to be fundamental in the implementation of adaptive management strategies. Implementing decision-making theories in adaptive management has served to elide the bifurcated reality of active and passive adaptive management, a distinction that is less than academically solid when both approaches rely on judgement.[84] Trade-offs are essential due to the long time spans of management projects, the uncertainty inherent to them, and also the opportunity costs of any given action (costs caused by the fact that only one management option can be trialled at once, leaving others unused, or from the fact that testing and trialling, in general, generates costs). Reducing uncertainty costs – especially in large-scale adaptive management projects such as river basin management with numerous variables – and hence trade-offs are a basic function of management.[85] This

79 Keeney (n 73) 7, 24–5.

80 The former differentiation, again, is reflected in the CJEU's practice over objectives in environmental regulation; text to n 32 in ch 4; see also text to n 37.

81 Keeney (n 73) 64, 77.

82 Keeney (n 73) 69, 127. Setting the value model is seen as 'art and science.'

83 Keeney (n 73) 129–30.

84 Robin Gregory, Lee Failing, and Paul Higgins, 'Adaptive Management and Environmental Decision Making: A Case Study Application to Water Use Planning' (2006) Ecol Econ 58(2) <https://doi.org/10.1016/j.ecolecon.2005.07.020>, 434, 435–6. More on the challenges with active and passive adaptive management see text to n 166 ff.

85 Gregory, Failing, and Higgins (ibid) 438–9. Trade-offs are also offered as a solution to better facilitate interaction between the different but overlapping concepts of vulnerability and resilience; BL Turner II, 'Vulnerability and Resilience: Coalescing or Paralleling Approaches for Sustainability Science?' (2010) Global Environ Change 20(4) <https://doi.org/10.1016/j.gloenvcha.2010.07.003>, 570.

reality has prompted a suggestion to implement a structured evaluation pattern consisting of step-by-step instructions to managers.[86]

A yearning after order unites the approaches or developments described above: all seek to solve the problems of adaptive management through better-structured management praxis. The examples have naturally been hand-picked to serve the needs of adaptive management and law – the latter of which is systematic in essence – and are more closely examined in Chapter 4, in which solutions to the deadlock of the WFD after the Weser ruling are drafted.[87]

The Apprehensive Setting of Objectives

Many of the central features of leading paradigms are contested. This is also the case with management objectives: the ability to set appropriate objectives is called into question in soft systems thinking or methodology (SSM), which simultaneously brings social learning to the table. This approach promulgates the idea that setting adaptive management goals is 'an emergent property of complex social situations' and pays attention to the challenges that adaptive management faces in this objective-setting phase. Concurrently, the emphasis is placed on how the learning process intrinsic to adaptive management hinges on the social context of the project.[88] The socio-political reality is brought to the fore by concentrating on the adaptive management process, i.e. how the process itself affects its outcomes.[89] SSM abandons objective-focused management and builds on the understanding that no system that includes people can be managed towards an objective. Adaptive management study takes a hard-systems perspective in which uncertainty is caused by multiple, layered systems working in unpredictable manners – a picture that can indeed be recognised from earlier adaptive management literature.[90] The hard-systems perspective is

86 Gregory, Failing, and Higgins (n 84) 445–6. Keeney's understanding of trade-offs focused on the value decisions – in the trade-offs of this structured pattern value choice serves as a stepping stone to the scheme but it is not seen elementary for everyday management decisions. Thus structured evaluation pattern complements Keeney's theory but does not replace it.

87 Temporal aspects are considered in text to n 143 in ch 4; questions of facts and values are returned to at text to n 19 and 67 in ch 5.

88 G Cundill and others, 'Soft Systems Thinking and Social Learning for Adaptive Management' (2012) Conserv Biol 26(1) <https://doi.org/10.1111/j.1523-1739.2011.01755.x>, 13, 18. Cundill and others studied adaptive management implemented to conservation, in which adaptive management has been widely used. Due to the more general viewpoint of elaborations here the differences in research theme are not of much significance.

89 Cundill and others (ibid) 15.

90 In a hard-systems approach, the system under enquiry is itself understood as being composed of subsystems; in a soft-systems approach the object of inquiry is taken as complex and fuzzy but the process of inquiry can be systematic; Peter Checkland, 'Soft Systems Methodology: A Thirty Year Retrospective' (2000) Syst Res Behav Sci S 17(S1) <https://doi.org/10.1002/1099-1743(200011)17:1+<::AID-SRES374>3.0.CO;2-O>, 17–18.

not fully abandoned, though, but SSM is comprehended as an adjunct to it. The methodological shift towards SSM is a way out of the challenges that the previous era was unable to resolve.[91] The theory behind it is that of 'appreciative systems' emphasising the open expression of worldviews underpinning management objectives, collaborative decision-making observing the individual histories, cultures, and aspirations of the deciding parties, and identifying the purposes motivating those who decided the issue.[92] The aim, in general, is to facilitate the learning process inherent to adaptive management and to do it in a non-authoritative manner, inevitably resulting in procedural considerations on how to best enable people's engagement.[93]

Seeing learning as a permanent part of goal-setting is fundamental to the approach, as is an appreciation for gaining knowledge and understanding goal-setting as an unending endeavour. Learning is fostered by a five-step approach applied at the level of adaptive management praxis.[94] The objective-setting phase of adaptive management begins with 'a process of orientation and exploration.' Since the stakeholders view and categorise the problem(s) differently, iterating for the most common shared viewpoint is needed. Crucially, this step is not only about what the participants express but also – and even more so – about the relationships they share, their past experiences, and the effect of those relationships and experiences on the decision-making process.[95] The link to the frames of reference or mental models of the participants is clear, referring to the participants' assumptions, beliefs, and values that affect their decisions. Even though the human-influenced process cannot be managed with objective-focused patterns, the goal set for this phase is to carve out a common frame of reference, a process in which disagreements are taken as stimuli for learning. Some intense compromising is also to be anticipated since no decision can be made without all parties' approval. Accordingly, the reflection required ought to take place among all the collaborating parties, not by one or some, to facilitate everybody's transformative learning and perpetual change of their frames of reference.[96] It seems that the contribution of SSM to adaptive management is the humane touch in its determination of the collaborative partners' personal

91 Cundill and others (n 88) 16.

92 Cundill and others (n 88) 15; Checkland (n 90) 17–18. Appreciative systems are presented as a polar opposite of those management theories more keen on acquiring set objectives.

93 Arjen EJ Wals, 'Learning in a Changing World and Changing in a Learning World: Reflexively Fumbling Towards Sustainability' (2007) Southern African Journal of Environmental Education 24(1) 35, 39, 42.

94 The stages are acknowledging that management situation takes place in socio-ecological context and that multiple solutions exist; endorsing enquiries and even deconstructions of the frames of reference used to solve the existing problems; advocating collaborative activities, and reflecting on the learning outcomes; Cundill and others (n 88) 16.

95 Cundill and others (n 88) 16–17.

96 Cundill and others (n 88) 17; Wals (n 93) 42. Thus here the question of 'who learns' is addressed, see text to n 29 ff.

history – or maybe better, partners' legal-personal history.[97] It also illustrates clearly the challenges in setting the management objectives, which, however delusional, are part of any management praxis.

'SOCIO' – Acknowledging the Human Touch

Some advocates of the 'social' aspect of adaptive management may even have excessive trust in the local governances' ability to solve management problems – similarly, the protagonists of the sustainability aspect may ignore the need for economic development or social justice issues. Panarchy thesis seeks to promulgate a view in which a balance is found among the different desires.[98] Even though the social side of adaptive management might not grant all the wishes made upon it, a closer look at the social aspects may help in understanding how adaptive water governance ought to perform.

Denouncing Command and Control

Social learning calls for better incorporation of the affected groups in the management process. Similar thinking is present in the understanding of socio-ecological systems, referring to the integrated manner in which humans and nature interact in an attempt to stress that the divide between the social and ecological is arbitrary and man-made.[99] Both experiential and experimental learning and vertical and horizontal collaboration are included in *adaptive co-management*, a contemporary version of adaptive management that amalgamates co-management theory with adaptive management. Adaptive co-management finds that traditional (i.e. command and control) environmental regulation neglects culture and is slow to react to socio-ecological changes.[100] Instead of subjecting institutions and organisations to their own separate scrutiny, they ought to be examined as closely as the ecological prerequisites, and since the

97 Cundill and others (n 88) 17. The SSM was suggested for adaptive management in conservation, the most significant anticipated challenge was that of bringing change to the often-strained relationships between natural resource managers and stakeholders. Unfortunately, hardened attitudes are not unique to conservation projects only.

98 Gunderson, Holling, and Ludwig (n 48) 7–8. Supporting the categorisation here, uncertainty can also be categorised as an ecological and social one; addressing both secures better management outcomes, Elisa Kochskämper, Tomas Koontz, and Jens Newig, 'Systematic Learning in Water Governance: Insights from Five Local Adaptive Management Projects for Water Quality Innovation' (2021) Ecology and Society 26(1) <https://doi.org/10.5751/ES-12080-260122>, 22.

99 F Berkes and C Folke (eds), *Linking Social and Ecological Systems: Management Practices and Social Mechanisms for Building Resilience* (Cambridge Univ. Press 1998). Thoughts of socio-ecological adaptive management are concretised in a 'Man and Biosphere Reserve' in Sweden, being first of its kind; Folke and others (n 68) 459.

100 Armitage (n 63) 95–6. Socio-ecological system is defined to mean integrated, coupled systems of people and environments; ibid 96, panel 1.

traditional management projects easily became adversarial, only worsening the relationships between the parties, this all-inclusive approach serves as a method of risk-sharing.[101]

Adaptively managed, resilient systems have been offered as an alternative to command and control, claiming that due to its stagnant elements, the latter leads to unforeseen and unwanted consequences since where reliability, predictability – and, often, according to the underlying desire, productivity – profit, and natural variation suffer.[102] Command and control does not refer merely to a common method of natural resources governance but to a philosophy according to which a successful selection can be made to favour one particular component of natural systems. The chosen element ought to be altered while the rest of the manipulated system remains undisturbed.[103] The critique is summarised in a maxim 'when the range of natural variation in a system is reduced, the system loses resilience.'[104]

Resilience has two contexts, equilibrium resilience being the traditional one, in which stability close to equilibrium is desired – in its search for efficiency and predictability, it is compatible with command and control. In the other, ecosystem resilience, the focus is on surveying the amounts of disturbance a system can absorb or accommodate before changing its structure, its variables, and its processes. Resiliency needs to be held apart from adaptability, which is built upon the former, being the capacity to which actors in a system can influence resilience.[105] On top of that, socio-ecological resilience includes notions of the 'degree to which the system is capable of self-organisation' and 'the degree to which the system can build and increase the capacity for learning and adaptation.' Resiliency is, however, a concept so broad that when needed, it serves also as a metaphor – in the more concrete interpretations, 'defining resilience *of* what *to* what' aids in analysing the system.[106]

101 Olsson, Folke, and Berkes (n 69) 75, 87. A socio-ecological system is defined to mean integrated, coupled systems of people and environments; ibid 96, panel 1. The managers' risk is limited, hence adaptive co-management represents a top-down approach to natural resources management; Armitage and others (n 63) 100. Risk limiting is not explicated in the source but interpreted here.

102 Holling and Meffe (n 21) 329–30. Use of pesticides in agriculture is given as one illustrative example.

103 Holling and Meffe (n 21) 330.

104 Holling and Meffe (n 21) 330.

105 Adaptability is defined in text to n 52 ff; Holling and Meffe (n 21) 330. Scientifically, resilience has basic rudiment aspects. They are: (1) latitude; (2) resistance; (3) precariousness; and (4) panarchy; Walker and others (n 48) 2–3.

106 Steve Carpenter and others, 'From Metaphor to Measurement: Resilience of What to What?' (2001) Ecosystems 4(8) <https://doi.org/10.1007/s10021-001-0045-9>, 765–7. The last-mentioned aspect concerns systems' capacity to revive, reorganise, and develop – in this viewpoint the attractor is not seen as a threat but as a source of opportunities; Carl Folke, 'Resilience: The Emergence of a Perspective for Social–Ecological Systems Analyses' (2006) Global Environ Change 16(3) <https://doi.org/10.1016/j.gloenvcha.2006.04.002>, 253, 259.

In the concrete understanding of resilience, the multilevel and polycentric collaboration of stakeholders is of great value, with participants ranging from the local level to international organisations.[107] The 'daunting task' of creating a space for adaptive co-management requires the presence of five elements. First, with multilevel governance, all the various levels and cross-scale interactions existing in the socio-ecological sphere can be accounted for. Time – it might take as long as a decade to build up the trust needed for the network to function properly – and money are needed: market-based solutions and delicate analysis of the incentives used should ease the challenging process. Learning also has a leading role in co-management: objectives, approaches, outcomes, and risks should create a systematic learning process. Power asymmetries that hamper trust-building are also recognised.[108] Regarding assessment and monitoring, uncertainty and the gap between theory and practice prevails, especially in the terrestrial–marine interface, a prime example of which is agricultural runoff. This is coupled with the importance of scale: indicators vary among large- and small-scale socio-ecological systems. Last but not least, if the policymakers are not willing to support the inevitably slow adaptive co-management project and give it the needed time, failure is to be expected.[109] The task is formidable, to say the least – no wonder command and control still prevails.

Knowledge in Learning

A resilient socio-ecological system is one that, upon being disturbed, can retain equilibrium and develop with the attractor instead of taking the path of transformation into a new socio-ecological system.[110] Whether the system is self-reliant and able to learn without much interference is relevant to how one should regulate the system. Resilience is built by deliberate knowledge generation that considers the organisations and institutions involved in management: in adaptive co-management, systems are in essence understood as multilevel, collaborative, and site-specific.[111] The development lies in how institutional arrangements are included in the learning process. While one elementary part of adaptive management is gaining scientific (i.e. ecological) knowledge,

107 Folke and others (n 68) 448–9. Multi-level collaboration in the Baltic Sea Region is examined above in ch 2.

108 Armitage (n 63) 97–8.

109 Alongside these five parameters, Armitage and others suggest ten conditions under which adaptive co-management is most likely to succeed; Armitage (n 63) 99. Regarding adaptive management with the WFD, the time span of six years acknowledges the tardiness of adaptive co-management process.

110 Folke and others (n 68) 457.

111 They are '[f]lexible community-based systems of resource management tailored to specific places and situations and supported by, and working with, various organisations at different levels'; Olsson, Folke, and Berkes (n 69) 75.

a similar increase in knowledge is expected of the participating institutions and organisations.[112] Resilience is not built simply by focusing on mere knowledge of institutions, but knowledge of and emphasis on processes occurring between institutions is needed – working rules and organisational dynamics being the telltale signs. The knowledge needed for adaptive management is both scientific and indigenous, and neither process exists without proper institutional frameworks. [113]

Even though traditional co-management might have been about formal arrangements organised in a top-down manner, it is now understood as *an emergent property* of management systems, emphasising its self-organisational aspects.[114] That does not mean complete anarchy: leadership is fundamental to the process, prioritising the shared vision over the management project. In smaller-scale adaptive co-management projects, leadership can also emerge from the communities joining the process. This philosophy rejects novel institutions: the process ought to emerge from those already existing.[115] This process can and, according to some, ought to be supported or facilitated through means including legislative actions enabling suitable social space, appropriate funding, facilitating monitoring, feedback, and learning, and minding the information flow and various combinations of information sources. In governance terminology, the process is at least multicentred, if not polycentric, which explains why adaptive co-management enhances resilience: bridging the gap of socio-ecological knowledge serves as a buffer zone protecting the managers from failure by increasing stability through the region's different levels.[116]

Tackling uncertainty with (social) learning began from the notion that the wider the origins of knowledge, the better its quality. Coupling local knowledge with scientific knowledge, a process called bridging, requires collaboration between various knowledge providers to succeed. Bearing in mind the tradition of one-way knowledge sharing and centralised governance in water

112 This aspect comes when the dynamic learning process of adaptive management is joined with the so-called linkage aspects of co-operative management; Olsson, Folke, and Berkes (n 69) 75.

113 Olsson, Folke, and Berkes (n 69) 76.

114 Emergent properties are such that evolve without external intervention and do not counteract a system's resilience – of these, Adam Smith's 'invisible hand' is the most common example. Whether adaptive co-management is even an emergent strategy has been studied at least in the context of forestry; Jack Ruitenbeek and Cynthia Cartier, 'The Invisible Wand: Adaptive Co-Management as an Emergent Strategy in Complex Bio-economic Systems' (2001) CIFOR Occasional Paper, (34) 16–17. Olsson, Folke, and Berkes (n 69) 83.

115 A distance from rational choice theory is presupposed. When systems are complex and participants of collaborative action myriad, this naturally requires them to be skilled in problem recognition, communication, and ability to place an agenda, to name but a few areas; Bonnie J McCay, 'Emergence of Institutions for the Commons: Contexts, Situations, and Events' in E Ostrom and others (eds), *The Drama of the Commons* (National Academy Press, Washington, DC 2002) 361, 366.

116 Olsson, Folke, and Berkes (n 69) 83–7 and Table 1.

management, bridging might not be the easiest task.[117] However, four factors fundamental to the coping of socio-ecological systems are tolerating uncertainty, combining different sources of knowledge, finding ways to facilitate self-organising, and resilience.[118] Social memory, actor groups, and teams are important in acquiring resilience. Social memory is a combination of previous experience and underlying values manifested in the deliberate decision-making processes. When it comes to adaptive management, diversity of experiences often accumulates. The question of social memory is highly individualised, boiling down even to key persons responsible for passing on the knowledge.[119] It is as if human networks formed traits: many social roles are needed for the formation of social networks that tolerate change and novel conditions. They can build barriers instead of bridges, though, if the underlying worldviews of alternative management options are too wide apart.[120]

Where this leadership takes place is not a trivial concern. Informal networks (also called shadow networks or 'skunkworks') are crucial as incubators of novel, daring ideas, fostering learning and creative problem-solving.[121] In some examples, the informality is taken to the level where a local governmental organisation is run entirely by volunteers. These institutions have been named bridging organisations; their elementary characteristics include the ability to enhance knowledge sharing, trust-building, the identification of common interests, the filtering of external threats, and only requiring flexible and open institutions to thrive. This has led to the concept of 'distribution of powers' at the local administrative level: since informality enhances resilience, separating enforcing administration from collaborating ones might be a reasonable solution.[122]

117 Bridging takes place most often between indigenous and scientific knowledge on, e.g. wildlife management, even though its benefits are wider, including trust-building and conflict-solving. Fikret Berkes, 'Evolution of Co-Management: Role of Knowledge Generation, Bridging Organizations and Social Learning' (2009) J Environ Manage 90(5) <https://doi.org/10.1016/j.jenvman.2008.12.001>, 1694, 1696.

118 Folke and others (n 68) 452.

119 Folke and others (n 68) 453; Berkes and Folke (n 99) 352–87.

120 Thus even single individuals can be crucial for a resilient socio-ecological network, emphasising leadership of institutions and organisations. Valuable characteristics of leaders include eye for opportunities and ability to manage inevitable conflicts between participants. Folke and others (n 68) 456–7, 459.

121 Folke and others (n 68) 459. Lance Gunderson, 'Resilience, Flexibility and Adaptive Management—Antidotes for Spurious Certitude?' (1999) Conserv Ecol 3(1) <https://www.jstor.org/stable/26271703>, 7. Concept 'shadow network' was introduced by L Gunderson, CS Holling, S Light (eds), *Barriers and Bridges to the Renewal of Ecosystems and Institutions* (Columbia Univ. Press 1995).

122 Folke and others (n 68) 460–2; Thomas Hahn and others, 'Trust-Building, Knowledge Generation and Organizational Innovations: The Role of a Bridging Organization for Adaptive Comanagement of a Wetland Landscape Around Kristianstad, Sweden' (2006) Hum Ecol 34(4) <https://doi.org/10.1007/s10745-006-9035-z>, 590.

Adaptive water management seeks to better incorporate learning, especially in the monitoring phase. Monitoring learning is similar to the adaptive cycles familiar from general adaptive management theory: when reflecting on learning, the focus is not on the success of the management but whether the learning itself has been successful. When monitoring is collaborative, management is 'easier to digest' – collaborative monitoring increases the experienced validity of collected data among the stakeholders and makes it more understandable and thus better exploited in the process.[123] In other words, the pattern acts as a meeting point of two governance models, adaptive management and collaborative governance, thus integrating collaborative monitoring with the ongoing monitoring systems.[124]

Social Learning in European Water Management

The challenge of adaptive water management has also brought up questions of boundaries: how the lines between policy, knowledge, and management practice are drawn. The governance of management must itself be adaptive, especially to enable social learning. Both informational and normative sources of uncertainty are of great importance and require different methods of scrutiny. Cognitive learning, which tends to be only one way, alleviates informational uncertainty: coming from experts (of, e.g. hydrology) or officials and going to stakeholders and local users. Thus, focusing on communication can impact cognitive learning. Normative learning is also an interesting endeavour in itself: when it comes to values and norms, not much more is acquired than acknowledging them. Wide-based collaboration might benefit this aspect of learning but when it comes to holistic management of hydrological systems, there are so many parties that it is rare to have management inclusive enough for comprehensive collaboration. (One of the main points of criticism in the WFD has been the assessment criteria.) Agreeing on the criteria does not save the managers – or politicians – from the controversy over whether a planned project complies with it, but discussions over whether hydropower overcomes household water needs continue even when assessment criteria have been agreed upon among the stakeholders.[125]

123 Georgina Cundill and Christo Fabricius, 'Monitoring in Adaptive Co-Management: Toward a Learning Based Approach' (2009) J Environ Manage 90(11) <https://doi.org/10.1016/j.jenvman.2009.05.012>, 3208. Also participatory adaptive management advances learning; Marie Fujitani, Andrew McFall, Christoph Randler, and Robert Arlinghaus, 'Participatory Adaptive Management Leads to Environmental Learning Outcomes Extending Beyond the Sphere of Science' (2017) Science Advances 3(6) <https://doi.org/10.1126/sciadv.1602516>.

124 Cundill and Fabricius (ibid) 3209.

125 Louis Lebel, Torsten Grothmann, and Bernd Siebenhüner, 'The Role of Social Learning in Adaptiveness: Insights from Water Management' (2010) International Environmental Agreements: Politics, Law and Economics 10 <https://doi.org/10.1007/s10784-010-9142-6>, 346–8. Another

As in other water management projects, learning in the WFD forms a three-tiered structure. The shortest is the collaboration between stakeholders (microlevel). The second tier, taking place across medium to long time spans, is learning in the actor networks (mesolevel), and the longest time is required for learning to affect the governance structure itself (macrolevel). The tiers are independent of each other, and learning among them follows the familiar pattern of single- or double-loop learning. In the WFD, the second and third tiers are strongly linked, not only formally but also informally, and interaction is two-fold: on one side, learning on informal platforms can add to the adaptivity of the management, and on the other, the structural context of the governance affects said informal platforms.[126] The model applies a broad understanding of learning and also often enables disregarded tacit knowledge.[127] This is fundamental in water management since expert knowledge is not necessarily as objective as could be desired for the management to be truly collaborative, and the issue is concretised in, e.g. agriculture. The farmers' knowledge of, for example, the soil conditions may be profound and could benefit management if the more abstract and less local scientific knowledge only allowed it.[128] In ten cases of social learning across the Union, enhanced collaboration benefitted the WFD's practical implementation, water management became more collaborative, and management became more widely accepted. However, and as can be expected, studies discovered management practices that effectively hindered collaboration: authorities were reluctant to open management to the public for fear of confidentiality loss or hid behind technical expert knowledge, a strategy readily available in the case of the WFD.[129]

Informality refers to the fact that participants of the platforms gather and negotiate freely and without contribution from formal institutions. Due to the two-fold interaction, originally, informal platforms could become permanent parts of the formal structure and still manage to sustain their informality. Even

---

aspect of social learning is relational learning that emphasises trust-building among stakeholders. Due to the acknowledged challenges of adaptive water management, this can be quite a challenge: when information flow is often one-way only, bringing different levels of stakeholders to the same table in order to develop trustful relations might be easier said than done. Ibid 346.

126 As illustrated in Figure 2 in Claudia Pahl-Wostl and others, 'Social Learning and Water Resources Management' (2007) Ecology and Society 12(2) <www.ecologyandsociety.org/vol12/iss2/art5/>, 5. Communities of practice are exploited when examining the layers. E Wenger, *Communities of Practice; Learning, Meaning, and Identity* (CUP 1998).

127 Tacit knowledge is not a counterpart to explicit knowledge. It attempts to – even when grounds for differentiation exist – avoid a dichotomy between 'soft' and 'hard' knowledge and clear room for broader understanding of knowledge affecting the stakeholders and formation of their opinions. Pahl-Wostl and others (n 126).

128 Erik Mostert, Marc Craps, and Claudia Pahl-Wostl, 'Social Learning: The Key to Integrated Water Resources Management?' (2008) Water Int 33(3) <https://doi.org/10.1080/02508060802275757>, 293, 301.

129 Mostert, Craps, and Pahl-Wostl (ibid) 299.

modest formalisation can obstruct the benefits of the informal platforms. In the context of the WFD, a modest level of institutionalisation is valuable since it bridges boundaries, work much needed due to the complexity of the WFD and the rapid macrolevel changes that affect local organisations. In the implementation of the WFD, national cultures had a strong impact on how successful implementation was in this respect: Germany is mentioned as a country that foresaw the need for bridging organisations and thus succeeded well in the implementation.[130] Facilitating social learning is nonetheless a question of power. Existing power structures are not often contested in hands-on water management projects. The one single factor that can be distinguished from successful management practices is clarity in the role of stakeholder involvement: the clearer the role, the better the stakeholders' understanding of the significance of their participation.[131]

A Call for Clarity Amidst Conflated Concepts

Clarity is called for elsewhere as well. Regardless of how often 'social learning' has been referred to in various adaptive management studies, the content of the concept has yet to be clarified. At least two distinctions are needed: separating individual and wider learning from each other and distinguishing participatory rights from social learning.[132] Conceptual blurriness most likely does not stem from the differences between governance and adaptive co-management approaches since these research frameworks are so much alike.[133] Misunderstanding regarding participatory rights is fuelled by the inability to distinguish between social learning and the conditions needed to facilitate it. There is a correlation between social learning and participation, but causality has not been established. The fulfilment of participatory rights may aid in social learning, but social learning can occur even without participatory processes – some projects published as successful social learning experiments have consisted of nothing but active stakeholder participation. A similar amalgamation of concepts appears with learning itself: distinguishing between learning and its consequences has proved tricky. Phenomena such as pro-environmental

130 Pahl-Wostl and others (n 126).

131 Erik Mostert and others, 'Social Learning in European River-Basin Management: Barriers and Fostering Mechanisms from 10 River Basins' (2007) Ecology and Society 12(1) <http://www.ecologyandsociety.org/vol12/iss1/art19/>, 19.

132 Mark Reed and others, 'What is Social Learning?' (2010) Ecology and Society 15(4) <http://www.ecologyandsociety.org/vol15/iss4/resp1/>.

133 Questions of participation and collaboration are mentioned as crucial in the interaction of the two research fields. Dave Huitema and others, 'Adaptive Water Governance: Assessing the Institutional Prescriptions of Adaptive (Co-) Management from a Governance Perspective and Defining a Research Agenda' (2009) Ecology and Society 14(1) <www.ecologyandsociety.org/vol14/iss1/art26/>.

behaviour, enhanced trust among stakeholders, stakeholder empowerment, adaptive capacity, or stakeholders' behavioural change are conflated with social learning even though they are potential outcomes of it, not characteristics of learning itself. Distinguishing between individual and wider learning is also absent.[134]

The concept of social learning is so conflated that impact analysis of management becomes challenging, as duly noted in adaptive management experiments. Unsurprisingly, when it comes to adaptive management, the results consist of differentiation between single, double-loop, and triple-loop social learning, which does not aid evaluation. The first stage means acknowledging the consequences of the actions. The second exposes the presuppositions behind decision-making, resulting in changing attitudes or social norms. The third phase affects values, norms, and thinking processes and fabricates the objects of previous phases. Since learning can occur independently at any or all of these levels, claims that, e.g. meagre progress in values equates to limited social learning would be an imprecise generalisation.[135] Social learning consists of two interdependent spheres: measurable changes in the knowledge of individuals and a measurable shift of this change from the individual level to a wider one. Learning among individuals ought to diffuse to wider institutional levels before social learning takes place. 'Wider institutional levels' refers to social units or communities. Transformed attitudes in a small group do not remain there but are funnelled further via 'learning through interaction,' which can take place in networks and even network structures.[136] It is beneficial to learning if networks consist of groups whose knowledge systems and worldviews vary – but, interestingly, whose epistemological beliefs are rather alike. The result implies that groups with contradicting worldviews can accommodate and learn from each other as long as they share certain underlying premises on the possibility of knowledge; that is, as long as they have sufficient epistemological ground in common.

It is also worth noting that high levels of interaction do not equate to high levels of social learning. Power structures can hinder learning by constraining interaction and replacing local knowledge with the knowledge of the most influential groups.[137]

134 Or maybe it ought to be seen as a natural consequence of the blurry concept: if social learning is not adequately determined from its facilitators and its consequences, it would be surprising to find it able to differentiate between different stages of learning. Reed and others (n 132).

135 Reed and others (n 132).

136 This mechanism is illustrated by a successful media campaign that popularises certain environmental issues, bringing them to the knowledge of wider communities. This cannot be counted as social learning if information is not distributed individually from one person to another. Reed and others (n 132).

137 Text to n 131. Reed and others (n 132).

Institutional Configurations from Robustness Framework

Social and ecological systems ought to be studied as one without hampering the understanding of the individual parts. The attempt has been criticised, however, based on the fact that the most successful case studies of adaptive co-management have been from primitive, homogenous societies with little financial or technological means; these communities possess the prerequisites for success in joining social and ecological management.[138] Practical solutions on how the same could be reached when economic development becomes the attractor have not been widely distributed.[139] Since regulation of adaptive management has also proved to be difficult, one is left to wonder whether adaptive socio-ecological management experiments follow the theory as long as nothing fixed is included, be they fixed economic realities or normative rules. Even while practical solutions on how the desired resilience could be exported to standard Western society are yet to be presented, the discussion has acknowledged the role of institutions and administration in the process.[140] When studying the 'institutional configurations' needed for socio-ecological systems to become sturdier, the robustness of the system hinges on one relationship: that between public infrastructure providers and natural resource users. The socio-ecological network system can be defined as consisting of resources and their users and public infrastructures and their users.[141] Layers of resources, their governance, and the institutional infrastructure involved form a robustness framework. Question-setting in this kind of institutional analysis is familiar to that which initiated adaptive management in the first place, focusing on enhancing the resilience of the ecosystem instead of seeing it as a management object. The aim is to move beyond descriptive examinations, complement resilience, and explicate the cost–benefit trade-offs inevitable in the era of

138 Though presented as a challenge in the context of this study, the finding was transformative in its time, exposing the feeble foundations of the then-paradigmatic tragedy of the commons theory; Elinor Ostrom and others (eds), *The Drama of the Commons* (National Academy Press 2002).

139 Christopher M Holmes, 'Navigating the Socioecological Landscape' (2001) 15(5) Conserv Biol <https://doi.org/10.1111/j.1523-1739.2001.01552.x>, 1467.

140 Including the question of or assumption that the required institutions already exist, John M Anderies, Marco A Janssen, and Elinor Ostrom, 'A Framework to Analyze the Robustness of Social-Ecological Systems from an Institutional Perspective' (2004) Ecology and Society 9(1) <http://www.ecologyandsociety.org/vol9/iss1/art18>, 18. For a more critical stance on the understanding of institutionalism in mainstream adaptive governance, Frances Cleaver and Luke Whaley, 'Understanding Process, Power and Meaning in Adaptive Governance' (2018) Ecology and Society 23(2) <https://doi.org/10.5751/ES-10212-230249>, 49.

141 Public infrastructure consists of physical and social capital, the latter referring to the rules used 'in governing, managing and using the system' and factors reducing the transaction costs of said activity and its enforcement. Anderies, Janssen, and Ostrom (n 140). See also John M Anderies, Olivier Barreteau, and Ute Brady, 'Refining the Robustness of Social-Ecological Systems Framework for Comparative Analysis of Coastal System Adaptation to Global Change' (2019) Reg Environ Change 19 <https://doi.org/10.1007/s10113-019-01529-0>, 1891.

uncertainty.[142] The robustness framework is particularly suited to investigating the last-mentioned goal.

Robustness is defined as 'the maintenance of some desired system characteristics despite fluctuations in the behaviour of its component parts or its environment.'[143] It is meant to tackle uncertainty, identified as the system's capacity to handle external and internal disturbances. The former include biophysical ones, such as floods or climate change, impacting either the resource itself or the public infrastructure, and socio-economic ones, e.g. economic or major political changes, impacting the resource users or public infrastructure providers. Internal disturbances include 'rapid reorganisations' of social or ecological systems that are caused by changes in the subsystems they consist of.[144] The definition of robustness is linked with the demise of the human population or its long-term suffering: if the ecological systems do not move 'into a new domain of attraction' in which these occur, the system is robust. Features of robustness consist of strategic interactions between parties, the rules governing these actions, and the collective choices made to create those rules. Since the robustness framework consists of four parties, it generates multiple possible interactions.[145] The ability to account for all these is how the robustness framework contributes to studies on adaptive socio-ecological management. Even though a single integrated model including all the factors and their interactions might not be feasible, a more nuanced analysis is enabled.[146] The robustness framework allows for simultaneously acknowledging the operational level practising adaptive management (the resources) and the collective-choice level at which the management is decided (the public infrastructure providers).[147] As such, the approach goes beyond multilevel analysis – it not only describes the multilevel aspects but also attempts to address the issues at stake.

One advantage of the robustness framework is its ability to elucidate the choices of the 'social' part of socio-ecological management. In cases when the ecological base might partially collapse or show signs of collapsing, the social system does not necessarily react to the decline by trying to sustain the deteriorating component with all the available means. It can also, in the wake of low adaptive capacity, turn to other resources capable of replacing the losses

142 Anderies, Janssen, and Ostrom (n 140). On trade-offs see text to n 63 ff.

143 Anderies, Janssen, and Ostrom (n 140), referring to definition by JM Carlson and John Doyle, 'Complexity and Robustness' (2002) PNAS 99 (suppl 1) 2538, 2539.

144 Anderies, Janssen, and Ostrom (n 140); Holling and Meffer (n 21) 330, Folke (n 106) 259.

145 Anderies, Janssen, and Ostrom (n 140) Table 2.

146 As a summary of the others, see Folke (n 106) 253.

147 Anderies, Janssen, and Ostrom (n 140).

occurring elsewhere.[148] This capacity can lead to a 'sequential destruction,' a notable risk for the long-term sustainability of the socio-ecological system.[149]

Another benefit of the robustness framework is the multi-agent models developed that may help in finding practical solutions – instead of only describing the complex systems at an abstract level – and maybe even benefit large-scale experiments. By exploiting the great advances in computing power, multi-agent models might fill the gaps previously filled with assumptions or even guesswork.[150] In essence, they are not necessarily anything new. Any form of management of ecosystems can be divided into actions taken by certain agents and their behaviour restricted by certain rules.[151] As with any dichotomy, the one between actors and rules can also be challenged, regardless of how entwined they are. At the end of the day, it all boils down to the rules; distinguishing the actors is a choice conducted due to practical reasons.[152] However, an obvious benefit from the shift is that analysis becomes more nuanced; yet another benefit of the robustness framework. Instead of having humans who have human aspirations and objectives, the various models that humans have in their decision-making become elucidated. Instead of assuming people have only one position, the various alternatives that people might have are acknowledged. The result of the analysis changes accordingly, as does its representativeness of the real-life systems modelled.[153] When applying multi-actor modelling in socio-ecological systems, an analogy is required: in the dichotomy of actors and rules, institutions take the place of rules. Institutions in this sense can be either formal, such as law, or informal, such as social norms.[154]

148 Anderies, Janssen, and Ostrom (n 140).

149 The choice available for the 'social' of the system remains unseen in more straightforward approaches – and proves how social systems rely on the ecological ones.

150 John M Anderies, 'The transition from local to global dynamics: a proposed framework for agent-based thinking in social-ecological systems' in Marco A Janssen (ed), *Complexity and Ecosystem Management: The Theory and Practice of Multi-Agent Systems* (Edward Elgar 2002) 13, 16–18.

151 Such as boundary, position, authority, scope, aggregation (or transformation), information, and payoff; Anderies (n 150) 18–19. Definition of rules is that of Ostrom.

152 That is not to claim that these two sides of the socio-ecological system would be alike or that pieces of the ecosystem would be setting objectives like people do. The behaviour of animals is *described as if* they would or could have goals and exploit resources like humans. A distinction between human and non-human actors is not required to successfully examine the resource allocation but relinquishing the human/non-human dichotomy contextualises multi-agent modelling better; Anderies (n 150) 19–21, 23–5.

153 Anderies (n 150) 29–30. When the framework is combined with the rules, a taxonomy for models is created. Thus, apart from being classified, compared, and contrasted, they can also be related to certain interests; Anderies (n 150) 31.

154 Both express cultural rules, which are products of group selection, being the opposites of individual rules produced by individual selection. Marco A Janssen, 'Changing the rules of the game: lessons from immunology and linguistics for self-organization of institutions' in Marco A Janssen (ed), *Complexity and Ecosystem Management: The Theory and Practice of Multi-Agent Systems* (Edward Elgar 2002) 35, 35–6.

These models allow for self-organised systems, hence avoiding the common mistake of assuming that governmental intervention is the most desirable solution. This assumption is based on the understanding that the governmental body has the perfect information needed for making optimal management decisions or that governments would be best equipped with the trust needed for co-operative management. A closer explanation of the self-organisation of institutions can be delivered, resulting in governmental intervention not even being needed for successful management.[155] The self-organisation model consists of four stages. First, the possible rules are coded, being founded on the integrated understanding or grammar of the institutions in which they are deciphered as rules, norms, and strategies, not just one of them. Second, the emergence of rules is described as a process of experimentation, including contact with different institutions in order to increase diversity. New rules are created in the process of tinkering instead of engineering. They are developed using whatever means the socio-ecological system provides under uncertainty regarding the course of the development.[156] After the rule is conceived comes the third stage – either by an external factor or endogenously: a group selection in which the emergent rule is dismissed or retained. The selection is based on an existing set of rules, either formal or informal. The latter is dependent on the amount of trust in the socio-ecological system, levels of which are higher in denser networks.[157] Last but not least, emergent and approved rules are needed: socio-ecological systems sustain a memory of useful responses.[158]

Working as a counterargument for the universal betterment of governmental interventions – and thus being founded on contemporary understanding of governance – multi-agent model methodologies serve as useful reminders of how it is not the scientific part of adaptive management that obstructs its regulation. Detailed analysis of socio-ecological systems and their development can be acquired even if resilience studies or adaptive management paradigms may appear obscure.[159] But how does the legal reply to the challenge of establishing

155 Janssen (ibid) 37. This evolution of the self-organisation of institutions (in the understanding of cultural rules) is concretised in a model facilitated by analogies from linguistics and immunology. Linguistics emphasises the aspect of learning a newcomer needs to undergo prior to being understood in new surroundings – or in analogy, the way in which the attractor and socio-ecological system need to become accustomed to each other. Even though socio-ecological systems are not organisms, the success of traditional ecosystems management is built on aspects familiar to immunology: detecting anomalies, developing effective policies, and learning lessons by remembering the previous wise choices; ibid 37–8.

156 Janssen (n 154) 45.

157 Janssen (n 154) 46. Serving to explain why a significant amount of adaptive management experiments have worked better on small-scale projects.

158 Janssen (n 154) 46–7.

159 See critique by text to n 36 ff. The greatest of the problems of our time are of course also multiscalar and multilevel, John M Anderies and others, 'Aligning Key Concepts for Global Change

a socio-eco-legal system? The rest of this chapter and Chapter 4 are reserved for answering the question.

'LEGAL' – Managing Adaptivity

We have learned that socio-ecological systems are tremendously complex, their management and scrutiny undergo unending learning cycles, and obstructing this flux of change with fixed boundaries sullies the novelty that the adaptive paradigm brought in comparison with its predecessor. These conclusions stem from scientific reality and ought to be treated as such in proceeding to the realms of the legal. Paying full attention to the social half does not reduce the uncertainty inherent in the adaptive paradigm – on the contrary, adding sociological knowledge to adaptive management only increases the amount of uncertainty that ought to be managed, intensifying the system's complexity.[160] On a high level of abstraction, the pursuits of adaptive management appear to be in conflict with those of any legal system: predictability and stability.[161] The command-and-control approach in ecology was doomed to fail, and it is highly likely that the same fate awaits those who wish to regulate socio-ecological systems towards predictability or certainty.[162] Or do these difficulties exist only in the eye of the beholder? After all, CS Holling himself has welcomed the legal to join the project of socio-ecological management: law, as a mechanism for harmonising human interactions in large areas, would be well suited to tackle the joint challenges.[163]

By default, environmental law encompasses features that promote adaptivity, and it is well versed in operating with future-oriented decision-making that requires estimates, risk assessment, and the accommodation of various uncertainties.[164] More specifically to the theme at hand, recent years have witnessed a rise in research on the role of law in adaptive management, probing the US-originated theorem in the European context as well, focusing on specific

Policy: Robustness, Resilience, and Sustainability' (2013) Ecology and Society 18(2) <http://dx.doi.org/10.5751/ ES-05178-180208>, 8.

160 John M Anderies and Marco A Janssen, 'Robustness of Social-Ecological Systems: Implications for Public Policy' (2013) Policy Studies Journal 41(3) <https://doi.org/10.1111/psj.12027>, 513.

161 Combining flexibility and stability is challenging not only in the broader governance regime but also – and especially – regarding the rudimentary questions of normativity, which should not be eclipsed. Andreas Duit and others, 'Governance, Complexity, and Resilience' (2010) Global Environ Change 20(3) <https://doi.org/10.1016/j.gloenvcha.2010.04.006>, 363, 367.

162 Holling and Meffe (n 21) 330. See also Folke (n 106) 263.

163 C Holling, 'Response to "Panarchy and the Law"' (2012) Ecology and Society 17(4) <http://dx.doi.org/10.5751/ES-05402-170437>.

164 Elizabeth Fisher, 'The Rise of Transnational Environmental Law and the Expertise of Environmental Lawyers' (2012) TEL 1(1) <https://doi.org/10.1017/S2047102511000021>, 43–52; text to n 1 in ch 5.

environmental problems or discussing it in more abstract and traditional terms, focusing on roles of legal certainty or flexibility in promoting adaptivity.[165] At times, the facilitatory role that the law could entail in the totality is emphasised.[166] As we will learn in detail in the next chapter, European water governance relies on heavy, decentralised administrative structures within which regional authorities across the continent conduct iterative water management cycles.[167] Also, as promised earlier, I give a full account of the details of these arrangements at the Union level in general and in one legal system in particular to establish the legal landscape in which the management is conducted. This book began with a bid for contingency: legal instruments, concepts, or practices are best analysed in their context, where the closer meaning of ubiquitous and vague concepts can best be defined.[168] Not paying due attention to the differences between legal systems may result in misinterpretations and overemphasis on assumed similarities: closer scrutiny may reveal that common and unifying abstractions are only ostensible.[169] Similar arguments about placing excessive trust on the unifying force of broad and vague concepts have also been presented in the adaptive management scholarship. Adaptive management has been popular for a long time, and for decades it has been 'something of a mantra' among managers of natural resources.[170] As the saying suggests, the concept is both value-laden and indeterminate, even to the extent of lacking substance. Uttering generalisations on what 'adaptive management' is and is not might be hasty, especially when one acknowledges the various ways in

165 Antti Belinskij and others, 'From Top-Down Regulation to Bottom-Up Solutions: Reconfiguring Governance of Agricultural Nutrient Loading to Waters' (2019) Sustainability 11 5364; N Soininen and FM Platjouw, 'Resilience and Adaptive Capacity of Aquatic Environmental Law in the EU: An Evaluation and Comparison of WFD, MSFD and MSPD' in D Langlet and R Rayfuse (eds), *The Ecosystem Approach in Ocean Planning and Governance – Perspectives from Europe and Beyond* (Brill 2018) 17.

166 Barbara A Cozens, Lance Gunderson, and Brian C Chaffin, 'Introduction to the Special Feature Practicing Panarchy: Assessing legal flexibility, ecological resilience and adaptive governance in regional water systems experiencing rapid environmental change' (2018) *Ecology and Society* 23(1) <https://doi.org/10.5751/ES-09524-230104>, 4; Miguel F Frohlich and others, 'The Relationship Between Adaptive Management of Social-Ecological Systems and Law' (2018) Ecology and Society 23(2) <https://doi.org/10.5751/ES-10060-230223>, 23.

167 If expressed as a brute simplification; more nuanced analysis in text to n 4 in ch 4.

168 Text to n 3 in ch 1. In other words, most appropriate scalar fit is searched to secure proper understanding of the institutional interplay at hand. Claudia Pahl-Wostl and others, 'Scale-Related Governance Challenges in the Water–Energy–Food Nexus: Toward A Diagnostic Approach' (2021) Sustain Sci 16 <https://doi.org/10.1007/s11625-020-00888-6> 615, 618, 622.

169 This being the contextualist's argument. Jorge E Viñuales, 'Comparative Environmental Law: Structuring a Field' in Jorge E Viñuales and Emma Lees (eds) *The Oxford Handbook of Comparative Environmental Law* (OUP 2019) 3, 15–16.

170 Bradley C Karkkainen, 'Adaptive Ecosystem Management and Regulatory Penalty Defaults: Toward a Bounded Pragmatism' (2002a) Minnesota Law Review 87 943, 945.

which adaptive management is referred to in scientific work.[171] The role of adaptive management appears to have bifurcated: the approach is either seen as an effective tool for natural resources management or as a great sham, its implementation burdened with challenges so great that one is left in permanent uncertainty over whether the desired aims will ever be met.[172] The extremes have emerged from a tendency to oversimplify adaptive management, a misunderstanding that still prevails, and the desire to regard adaptive management as a learning-by-doing method. However, neither of the perspectives is accurate enough. What is commonly cited as a failure of adaptive management is not necessarily a failure of adaptive management in particular but a failure of the management system itself. Understandably, not distinguishing between the two hampers a reliable assessment of the method's effectiveness.

The lack of specificity is a two-way street: the effectiveness of adaptive management has not yet been sufficiently evaluated, in spite of vigorous activity in the field.[173] Even the term 'adaptive management' itself has been given various meanings, some of them hardly dignifying the original concept. To some extent, this is understandable – adaptive management is employed in very diverse settings – but ambiguity appears to be the origin of the confusion. The worst-case scenarios have been realised too, when adaptive management is used as a mere buzzword without taking into account the original definition and requirements of the model.[174] Whether conceptual clarity could have aided in avoiding these challenges remains unresolved, but some have suggested nonetheless that, instead of applying adaptive management to large-scale and complex situations, the method might suit smaller and simpler applications better.[175] Whether such suggestions only add yet another layer of abstraction to the saga is a worthy question.

Pragmatic Orientation to Factual-Evaluative Complexes

However, ambiguity does not necessarily result in futility – and even though vagueness might be the status quo, serious attempts have been made and are

171 Rist, Campbell, and Frost (n 1) 5–7. The analysis is of published research papers, mainly relating to nature conservation on terrestrial systems – waters consisted of approximately one-fifth of the analysed works.

172 Rist, Campbell, and Frost (n 1) 7.

173 Rist, Campbell, and Frost (n 1) 14. 'Seemingly vivid' due to the ambiguous use of the concept – not all projects claiming to employ adaptive management are actually doing what they claim. Ibid, 13.

174 Rist, Campbell, and Frost (n 1) 10, 13. Even misunderstandings of the core concepts can occur. The challenges can be dissected as those relating, first, to logistical, financial, and personnel questions; second, to institutional environment; third, to experimentation within a management framework; or, finally, to spatial and temporal scale. The importance of spatial and temporal scale in EU water management is discussed in text to n 143 and 158 in ch 4.

175 Rist, Campbell, and Frost (n 1) 8, 14.

being made to solidify the concept. Adaptive management is not the sole concept in environmental studies plagued by these aspects: ecological services, keystone species, or ecological restoration have been cited as similar concerns. In contemporary conservation biology, these concepts are considered normative, as ones that 'set the agenda for conservation efforts,' resembling aims or objectives in environmental regulation.[176] Unsurprisingly, one of the main concerns that the fashionableness of the concepts has brought is the obvious conflict between the predictability and accuracy required by the rule of law and the praxis of adaptive management.[177] The claim is that no matter how much the panarchy loops evolve, predictability and certainty are not to be expected.

Adaptive management represents a functional approach to natural resources management. Unlike their counterpart, compositionalism, functionalist approaches share a humanity-nature doctrine in which humans are part of nature and their dependence on the ecosystem is seen as tenuous and even haphazard. Functionalism and compositionalism are antithetical only to the extent that they are ends of one continuum: compositionalists aim to de-anthropocentrise the ages-old preservationist agenda by, e.g. redefining national parks as biodiversity reservoirs. Functionalism might better serve the purposes of the exploited areas of the earth by embedding human economies with nature's in order to produce a mutually sustaining relationship.[178] This bifurcated comprehension of conservative biology, and the synthesis promulgated based on it, has inspired strong objections, even to the extent of claiming that the model is based on an erroneous reading of basic literature in a way that would not be recognised by the original authors. The critique finds that the above-mentioned continuum and the envisaged resolution are not based on solid foundations, dismissing the conclusions particularly regarding the position of adaptive management. Unlike what the synthesis suggests, adaptive management will not lead to the amount of predictability needed for proper controls.[179] To suggest that it might develop into a mechanism subsuming adequate controls is sanguine.[180] Claiming that the development of adaptive management culminates with a secure controlling mechanism is unrealistic.[181]

176 J Baird Callicott, Larry B Crowder, and Karen Mumford, 'Current Normative Concepts in Conservation' (1999) Conservation Biology 13(1) <https://doi.org/10.1046/j.1523-1739.1999.97333.x>, 23. Or, as expressed in Bill Willers, 'A Response to "Current Normative Concepts in Conservation" by Callicott et al.' (2000) Conservation Biology 14(2) <https://www.jstor.org/stable/2641623>, 572; normativity is referring to 'generally accepted standards of correctness.'

177 Karkkainen (n 170) 944.

178 To secure the fulfilment of both traditions, a synthesis that enables both to thrive is suggested, offering one way forward. Callicott, Crowder, and Mumford (n 176) 24, 32.

179 Willers (n 176) 570. Based on the chapters above, this ought to be obvious.

180 Willers (n 176) 570–1.

181 Opinion shared by Willers (n 176) 570.

If the paradigm itself does not offer easy answers, could harsh enough punishment mechanisms rooted in pragmatism help the struggling regulator who wishes to corner the paradigm and regulate it? Adaptive management is not a stranger to philosophy: after all, in its functionality, it can represent 'Deweyan pragmatism.' Dewey suggested that policy ought to be experimental in its essence: tested in practice, analysed, and remodelled when needed. Dewey believes – similarly to the adaptive management paradigm – that evolutionary adaptation occurs in societies, and policy-makers ought to cherish this 'experimental method of inquiry.'[182] Dewey's philosophy of law has been a fruitful guide in attempts to regulate adaptive management but only when coupled with 'regulatory penalty default' to encourage stakeholders in their negotiations to pursue better management. The punishment is applied by default if the parties fail to meet the objective of the negotiations. The model aims to introduce accountability to adaptive management without excessively hindering its flexibility with administrative restraints – accountability might increase if threshold standards of environmental performance were included in the decisions reached.[183] With regulatory penalty default, regulators can also affect where negotiations focus in the first place – if negotiations do not reach an agreement on certain themes, the default option is exercised. (It is a good question whether this kind of agreement is consensual or whether it should be described with an oxymoron of being 'forced voluntary.')[184] Regulatory penalty defaults offer an interesting viewpoint on how adaptive management can be fostered but is best applicable in legal systems with limited central governance. In the reality of the WFD, where the states' (regional) administration is made responsible for management praxis, regulatory penalty defaults can hardly become critical in the European context.

The key difficulty that regulation of adaptive water management faces is essentially that of the fact/value dichotomy. If the choice over facts was better differentiated from normative decision-making, regulation would be a much easier task. Challenging this presupposition might be the first step to a solution and can be done if Putnam's views on disregarding the dichotomy between facts and values are adopted (which, in doing so, builds on the work of Dewey).[185]

182 John Dewey, *Logic: The Theory of Inquiry* (1938) 508–9; Karkkainen (n 170) 956–9. The comparison may be hasty since adaptive management is more thorough and diverse as its average implementation would lead us to believe. The thought is elaborated with this prerequisite in mind.

183 Regulatory penalties ought to enhance information sharing. Karkkainen (n 170) 965. The model was developed in the US regulatory system where similar approaches had already been implemented in the 1970s: if states failed to develop decent enough implementation plans for the Clean Air Act, a federal implementation standard was imposed. The threat of applying the federal approach is believed to form an incentive for states to take matters into their own hands. Karkkainen (n 170) 956–6, fn 73.

184 Karkkainen (n 170) 967, 970. Whether the suggestion is overtly optimistic is another question.

185 Hilary Putnam, *The Collapse of the Fact/Value Dichotomy and Other Essays* (Harvard University Press 2002) 190, 9.

The emphasis is on the word 'dichotomy': differentiation as such does not need to be eliminated, only the notion that they are opposites. Some concepts of law are simultaneously both descriptive and evaluative and ought to be used as such. The reason for disregarding the dichotomy is that often the dichotomy comes hand in hand with 'a highly contentious set of metaphysical claims.'[186] Preserving the dichotomy may also result in belittling values and decisions based on values: when compared to decision-making based on facts, the former might be perceived as outcomes of subjectivity. Disregarding the dichotomy and retaining only the distinction enables the 'factual-evaluative complexes' in which the two aspects are entangled. What is factual and what is evaluative in these complexes is dynamic and changes in relation to time and association, allowing the development and learning of the concept in question.[187]

There is much in factual-evaluative complexes, developed by Del Mar for the needs of relational jurisprudence, to equip the regulator of adaptive management. Assessment of adaptive management regulation might be easier if the field was understood as factual-evaluative instead of either strictly empirical or normative. Relational jurisprudence calls for a holistic understanding of law: instead of scrutinising individual agencies and their positions in law, the focus should be shifted to the relations between individuals (or individuals and communities) and the quality of their interactions. In this analysis, the law is a particle affecting the relations, a reality that makes it necessary to apply both empirical and normative methods of inquiry. Relational jurisprudence consists of three phases, reminiscent of the panarchy loops of adaptive management: first, the decision to focus specifically on relations; second, the decision to examine the quality of those relations; and third, taking some of the relations into closer scrutiny in order to evaluate how an individual factor affects the quality of the examined relations.[188] The approach is introduced with an example, vulnerability, illustrating features in which relational jurisprudence differs from preceding perceptions of law. The example emphasises mutual dependency over the autonomy of individuals and acknowledges that management of the examined concepts diverges in different relations: some contain more risk than others, which ought to be reflected in the management process.[189] The role of the law in the protection of vulnerability (or, *mutatis mutandis*, the environment) is proactive and prophylactic, creating structures in which vulnerability (or the environment) can best be protected from even tentative

186 Maksymilian Del Mar, 'Relational Jurisprudence – Vulnerability between Fact and Value' (2012) 2(2) Law and Method <https://doi.org/10.5553/ReM/221225082012002002005>, 66–7.

187 To claim something as entangled presupposes a distinction but saves from the metaphysical commitments dichotomy would incorporate. Del Mar (n 186) 69–71.

188 Del Mar (n 186) 72–3.

189 Del Mar (n 186) 74–5.

disruptions.[190] Relational jurisprudence elegantly describes the role that the legal ought to possess in the regulation of adaptive management. The legal has its part in managing the environment: it is not only an instrument for protection but a part of a mutually dependent system. Both normative and empirical methods are required for a full picture of adaptive water management regulation. By letting go of the strict fact/value dichotomy, the observer gains, if nothing else, a viewpoint from which the complexity of the situation is seen in its broadest.[191] With the help of relational jurisprudence, the legal takes its place in the system: the complex system to be managed becomes not socio-ecological but socio-eco-legal.[192]

In the following chapters, the challenge of this endeavour is dissected in the context of European water management praxis.[193] It is not exceptional for waters to necessitate a re-evaluation of concepts: water rights – water abstraction and water stewardship – also emphasise the need to rethink traditional concepts in order to enable holistic and integrated management.[194] In the evolution of property rights, the economic underpinnings of the complex system resemble the ecological underpinnings of socio-ecological systems: the understanding of conceptions of water rights is enriched if the institutional and legal framework, the natural surroundings, and the economic foundation are all fully considered. Instead of seeing rights and regulation as competing or exclusive, they can be seen to complement each other, the WFD being an illustrative example thereof: it is holistic not only regarding the physical surroundings it aims to govern but also regarding the institutional or legal mechanisms it employs.[195]

The Unavoidable Legal Fictions

By turning to the concept of legal fictions, relational jurisprudence can make a difference in adjudication as well as (socio-eco-)legal self-understanding.[196] The original purpose of legal fictions was to make visible the relation between

190 Del Mar is naturally not the first to promulgate law's reactivity: within environmental legal scholarship, Westerlund can be cited as a forefather. Staffan Westerlund, 'Rätt och riktigt vetenskap' (2010) (1) Nordic Environmental Law Journal 3, 9–10; Staffan Westerlund, 'Theory of Law for Sustainable Development – Towards or Against?' in HC Bugge and Christina Voigt (eds), *Sustainable Development in National and International Law* (Europa Law Publishing 2008).

191 Del Mar (n 186) 63, 80.

192 In line with Bettina Lange and Mark Shepheard, 'Changing Conceptions of Rights to Water? An Eco-Socio-Legal Perspective' (2014) JEL 26(2) <https://doi.org/10.1093/jel/equ013>, 215.

193 Ch 4 and also ch 5.

194 Lange and Shepheard (n 192) 216–8, 220–1.

195 Lange and Shepheard (n 192) 216–8.

196 Maksymilian Del Mar, 'Legal Fictions and Legal Change' (2013) International Journal of Law in Context 9(04) <https://doi.org/10.1017/S1744552313000244>, 442; Maksymilian Del Mar, 'Legal Fictions and Legal Change in the Common Law Tradition' in Maksymilian Del Mar and William Twining (eds), *Legal Fictions in Theory and Practice* (Springer 2015) 225, 226. Legal fictions

concepts and reality, to evoke their complexity and to explain how seemingly distinct fields such as physics and jurisprudence could find common ground.[197] The trend towards holistic systems prompted the development of the concept, and the systematic features of the examined topic are crucial in attaining a comprehensive view – which is why legal fictions should help in adaptive management regulation.[198] Others have defined the concept in greater detail, discussing how at times, assumption of fact can be 'deliberately, lawfully and irrebuttably made contrary to the facts proven or probable': assumptions are, however, justified by the desire to operationalise legal rules.[199]

In the marriage of legal fictions and adaptive management regulation, the first step is to expand and alter the concept of legal fictions to refer to 'any *suspension* of one or more of the required operative facts leading to the imposition of an associated normative consequence,' as Del Mar has proposed, disregarding the idea of assumption.[200] As a vehicle for legal change, the suspension can occur for two reasons: proof of a required fact is inadequate or the presence of proof to the contrary. By paying full account to uncertainty, legal fictions become forms of tentative cognition, a dynamic resource to courts, aiding adjudication, including adaptive management in a similar manner to how relational jurisprudence aids the understanding of its regulation.[201] One must be cautious, however, since in these developments, legal fictions are examined in relation to the question of evidence, a concept of marginal use in administrative environmental law.[202] The risk must not be overstated, though. Regarding evidence, the claim is more of how the burden of causation ought to be loosened.[203] The situation resembles the uncertain and forward-looking facts fabricated in environmental litigation. Suspended facts enable discourse between judges (or rulings): a once suspended fact can be reinstated in some later proceeding to evaluate whether the evidence is already sufficient. Epistemologically speaking, legal fictions, in the sense adopted here, fits well in the common law system, which is reluctant to adopt firm rules but instead views itself as a 'practised

appear to be experiencing a renaissance, see e.g. Reece Lewis, *Legal Fictions in International Law* (Edward Elgar 2021).

197 Lon L Fuller, *Legal Fictions* (Stanford University Press 1967) ix.

198 Ibid, xi. When probing the boundary between science and law, turning to legal fictions is not unusual, see e.g. Sheila Jasanoff, 'Judicial fictions: The Supreme Court's quest for good science' in Jonathan B Imber (ed) *Searching for Science Policy* (Transaction Publishers) 97.

199 Pierre Olivier, *Legal Fictions in Practice and Legal Science* (Rotterdam University Press 1975), 81.

200 Del Mar 2013 (n 196) 442.

201 Del Mar 2015 (n 196) 229–30. Del Mar continues by deliberating on Olivier's definition and understanding of legal fictions, explaining why the assumption would be dangerous and ambiguous definition to accept; ibid 230–1.

202 Text to n 1 in ch 5.

203 Del Mar 2013 (n 196) 442.

framework of practical reasoning.'[204] Common law reasoning is a process of unending experiments constantly transforming what is regarded as law. It is justified to consider the process as relational, and hence employing relational jurisprudence to common law adjudication does not require an excessively critical approach.[205] Thus, in common law systems, legal fictions have an established position as a vehicle for transformation – constant transformation, or learning, being also characteristic of adaptive management.

Legal fictions are traditionally portrayed in a negative light. They are even seen as dishonest tools of immature legal systems, the use of which diminishes when the system matures into a more structured form. Legal fictions are one manner of growth for the system, often perceived as a phase in the development of a norm, enabling its gradual progress.[206] However, rather than being a box of unpredictable tools in the wrong hands, legal fictions can be construed as an imperative mechanism for a system that holds dynamic balancing dear because, along with other mechanisms, fictions can secure the attainment of the correct balance between flexibility and stability.[207] This is especially so if legal fictions are comprehended as affecting the evaluation of the factual side of the case, becoming a form of tentative cognition. Deployed in this manner, fictions influence the causation (or proof of it), adding to the flexibility and enabling case-by-case development. Thus, fictions are employed when there is inadequate proof, and the line of the preceding cases justifies their use. When legal fictions are examined separately, power abuse claims might be correct but putting the rulings in chronological order alters the assessment. As noted by Del Mar,

> [t]he suspension of a required operative fact is assisted by the analogical extension of a string of cases now asserted to be relevant to the present problem. Facts extended by analogy are like the bricks in the bridge of the fiction.[208]

The judicial system hence learns, and the learning aspect justifies the otherwise suspect procedure. Thus, if accepting pragmatism as the starting point, intellectual tools for advancing adaptive socio-eco-legal systems exist. The legal system can be comprehended as a complex system under experimental development, consisting of case-by-case learning and evolving towards a more balanced

204 Del Mar 2015 (n 196) 238, citing Gerald Postema, 'Classical common law jurisprudence (Part II)' (2003) *Oxford University Commonwealth Law Journal* 3(1) 1–28.

205 Del Mar 2015 (n 196) 227, 238.

206 Del Mar 2015 (n 196) 239–40. Their role as evolutionary device was constructed as an obstruction to legislatural intervention, distributing power to the courts where its rightful holder was deemed to be found. The legislature's initiative even described this as even 'stealing of power.' Ibid 241.

207 Del Mar 2015 (n 196) 245–6.

208 Del Mar 2015 (n 196) 248, 250. Another context in which this feature of legal fictions reoccurs is intention.

reality. In the part of judicial review, these features are most pronounced and hence, in the following chapter, the examination constantly returns to the works of the judiciary. Environmental adjudication is a forward-looking balancing act between desired undertakings and their undesired consequences. In the following chapter, I turn to the practical administrative and procedural constraints under which these balancing acts are conducted. The analysis covers the European level, explaining the realities of its contemporary water governance, but as the volume at hand has pledged to offer a contingent analysis of its object of study, it also elaborates on the implementation of a single Member State and the possibilities of its judicial system to address the challenge. As we will learn, adequate judicial review may become crucial to the European adaptation of adaptive management.[209]

Bibliography

Alexy R, 'On Balancing and Subsumption. A Structural Comparison' (2003) 16(4) Ratio Juris 433–49.

Anderies JM, 'The Transition from Local to Global Dynamics: A Proposed Framework for Agent-Based Thinking in Social-Ecological Systems' in Janssen MA (ed), *Complexity and Ecosystem Management: The Theory and Practice of Multi-Agent Systems* (Edward Elgar 2002).

——— and Janssen MA, 'Robustness of Social-Ecological Systems: Implications for Public Policy' (2013) 41(3) Policy Studies Journal 513 <https://doi.org/10.1111/psj.12027>.

——— and others, 'Aligning Key Concepts for Global Change Policy: Robustness, Resilience, and Sustainability' (2013) 18(2) Ecology and Society 8 <http://doi.org/10.5751/ ES-05178-180208>.

——— Barreteau O and Brady U, 'Refining the Robustness of Social-Ecological Systems Framework for Comparative Analysis of Coastal System Adaptation to Global Change' (2019) 19 Reg Environ Change 1891 <https://doi.org/10.1007/s10113-019-01529-0>.

——— Janssen MA and Ostrom E, 'A Framework to Analyze the Robustness of Social-Ecological Systems from an Institutional Perspective' (2004) 9(1) Ecology and Society 18 <http://www.ecologyandsociety.org/vol9/iss1/art18>.

Armitage D, Marschke M and Plummer R, 'Adaptive Co-Management and the Paradox of Learning' (2008) 18(1) Global Environ Change 86 <https://doi.org/10.1016/j.gloenvcha.2007.07.002>.

Armitage DR and others, 'Adaptive Co-Management for Social-Ecological Complexity' (2009) 7(2) Frontiers in Ecology and the Environment 95 <http://www.jstor.org/stable/25595062>.

Belinskij A and others, 'From Top-Down Regulation to Bottom-Up Solutions: Reconfiguring Governance of Agricultural Nutrient Loading to Waters' (2019) 11 Sustainability 5364.

209 Text to n 3 in ch 1 and text to n 186 in ch 4. The interaction ought, however, to be a two-way street: the socio-ecological sustainability studies might also benefit from the lessons learned on resilience in law, Jonas Ebbesson, 'The Rule of Law in Governance of Complex Socio-Ecological Changes' (2010) Global Environ Change 20(3) <https://doi.org/10.1016/j.gloenvcha.2009.10.009>, 417, 421.

Berkes F, 'Evolution of Co-Management: Role of Knowledge Generation, Bridging Organizations and Social Learning' (2009) 90(5) J Environ Manage 1692 <https://doi.org/10.1016/j.jenvman.2008.12.001>.

Berkes F and Folke C (eds), *Linking Social and Ecological Systems: Management Practices and Social Mechanisms for Building Resilience* (Cambridge University Press 1998).

Callicott JB, Crowder LB and Mumford K, 'Current Normative Concepts in Conservation' (1999) 13(1) Conservation Biology 22 <https://doi.org/10.1046/j.1523-1739.1999.97333.x>.

Carlson JM and Doyle J, 'Complexity and Robustness' (2002) 99(Suppl 1) PNAS 2538.

Carpenter S and others, 'From Metaphor to Measurement: Resilience of What to What?' (2001) 4(8) Ecosystems 765 <https://doi.org/10.1007/s10021-001-0045-9>.

Checkland P, 'Soft Systems Methodology: A Thirty Year Retrospective' (2000) 17(S1) Syst Res Behav Sci S11 <https://doi.org/10.1002/1099-1743(200011)17:1+<::AID-SRES374>3.0.CO;2-O>.

Cleaver F and Whaley L, 'Understanding Process, Power and Meaning in Adaptive Governance' (2018) 23(2) Ecology and Society 49 <https://doi.org/10.5751/ES-10212-230249>.

Costanza R, Graumlich LJ and Steffen W, 'Sustainability or Collapse: Lessons from Integrating the History of Humans and the Rest of the Nature' in Costanza R, Graumlich LJ and Steffen W (eds), *Sustainability or Collapse? An Integrated History and Future of People on Earth* (MIT Press 2007).

Cozens BA, Gunderson L and Chaffin BC, 'Introduction to the Special Feature Practicing Panarchy: Assessing Legal Flexibility, Ecological Resilience and Adaptive Governance in Regional Water Systems Experiencing Rapid Environmental Change' (2018) 23(1) Ecology and Society 4 <https://doi.org/10.5751/ES-09524-230104>.

Cundill G and Fabricius C, 'Monitoring in Adaptive Co-Management: Toward a Learning Based Approach' (2009) 90(11) J Environ Manage 3205 <https://doi.org/10.1016/j.jenvman.2009.05.012>.

Cundill G and others, 'Soft Systems Thinking and Social Learning for Adaptive Management' (2012) 26(1) Conserv Biol 13 <https://doi.org/10.1111/j.1523-1739.2011.01755.x>.

Dearing JA and others, 'Group Report: Integrating Socioenvironmental Interactions Over Centennial Timescales' in Costanza R, Graumlich LJ and Steffen W (eds), *Sustainability or Collapse? An Integrated History and Future of People on Earth* (MIT Press 2007).

Del Mar M 'Relational Jurisprudence – Vulnerability between Fact and Value' (2012) 2(2) Law and Method 63 <https://doi.org/10.5553/ReM/221225082012002002005>.

——— 'Legal Fictions and Legal Change' (2013) 9(4) International Journal of Law in Context 442 <https://doi.org/10.1017/S1744552313000244>.

——— 'Legal Fictions and Legal Change in the Common Law Tradition' in Del Mar M and Twining W (eds), *Legal Fictions in Theory and Practice* (Springer 2015).

Dewey J, *Logic: The Theory of Inquiry* (Henry Holt and Company, Inc. 1938).

Duit A and others, 'Governance, Complexity, and Resilience' (2010) 20(3) Global Environ Change 363 <https://doi.org/10.1016/j.gloenvcha.2010.04.006>.

Ebbesson J, 'The Rule of Law in Governance of Complex Socio-Ecological Changes' (2010) 20(3) Global Environ Change 414 <https://doi.org/10.1016/j.gloenvcha.2009.10.009>.

Fisher E, 'The Rise of Transnational Environmental Law and the Expertise of Environmental Lawyers' (2012) 1(1) TEL 43–52 <https://doi.org/10.1017/S2047102511000021>.

Folke C, 'Resilience: The Emergence of a Perspective for Social–Ecological Systems Analyses' (2006) 16(3) Global Environ Change 253 <https://doi.org/10.1016/j.gloenvcha.2006.04.002>.

——— and others, 'Adaptive Governance of Social-Ecological Systems' (2005) 30(1) Annual Review of Environment & Resources 441 <https://doi.org/10.1146/annurev.energy.30.050504.144511>.

Frohlich MF and others, 'The Relationship between Adaptive Management of Social-Ecological Systems and Law' (2018) 23(2) Ecology and Society 23 <https://doi.org/10.5751/ES-10060-230223>.

Fujitani M, McFall A, Randler C and Arlinghaus R, 'Participatory Adaptive Management Leads to Environmental Learning Outcomes Extending Beyond the Sphere of Science' (2017) 3(6) Science Advances <https://doi.org/10.1126/sciadv.1602516>.

Fuller LL, *Legal Fictions* (Stanford University Press 1967).

Gregory R, Failing L and Higgins P, 'Adaptive management and environmental decision making: a case study application to water use planning' (2006) 58(2) Ecol Econ 434 <https://doi.org/10.1016/j.ecolecon.2005.07.020>.

Gunderson L, 'Resilience, Flexibility and Adaptive Management—Antidotes for Spurious Certitude?' (1999) 3(1) Conserv Ecol 7 <https://www.jstor.org/stable/26271703>.

——— Holling CS and Light S (eds), *Barriers and Bridges to the Renewal of Ecosystems and Institutions* (Columbia University Press 1995).

——— Holling CS and Ludwig D, 'In Quest of a Theory of Adaptive Change' in Gunderson L and Holling CS (eds), *Panarchy: Understanding Transformations in Human and Natural Systems* (Island Press 2002).

Hahn T and others, 'Trust-Building, Knowledge Generation and Organizational Innovations: The Role of a Bridging Organization for Adaptive Comanagement of a Wetland Landscape Around Kristianstad, Sweden' (2006) 34(4) Hum Ecol 573 <https://doi.org/10.1007/s10745-006-9035-z>.

Holling C (ed), *Adaptive Environmental Assessment and Management* (Wiley-Interscience 1978).

——— 'Response to "Panarchy and the Law"' (2012) 17(4) Ecology and Society <http://doi.org/10.5751/ES-05402-170437>.

——— and Clark WC, 'Notes Towards a Science of Ecological Management' in van Dobben WH and Lowe-McConnell RH (eds), *Unifying Concepts in Ecology* (Dr. W. Junk B. V. Publ. 1975).

——— and Gunderson L, 'Resilience and Adaptive Cycles' in Gunderson L and Holling CS (eds), *Panarchy: Understanding Transformations in Human and Natural Systems* (Island Press 2002).

——— and Meffe GK, 'Command and Control and the Pathology of Natural Resource Management' (1996) 10(2) Conserv Biol 328 <https://doi.org/10.1046/j.1523-1739.1996.10020328.x>.

Holmes CM, 'Navigating the Socioecological Landscape' (2001) 15(5) Conserv Biol 1466 <https://doi.org/10.1111/j.1523-1739.2001.01552.x>.

Huitema D and others, 'Adaptive Water Governance: Assessing the Institutional Prescriptions of Adaptive (Co-)Management from a Governance Perspective and Defining a Research Agenda' (2009) 14(1) Ecology and Society <http://www.ecologyandsociety.org/vol14/iss1/art26/>.

Janssen MA, 'Changing the Rules of the Game: Lessons from Immunology and Linguistics for Self-Organization of Institutions' in Janssen MA (ed), *Complexity and Ecosystem Management: The Theory and Practice of Multi-Agent Systems* (Edward Elgar 2002).

Jasanoff S, 'Judicial Fictions: The Supreme Court's Quest for Good Science' in Imber JB (ed), *Searching for Science Policy* (Transaction Publishers 2002).

Karkkainen BC 'Adaptive Ecosystem Management and Regulatory Penalty Defaults: Toward a Bounded Pragmatism' (2002a) 87 Minnesota Law Review 943.

——— 'Collaborative Ecosystem Governance: Scale, Complexity, and Dynamism' (2002b) 21 Virginia Environmental Law Journal 189 <https://www.jstor.org/stable/24785995>.

——— 'Panarchy and Adaptive Change: Around the Loop and Back Again' (2005) 7 Minn JL Sci & Tech 59.

Keeney RL, *Value-Focused Thinking: A Path to Creative Decision Making* (Harvard University Press 1992).

Kinzig A and Starrett D, 'Coping with Uncertainty: A Call for a New Science-Policy Forum' (2003) 32(5) Ambio 330 <http://www.jstor.org/stable/4315393>.

Kochskämper E, Koontz T and Newig J, 'Systematic Learning in Water Governance: Insights from Five Local Adaptive Management Projects for Water Quality Innovation' (2021) 26(1) Ecology and Society 22 <https://doi.org/10.5751/ES-12080-260122>.

Lange B and Shepheard M, 'Changing Conceptions of Rights to Water? An Eco-Socio-Legal Perspective' (2014) 26(2) JEL 215 <https://doi.org/10.1093/jel/equ013>.

Lebel L, Grothmann T and Siebenhüner B, 'The Role of Social Learning in Adaptiveness: Insights from Water Management' (2010) 10 International Environmental Agreements: Politics, Law and Economics 333 <https://doi.org/10.1007/s10784-010-9142-6>.

Lewis R, *Legal Fictions in International Law* (Edward Elgar 2021).

Linkov I and others, 'From Comparative Risk Assessment to Multi-Criteria Decision Analysis and Adaptive Management: Recent Developments and Applications' (2006) 32(8) Environ Int 1072 <https://doi.org/10.1016/j.envint.2006.06.013>.

McCay BJ, 'Emergence of Institutions for the Commons: Contexts, Situations, and Events' in Ostrom E and others (eds), *The Drama of the Commons* (National Academy Press 2002).

Mostert E and others, 'Social Learning in European River-Basin Management: Barriers and Fostering Mechanisms from 10 River Basins' (2007) 12(1) Ecology and Society 19 <http://www.ecologyandsociety.org/vol12/iss1/art19/>.

Mostert E, Craps M and Pahl-Wostl C, 'Social Learning: The Key to Integrated Water Resources Management?' (2008) 33(3) Water Int 293 <https://doi.org/10.1080/02508060802275757>.

Olivier P, *Legal Fictions in Practice and Legal Science* (Rotterdam University Press 1975).

Olsson P, Folke C and Berkes F, 'Adaptive Comanagement for Building Resilience in Social–Ecological Systems' (2004) 34(1) Environ Manage 75 <https://doi.org/10.1007/s00267-003-0101-7>.

Ostrom E and others (eds), *The Drama of the Commons* (National Academy Press 2002).

Pahl-Wostl C and others, 'Social Learning and Water Resources Management' (2007) 12(2) Ecology and Society 5 <http://www.ecologyandsociety.org/vol12/iss2/art5/>.

Pahl-Wostl C and others, 'Scale-Related Governance Challenges in the Water–Energy–Food Nexus: Toward a Diagnostic Approach' (2021) 16 Sustain Sci https://doi.org/10.1007/s11625-020-00888-6.

Postema, G, 'Classical Common Law Jurisprudence (Part II)' (2003) 3(1) Oxford University Commonwealth Law Journal 1–28.

Pritchard L and Sanderson SE, 'The Dynamics of Political Discourse in Seeking Sustainability' in Gunderson L and Holling CS (eds), *Panarchy: Understanding Transformations in Human and Natural Systems* (Island Press 2002).

Putnam H, *The Collapse of the Fact/Value Dichotomy and Other Essays* (Harvard University Press 2002).

Rauscher HM and others, 'A Practical Decision-Analysis Process for Forest Ecosystem Management' (2000) 27(1–3) Comput Electron Agric 195 <https://doi.org/10.1016/S0168-1699(00)00108-3>.

Reed M and others, 'What is Social Learning?' (2010) 15(4) Ecology and Society <http://www.ecologyandsociety.org/vol15/iss4/resp1/>.

Rist L, Campbell BM and Frost P, 'Adaptive Management: Where are we Now?' (2013) 40(1) Environmental Conservation 5 <https://doi.org/10.1017/S0376892912000240>.

Robinson NA, 'Legal Systems, Decisionmaking, and the Science of Earth's Systems: Procedural Missing Links' (2000–2001) 27 Ecology L Q 1077 <https://www.jstor.org/stable/24114052>.

Ruhl JB, 'Regulation by Adaptive Management—Is it Possible?' (2005) 7 Minn JL Sci & Tech 21 <http://hdl.handle.net/1803/6643>.

Ruitenbeek J and Cartier C, 'The Invisible Wand: Adaptive Co-Management as an Emergent Strategy in Complex Bio-Economic Systems' (2001) (34) CIFOR Occassional Paper, 16–7.

Soininen N and Platjouw FM, 'Resilience and Adaptive Capacity of Aquatic Environmental Law in the EU: An Evaluation and Comparison of WFD, MSFD and MSPD' in Langlet D and Rayfuse R (eds), *The Ecosystem Approach in Ocean Planning and Governance – Perspectives from Europe and Beyond* (Brill 2018).

Turner BL II, 'Vulnerability and Resilience: Coalescing or Paralleling Approaches for Sustainability Science?' (2010) 20(4) Global Environ Change 570 <https://doi.org/10.1016/j.gloenvcha.2010.07.003>.

Viñuales JE, 'Comparative Environmental Law: Structuring a Field' in Viñuales JE and Lees E (eds), *The Oxford Handbook of Comparative Environmental Law* (OUP 2019).

Wahlberg L, *Legal Questions and Scientific Answers: Ontological Differences and Epistemic Gaps in the Assessment of Causal Relations* (Lund University 2010).

Walker B and others, 'Resilience, Adaptability and Transformability in Social–Ecological Systems' (2004) 9(2) Ecology and Society 5 <https://www.jstor.org/stable/26267673>.

Wals AEJ, 'Learning in a Changing World and Changing in a Learning World: Reflexively Fumbling Towards Sustainability' (2007) 24(1) Southern African Journal of Environmental Education 35.

Walters CJ, *Adaptive Management of Renewable Resources* (Macmillan 1986).

Wenger E, *Communities of Practice; Learning, Meaning, and Identity* (CUP 1998).

Westerlund S 'Theory of Law for Sustainable Development – Towards or Against?' in Bugge HC and Voigt C (eds), *Sustainable Development in National and International Law* (Europa Law Publishing 2008).

——— 'Rätt och riktigt vetenskap' (2010) 1 Nordic Environmental Law Journal 3.

Willers B, 'A Response to "Current Normative Concepts in Conservation" by Callicott et al' (2000) 14(2) Conservation Biology 570 <https://www.jstor.org/stable/2641623>.

Williams BK, 'Reducing Uncertainty about Objective Functions in Adaptive Management' (2012) 225 Ecological Modelling 61 <https://doi.org/10.1016/j.ecolmodel.2011.11.009>.

——— and Brown ED, 'Adaptive Management: From More Talk to Real Action' (2014) 53(2) Environ Manage 465 <https://doi.org/10.1007/s00267-013-0205-7>.

Chapter 4

To Frame Water

Introduction

This chapter analyses adaptive management in a particular context, the EU Water Framework Directive (WFD), focusing on the compatibility of the paradigm with the legal system in general and the requirements set for adequate judicial review in particular. The key components and short history of the development of the WFD are explained, but the solutions of the example Member State, Finland, are simultaneously covered. The chapter describes the continuum of normativity that takes place in WFD-related administrative-legal and judicial processes. The non-deterioration principle appears to be of greater importance in EU water governance than the good status objective, though as legal norms, both are central. Later, the chapter describes the four ways in which further congruence can be found between adaptive management and law. The roles of compensation or restoration mechanisms are discussed, too, as are temporal aspects and spatiality of integrated and holistic water management. The chapter concludes by focusing on the judicial review of matters with relevance to the WFD, positing that even in a legal system where judicial review is broad and in-depth and where the in-house expert judges provide scientific expertise in a court chamber, this expertise is not enough to secure adequate access to justice in EU water governance as it is implemented in Member States. The chapter thus argues that the *continuum of normativity* that the EU WFD has created poses a challenge to the legal systems in the Member States and in the EU.

The Ambitious Regulator of the WFD

Managing With Adaptive Management

As seen in the preceding chapter, adaptive management has constantly increased its importance in natural resources management over the past decades. Its relevance, from the lawyer's point of view, is that adaptive management should consist of well-managed experiments from which both scientists and managers can learn, uncertainty is not an impediment to it, and anything fixed fits poorly

DOI: 10.4324/9781003197829-4

with its strategy.[1] This approach has matured into research on socio-ecological systems in which sociological aspects are examined ostensibly equally with ecological ones.[2] What distinguishes adaptive management from the previous eras of natural resources management is its attitude towards change: instead of attempting to tame nature, social systems and their ineluctable patterns of change, the inevitability of change is cherished, and uncertainty is taken as the underpinning foundation of resource management.[3] The approach towards uncertainty is what induced avid learning in the first place. The socio-ecological system was understood to be too complex to be properly modelled; thus, generating knowledge in the traditional manner was either impossible or of no help. Learning is seen as a solution: even when firm knowledge might not be available, constant learning is yet achievable, enabling a gradual increase of knowledge.[4] The more resilient these socio-ecological systems are, the better. The concept of 'resilience,' used almost as a buzzword in contemporary natural resources research, refers to systems that can sustain changes without losing their characteristic features.[5] My characterisation of *the ambitious regulator* stems from the fact that the EU regulator adopted the adaptive management paradigm in the WFD as its holistic water governance instrument of the 21st century. As mentioned at the beginning of this work, one ought not to read too much from these epithets, especially when it comes to this characterisation. Some of its features undermine its zeal significantly.[6] Thus, although, on balance, the nickname is appropriate, it should be taken with a pinch of salt.

Much of the popularity of the adaptive management paradigm comes from the perception that it is intuitive, reasonable, and feasible. Successful examples of adaptive natural resources management come mostly from nature conservation projects run in confined areas and aimed at preserving a viable population of some specific species of flora or fauna. Successful large-scale management

1 Chapter 3.1.3; CS Holling (ed), *Adaptive Environmental Assessment and Management* (Wiley-Interscience 1978) 377.

2 To name just a few, Carl Folke and others, 'Adaptive Governance of Social-Ecological Systems' (2005) Annual Review of Environment & Resources 30(1) <https://doi.org/10.1146/annurev.energy.30.050504.144511>, 441; Marco A Janssen, 'Changing the rules of the game: lessons from immunology and linguistics for self-organization of institutions' in Marco A Janssen (ed), *Complexity and Ecosystem Management: The Theory and Practice of Multi-Agent Systems* (Edward Elgar 2002) 35; Per Olsson, Carl Folke, and Fikret Berkes, 'Adaptive Comanagement for Building Resilience in Social–Ecological Systems' (2004) Environ Manage 34(1) <https://doi.org/10.1007/s00267-003-0101-7>, 75.

3 At text to n 48 in ch 3 it is explained how the flux of change is currently understood in the panarchy thesis.

4 Not that adaptive management itself would not be one, see e.g. Bradley C Karkkainen, 'Adaptive Ecosystem Management and Regulatory Penalty Defaults: Toward a Bounded Pragmatism' (2002a) Minnesota Law Review 87 <https://scholarship.law.umn.edu/mlr/760>, 955 fn 40.

5 For resilience see text to n 104 and 19 in ch 3.

6 Text to n 31 ff; text at n 25 in ch 1.

projects have yet to present themselves. For this reason, water management at the scale it is attempted in the EU with the WFD is an ambitious endeavour not only with regard to its management target – all EU waters, inclusive of both surface and ground water – but also regarding its size: covering all the EU's waters in the same holistic management system is a vast venture seeking for comparison.[7] In principle, the WFD draws upon adaptive management and seeks to employ ecological knowledge at its fullest, but as is common, adaptive management is deployed in a limited manner that could be called 'passive' management. The passive version skips the scientists' and managers' constant learning but keeps the holistic understanding of ecosystems and integrated approach towards activities affecting them.[8] Whether this passive version is actually adaptive management at all, or whether it is the old natural resources management in new clothes, is a question worth pondering. However, the WFD is not the worst-case scenario of passive adaptive water management, for it retains glimpses of learning in it. In the structure created by the WFD, waters are categorised as water bodies and river basins, the quality of which are evaluated and assessed. The evaluations are compiled in the river basin management plans (RBMPs), which include the environmental status classification and programmes of measures (PoMs) adopted to promulgate the environmental objectives.[9]

The WFD cannot, however, be acclaimed for its flexibility, especially not after the Weser case in 2015 by the Court of Justice of the European Union (CJEU), which moulded the interpretations of the WFD into a more formalistic version. This chapter examines whether the implementation of the

7 The WFD was an EU reply to a global wave of holistic and intergrated enviromental management tools, taking place in the 1990s; Daniel Hering and others, 'The European Water Framework Directive at the Age of 10: A Critical Review of the Achievements with Recommendations for the Future' (2010) Sci Total Environ 408(19) <https://doi.org/10.1016/j.scitotenv.2010.05.031>, 4007–8.

8 Or as described by Williams, learning is a 'useful but unintended byproduct of decision making,' Byron K Williams, 'Passive and Active Adaptive Management: Approaches and an Example' (2011) Journal of Environmental Management 92(5) <https://doi.org/10.1016/j.jenvman.2010.10.039>, 1371, referring to CJ Walters, *Adaptive Management of Renewable Resources* (Blackburn Press 1986).

9 Adaptivity in the WFD is well illustrated as a circle in Figure 4.3 in Marleen van Rijswick and Andrea Keessen, 'The EU Approach for Intergrated Water Resource Management: Transposing the EU Water Framework Directive within a national context – key insights from experience' in Andrew Allan, Sarah Hendry, and Alistair Rieu-Clarke (eds), *Routledge Handbook of Water Law and Policy* (Routledge 2017) 51, 55. The circle begins with defining the river basins, continues with defining the good status objectives and assessment of river basins, compiling the RBMPs, establishing the PoMs, covering the monitoring and reporting. What could be added to the beginning is the stage of defining the water bodies according to Annex II of the WFD; see text to n 148 ff. The relationship between the PoMs and RBMPs has been ambivalent; Lasse Baaner, 'Programmes of Measures Under the Water Framework Directive – A Comparative Case Study' (2011) Nordisk miljörättslig tidsskrift 1 <https://ssrn.com/abstract=1813662>, 31.

post-Weserian WFD in the Member States could offer a way to reconnect the WFD with its roots, bringing back the aspects of constant learning and openness towards uncertainty. Are these aims such a poor match with the aims of the legal sphere as one might presume? Could law and adaptive management find common ground instead of either forcing adaptive management into unfamiliar rigidity or the management depriving the legal of its pivotal components? In this chapter, the question of compatibility between adaptive management and law is studied through three examinations. Each examination takes place in the jurisdiction of Finland, exemplifying a national administrative-legal system in which EU environmental law is enforced. The manner in which the WFD was originally implemented in Finland offers an interesting framework for the examinations. Unlike some of the other Member States, the country opted to emphasise the administrative part of the management strongly. This implementation choice was explicitly found inadequate in the Weser ruling by the CJEU, forcing the country – or rather its courts – to re-evaluate its interpretation of the WFD, reaching at least a temporary closure in 2019.[10]

Adaptive management systems are complex and resilient, and as such, they have proved to be a challenge for regulators. Lawyers have tended to recoil from adaptive management as it clashes fundamentally with predictability and certainty.[11] Establishing clear dividing lines between scientific knowledge, management decisions, and judicial decision-making becomes impossible in general and in the European water management context in particular. The WFD is an intentionally science-heavy regulatory instrument in which such boundaries are intentionally blurred: the management practice that it establishes relies on, e.g. environmental modelling on multiple points of its processes, modelling being an inferential process to begin with.[12] Adaptive management adds to the dilemma when its main objective is managers' and scientists' constant learning and the steady evolution of their actions. Understandably, regulating this undertaking is a challenge; predictability is part of law's epistemology, even if mechanisms of weighing and balancing are incorporated into the system. Balancing mechanisms are widely employed in environmental law, stemming from flexible norms, frequent use of principles, and securing

10 The development is explained in detail at text to n 50.

11 Bradley C Karkkainen, 'Collaborative Ecosystem Governance: Scale, Complexity, and Dynamism' (2002b) Virginia Environmental Law Journal 21 189.

12 Elizabeth Fisher, Pasky Pascual, and Wendy Wagner, 'Understanding Environmental Models in Their Legal and Regulatory Context' (2010) JEL 22(2) <https://doi.org/10.1093/jel/eqq012>, 256. The complexity of the WFD's science-policy interface is well illustrated in Figure 9 at Philippe Quevauviller and others, 'Science-Policy Integration Needs in Support of the Implementation of the EU Water Framework Directive' (2005) Environ Sci & Policy 8(3) <https://doi.org/10.1016/j.envsci.2005.02.003>, 210–11. The role of models in the WFD-related judicial review are analysed in Tiina Paloniitty and Niina Kotamäki, 'Scientific and Legal Mechanisms for Addressing Model Uncertainties: Negotiating the Right Balance in Finnish Judicial Review?' (2021) JEL 2 <https://doi.org/10.1093/jel/eqab001>.

participatory rights that expand the value (and knowledge) base of the administrative decision-making.[13] Elaborations on this and the following chapter are rooted in this ground.

As a point of departure, it can be summarised that the post-Weserian WFD is by and large incompatible with the defining features of the adaptive management paradigm. If we desire to develop this situation into better functioning forms, Finland's original point of departure may offer valuable insights into initiating congruence while also elucidating the aspects that are most difficult to address. Judicial review in Finland offers invigorating views on administrative authorisations of individual undertakings relevant to the WFD: the broad scope of review, in-house scientific expertise, and broad interpretation of 'legality' form a favourable setting to decide on matters that require both legal and scientific understanding – that, undoubtedly, matters relating to the WFD are. Nonetheless, as shown later on, even the Finnish version of judicial review might not allow for an inclusive enough examination that could resolve the challenge for access to justice that layers and layers of normative decisions may generate.[14] Though it eventually leaves the factual question unresolved, the approach adopted asserts a continuum of normativity shaped by these consecutive decisions. The continuum is elaborated on at the very end of this chapter.[15]

The Coming-of-Age Era of the WFD

The WFD's prime aim is that the quality of all water bodies should not deteriorate and that they should attain good ecological status, objectives that are meticulously defined in the Directive (Art. 4(1) and Annex V). From the beginning, there has been an ongoing discourse on whether the WFD encompasses only procedural obligations on the Member States or if it also contains substantial requirements. 'Proceduralisation' is taken as a mechanism for enhancing flexibility: instead of defining binding outcomes for environmental management, procedures in which the management is to be undertaken are detailed, as are the constraints for the activity.[16] Legal scholarship expressed keen interest in this 'good status' objective, deliberating over its normative impetus, in analysing the various manners in which the Member States have interpreted and

13 Text to n 28 and 160 in ch 3. The mechanisms with which law discusses the resilience are introduced in Jonas Ebbesson, 'The Rule of Law in Governance of Complex Socio-Ecological Changes' (2010) Global Environ Change 20(3) <https://doi.org/10.1016/j.gloenvcha.2009.10.009>, 414, whereas the manners in which judicial review can advance adaptivity are detailed in Brian J Preston, 'The Judicial Development of the Precautionary Principle' (2018) EPLJ 35 123.

14 Text to n 186.

15 Text to n 203.

16 William Howarth, 'Aspirations and Realities under the Water Framework Directive: Proceduralisation, Participation and Practicalities' (2009) JEL 21(3) <https://doi.org/10.1093/jel/eqp019>, 396ff.

implemented the environmental objectives of the WFD. The Member States opted for a variety of implementation strategies, analysed in research with a dichotomy cut out for presenting the WFD's obligations in relation to its normativity: the normativity of the 'good status' objective has been understood as either *objective of best effort* or *objective of result*, or an amalgamation of both. The so-called 'non-deterioration' principle has gained less visibility, perhaps partly because the Member States were not required to specifically transpose it, but interpreting the implementing legislation accordingly was considered sufficient.[17] Some also interpreted the obligation to refer to the quality of EU waters at the time the WFD was issued as a renewal of the previous EU water quality standards.[18] To the surprise of many, in the Weser ruling, this interpretation was shown to be mistaken.[19] Before embarking on a closer analysis of the Court case law on the WFD, the context is established by analysing the post-regulatory aspects of the WFD, challenging the role of the CJEU in defining the normative content of the WFD.[20]

The Post-Legislative Rule-Making

Illustrating the difficulty of combining ecological knowledge and the law, the WFD has suffered much criticism from scientists, managers, and legal scholars, including claims that the WFD does not make the best use of ecological knowledge. The ecological status of a water body is defined by biological 'quality elements' that are classified by scientists in the Member States and unified at the EU level. In gauging the 'good ecological status' of waters, these elements are nonetheless secondary features – quality is more about the structures and processes of aquatic ecosystems than the presence or absence of single elements. Ecological concepts such as trajectories or self-organisation have long been found challenging to the legal, and the manner in which the WFD's classification system is built only adds to the problem, resulting in a reality where fulfilling the WFD's obligations results in outcomes undesirable from

17 JJH van Kempen, 'Countering the Obscurity of Obligations in European Environmental Law: An Analysis of Article 4 of the European Water Framework Directive' (2012) JEL 24(3) <https://doi.org/10.1093/jel/eqs020>, 523, 532; Andrea M Keessen and others, 'European River Basin Districts: Are They Swimming in the Same Implementation Pool?' (2010) JEL 22(2) <https://doi.org/10.1093/jel/eqq003>, 210–11.

18 Howarth (n 16) 410–11. Also understanding that the non-deterioration principle obliged 'upon implementation of the measures' was presented; Giorgios Kallis and David Butler, 'The EU Water Framework Directive: Measures and Implications' (2001) Water Policy 3 <https://doi.org/10.1016/S1366-7017(01)00007-1>, 130.

19 See text to n 43 ff.

20 Henrik Josefsson, 'Ecological Status as a Legal Construct—Determining its Legal and Ecological Meaning' (2015) JEL 27(2) <https://doi.org/10.1093/jel/eqv009>, 257; Joanne Scott, 'In Legal Limbo: Post-Legislative Guidance as a Challenge for European Administrative Law' (2011) CML Rev 48 329.

the scientific point of view. All this while the WFD aims for an environment with as little anthropocentric impact as possible.[21] Even when the WFD incorporated a mature understanding (compared with previous regulatory attempts) that successful water management cannot occur without sympathetic land management, this well-considered stance remains absent in the mechanisms adopted in the WFD.[22] More importantly, the approach adopted in the WFD allows for acknowledging the complexity of various regions and water types burdened with multiple sources of pollutants, but in practice securing adequate harmonisation across the EU has been easier said than done.[23]

The Commission heard the criticism, and the Common Implementation Strategy (CIS) was generated to advise the implementation.[24] Annex V acts as the starting point for the Member States in their assessment and classification work, co-ordinating scientific work across the EU. Because of the strong link between the scientific assessment guided by the WFD's annexes and the – then political, nowadays also legal – environmental objectives laid down in the article, the variation between the Member States became a pressing issue.[25] The answer selected was intercalibration, designed to harmonise the Member States' interpretation of this scientific undertaking, identify inconsistencies, and strive to make the classification comparable between different Member States.[26] The CIS is an informal governance structure that publishes non-binding guidance documents to assist the Member States in their implementation work.[27] The intercalibration has proven to be more complex than originally predicted, but, in all likelihood, it would have been so even if the WFD had originally employed ecological knowledge better.[28] Even with harmonisation as the

21 Henrik Josefsson and Lasse Baaner, 'The Water Framework Directive—A Directive for the Twenty-First Century?' (2011) JEL 23(3) <https://doi.org/10.1093/jel/eqr018>, 468–70; Brian Moss, 'The Water Framework Directive: Total Environment or Political Compromise?' (2008) Sci Total Environ 400(1) <https://doi.org/0.1016/j.scitotenv.2008.04.029>, 33–5.

22 Moss distinguishes two flaws in the WFD, both too grand to overcome the goodwilling and correct fundamental understanding: on the one hand the WFD is absent of precisely defined key concepts, on the other it encompasses understanding that ecological variables could be expressed in simple ratios; Moss (n 21) 35, also Hering and others (n 7) 4008–9.

23 Hering and others (n 7) 4009.

24 The guidance documents are available online, Commission, WFD Guidance Documents, available at <https://ec.europa.eu/environment/water/water-framework/facts_figures/guidance_docs_en.htm>.

25 The WFD, Annex V (1.4.1); Hering and others (n 7) 4012.

26 Sebastian Birk and others, 'Intercalibrating Classifications of Ecological Status: Europe's Quest for Common Management Objectives for Aquatic Ecosystems' (2013) Sci Total Environ 454 <https://doi.org/10.1016/j.scitotenv.2013.03.037>, 491; Josefsson (n 20) 232;

27 Josefsson (n 20) 242. Due to these soft law features, the formal legal responsibility is retained by the Member States; Maria Lee, 'Law and governance of water protection policy' in Joanne Scott (ed), *Environmental Protection: European Law and Governance* (Oxford University Press 2009).

28 On the good side, the intercalibration mechanism has produced intense collaboration between scientists from different Member States; Birk and others (n 26) 498.

starting point, the role of this post-legislative rule-making can be criticised as undemocratic. This is primarily because neither the process nor its outcome meets the demands of access to justice when it has not been considered as falling under the CJEU's scope of review.[29] That is interesting as, among the reasons for establishing the CIS, there were concerns that the CJEU could disagree with some of the Member States' implementation due to the complexity and ambiguity of the WFD.[30]

As explained below, after the Weser ruling, the focus of the WFD's legal conundrums has to some extent moved from status classifications to the non-deterioration principle. However, the ambivalence created by the CIS round in the WFD and the CJEU's role in interpreting it has remained intact. The post-regulatory powers brought under the roof of the CIS process impact the role of the CJEU in the WFD significantly and, consequently, the gravity of the traditional legal processes and outcomes described in the following as well.[31] This is simultaneously the reason why adjoining the regulatory act known as the WFD with just one epithet need to be approached with caution. With this note, the examination next moves to the CJEU.

The CJEU's Path-Dependency

The technical nature of the WFD and the strong link between the scientific evaluations and normative objectives has, nonetheless, led the CJEU to decide on the normativity of the instrument, scientific analysis included. The first cases brought to the CJEU were about failures to transpose the WFD in a given timeframe.[32] In these, the CJEU established a rule that not only the definitions of the WFD but also the timeframes of management planning must be transposed to national legislations with adequate binding force.[33] Emphasising the importance of the management practice, the ensuing cases were not only about failures to provide required reports to the Commission but also about failures to carry out the analyses and studies necessitated by the WFD. The cases covered scientific analysis required in Article 5(1) on the characteristics of river basin districts, reviews on anthropogenic impact, and also the economic

29 Scott (n 20); Josefsson (n 20) 243; Linda Senden, 'Soft Post-Legislative Rulemaking: A Time for More Stringent Control' (2013) ELJ 19 <https://doi.org/10.1111/eulj.12013>, 57.

30 Josefsson (n 20) 239–40.

31 Emilia Korkea-Aho, 'Watering Down the Court of Justice? The Dynamics Between Network Implementation and Article 258 TFEU Litigation' (2014) ELJ 20 <https://doi.org/10.1111/eulj.12076>, 649; Josefsson (n 20) 240.

32 The cases were Case C-33/05 *Commission v Belgium* [2005] ECLI:EU:C:2006:48; Case C-67/05 *Commission v Germany* [2005] ECLI:EU:C:2005:791; Case C-85/05 *Commission v Italy* [2006] ECLI:EU:C:2006:33; Case C-118/05 *Commission v Portugal* [2006] ECLI:EU:C:2006:35

33 Case C-32/05 *Commission v Luxembourg* [2006] ECLI:EU:C:2006:749 paras 16, 17, and 65.

analysis of water use.[34] Thus the core of the WFD was not yet on the table, but the situation changed when the long time span of the WFD proceeded, and the CJEU was given an opportunity to decide on more substantial matters. First, in C-351/09, the CJEU found failure when a Member State had not first established, then made operational, the monitoring programmes required in Article 8 and Annex V.[35] The Member State, Malta, argued that the small size of the country and its water bodies ought to exclude it from the detailed monitoring system and intercalibration procedures, or that the fulfilment of the WFD's objectives was secured by other national mechanisms – but to no avail.[36] The CJEU insisted that the mechanisms laid down in the WFD are indeed to be used and reported, and failing to do so is a dereliction of the Member State's responsibilities.

The chosen path was followed in the infamous Nomarchiaci case, in which the CJEU found that even before the management plans are adopted, the Member State is bound not to allow undertakings that would cause deterioration.[37] In this case, the CJEU was also able to declare that the WFD covers not only administrative planning and programming measures but also individual undertakings, should they hinder the achievement of the WFD's environmental objectives, and given that no derogation is granted according to Article 4(7) of the WFD.[38] In retrospect, the decision in the Nomarchiaci case can be seen as setting the foundation for the exact legal norm established later in the Weser ruling. However, since the implementation of the WFD was as diverse as it was, and in the Nomarchiaci case, the questions of the referring court were rather case-specific (and, as such, perhaps not universal enough), the main proceedings necessitated focusing on the scope of derogation, the existence of which, at that time, was not automatically taken to refer to the saying 'exception proves the rule,' and the case also contained examinations of other environmental directives that might have fused the reader's understanding. The interested parties were left waiting for a few more years before the Weser case finally clarified the CJEU's interpretation of the WFD.[39]

Other cases further exemplify the CJEU's resolution to carve out a coherent interpretation of the WFD's complexities. In multiple cases from 2012,

34 Case C-85/07 *Commission v Italy* [2007] ECLI:EU:C:2007:822 and Case C-264/07 *Commission v Greece* [2008] ECLI:EU:C:2008:69. In one of the early cases, a Member State was found in infringement for it had not complied with Article 3 on designation of competent authorities; Case C-561/07 *Commission v Spain* [2009] ECLI:EU:C:2009:363.

35 Case C-351/09 *Commission v Malta* [2010] ECLI:EU:C:2010:815.

36 Ibid Case C-351/09 para 18.

37 Case C-43/10 *Nomarchiaki Aftodioikisi Aitoloakarnanias and Others* [2012] ECLI:EU:C:2012:560, paras 57 and 58 ('Case *Nomarchiaki*').

38 Case *Nomarchiaki* paras 61 and 69; Case C-43/10 *Nomarchiaki Aftodioikisi Aitoloakarnanias and Others* [2012] Opinion of Advocate General Kokott ECLI:EU:C:2011:651, para 62.

39 For details of the stance, see text to n 67ff.

the CJEU re-emphasised that vis-à-vis public participation, Member States are obliged to publish the RBMPs for the end-users to examine and comment on as well; failing to do so constitutes an infringement. Cases have also confirmed that the obligation to provide the Commission with the RBMPs is of a binding nature.[40] Since these cases covered the Member States' obligations in relation to either the public or the Commission, it might be understandable that the bystanders began to understand that those vertical relations are the WFD's core – and that what was decided in the Nomarchiaci ruling should not be overinterpreted.

For a long time, the Commission found success in the cases it brought to the CJEU. The tide turned in case C-525/12 concerning the concept of water services and the recovery of costs (Article 9 of the WFD), in which the CJEU dismissed the Commission's action. Even though the Member State's, Germany's, argument was found to be better reasoned, the victory came with a sour undertone.[41] In essence, the case discussed the scope of the concept of 'water service' in Art 2(38) of the WFD: in order to better preserve water resources, the Commission wished the CJEU to adopt a broad interpretation of the concept, whereas Germany insisted that only water abstraction and wastewater treatment are to be regarded as water services.[42] Germany considered the Commission's interpretation as single-minded and argued that even though pricing is one tool for efficient water use, it is only one among many provided in the WFD to secure reaching its objectives.[43] The CJEU embraced the understanding that the WFD establishes, first and foremost, principles to manage the river basins and that recovery of costs is, indeed, only one available means to an end.[44] Had the narrow interpretation of the concept hindered

40 Case C-233/11 *Commission v Portugal* [2012] ECLI:EU:C:2012:379; Case C-297/11 *Commission v Greece* [2012] ECLI:EU:C:2012:228; Case C-366/11 *Commission v Belgium* [2012] ECLI:EU:C:2012:316; Case C-403/11 *Commission v Spain* [2012] ECLI:EU:C:2012:612. For unknown reasons one similar case was adjudged as late as in 2014, Case C-190/14 *Commission v Denmark* [2014] ECLI:EU:C:2014:2341.

41 C-525/12 *Commission v Germany* [2014] ECLI:EU:C:2014:2202; Case 525/12 *Commission v Germany* [2014] Opinion of Advocate General Jääskinen ECLI:EU:C:2014:449. The author consulted Finland in the pre-litigation stage of this matter: multiple northern Member States were involved in the pre-litigation procedure even though the Commission eventually took Germany to the CJEU; Ibid para 42.

42 C-525/12 *Commission v Germany* paras 11, 29, and 30. The discussion of the WFD's wording went into the details, almost bordering debate over the 'Oxford comma,' ibid para 31. On the benefits of the broad interpretation: Sarolta Tripolszky, 'Water Services and Why a Broad Definition under the WFD is Needed to Ensure the Polluter Pays Principle' (2012) Elni Review (2) 59.

43 C-525/12 *Commission v Germany* para 36. Germany's argumentation was overall more holistic and structural; see e.g. ibid para 38.

44 C-525/12 *Commission v Germany* paras 53 and 55; Case 525/12 *Commission v Germany* Opinion of Advocate General Jääskinen para 72. This stance has a risk of limiting the potential of the concept; PE Lindhout and HFMW van Rijswick, 'The Effectiveness of the Principle of Recovery of the Costs of Water Services Jeopardized by the European Court of Justice - Annotations on the

the achievement of said objectives, the Commission's claim would have triumphed, but since such a claim had not been proven, the CJEU dismissed the action.[45] The CJEU thus ignored the parties' dispute over the scope of the concept, hence the bitter taste.

Even though the focal point of Case C-525/12 was not in the science-law-management nexus, it prepared the ground for the Weser ruling. The CJEU did emphasise the WFD's objectives and declared how the whole river basin management apparatus and the concepts detailed in Article 2 of the WFD are subordinate to the overall aim, good water quality. The Commission attempted to include most water uses, such as hydropower plants, irrigation or flood protection, in the concept: this was ambitious and in line with the 'holistic and integrated' mantra cherished in the WFD, but the CJEU was not willing to bind the Member States to just one mechanism, but allowed for leeway in their implementation.[46] The Commission returned to the scientific considerations in rulings given after the Weser case: concepts of good groundwater/surface water status must be clearly implemented in the Member State's legislation alongside the obligations for monitoring and assessment found in the WFD's annexes.[47] The CJEU held, again, that not just any administrative procedure will do: the monitoring must be conducted according to the specifications included in the WFD.[48] The CJEU also accepted the Commission's claim that when the measures adopted according to other EU legislation – here namely the Nitrates Directive – do not offer sufficient water protection, Article 10(3) of the WFD obliges the Member States to adopt stricter controls, confirming the order of priority of the two directives, should there have been uncertainty on it.[49]

A few conclusions are to be drawn from the CJEU's proceedings. First, the CJEU is determined in its understanding that the environmental objectives are the WFD's core. Second, river basin management is to be conducted in the precise manner detailed by the instructions given in the WFD's annexes – no haphazard administrative procedure will do. Third, the objectives bind the Member States; if they are not met with the existing measures, more stringent ones are to be enacted. As it should, the CJEU has developed these considerations in a resolute manner over more than ten years. The CJEU's interpretation

Judgment in C-525/12' (2015) JEEPL 12(1) <https://doi.org/10.1163/18760104-01201006>, 87.

45 Case 525/12 *Commission v Germany* paras 56 and 58. The reasoning in the case is such that it does exclude future litigation on the question, as is noted in an even fiercily critical analysis by Erik Gawel, 'Cost Recovery for Water Services in the EU' (2015) Intereconomics 50(1) <https://doi.org/10.1007/s10272-015-0523-5>, 40.

46 The same conclusion can be reached from the Schwarze Sulm case; see text to n 92ff.

47 Case C-648/13 *Commission v Poland* [2016] ECLI:EU:C:2016:490 paras 76–7 and 95.

48 Case C-648/13 *Commission v Poland* paras 109 and 111.

49 Case C-648/13 *Commission v Poland* paras 125 and 132.

of the WFD has also conveyed some of the desires of socio-ecological, resilient water management. In its emphasis on river basin management and meeting the objectives, the CJEU has highlighted the WFD as a long-term management instrument aimed at environmental benefits. However, in its task as interpreter of the legislature's outputs, the CJEU has been and is bound to the WFD in all its shortcomings. While the CJEU has rejected any other administrative mechanisms than the ones detailed in the annexes, it has bound the Member States to the scientifically much-denounced measures. It could not have done otherwise without overstepping its scope of review but while doing it generated a EU-wide and firm deadlock.

The question in what follows is partly speculative: how the WFD and/or one administrative-legal reality should be amended to better serve the needs of adaptive socio-ecological water management. Instead of being speculative in an abstract sense, the following examination seeks to embrace the details of the current legal system as thoroughly as the details of the underpinning scientific theorem.

The WFD in Finnish Administrative-Legal Reality

Along with most of the Member States, Finland's transposition strategy was strongly challenged by the Weser ruling. Due to the country's geographical realities as the 'land of the thousand lakes,' water law has long been pivotal in the country's economic life, inspiring elaborate regulation, and for the same reason, the demands of modern EU water law are pressing and central.[50] In reconnecting the WFD's system with its roots in adaptive water management, the implementation strategy of Finland can have surprising assets. In what follows, the existing Finnish system is first described, serving as an explanation for why Finland's administrative-legal system is such a prime example for the present enquiry. Then the researcher's liberty is exploited in the quest for the most reasonable socio-eco-legal solution that the system allows within its boundaries.

Water law has long traditions in Finland: since its vast water areas (but not the waters) are privately owned, the country has gained great experience in regulating water construction, balancing the needs and rights of end-users and in general governing water-related matters.[51] That being said, water management à la the WFD's definitions was not part of the Finnish system, so the

50 To be precise, Finland has 5,123 groundwater basins, 4,617 lake water bodies, and 1,913 river water bodies, Maanmittauslaitos, 'Suomi 57 000–168 000 järven maa' (12 July 2019) <https://www.maanmittauslaitos.fi/ajankohtaista/suomi-57-000-168-000-jarven-maa> as cited in Paloniitty and Kotamäki (n 12) 3 fn 15.

51 Pekka Vihervuori, *Environmental Law in Finland* (2nd edition, Wolters Kluwer Law International 2021), para 1038ff; Erkki J Hollo, Pekka Vihervuori, and Kari Kuusiniemi, 'Environmental Law and Administrative Courts in Finland' (2010) J. Ct. Innovation 51(3) 51, 52–3.

legislation was required to launch a novel administrative pattern to implement it. The work consisted of issuing a statute on the Organisation of River Basin Management and the Marine Strategy (RBM Act) along with three government decrees.[52] Similar to the WFD, in the RBM Act, the key concepts are defined, river basin districts are established, and certain regional authorities are entrusted with the obligations of assessment, evaluation, and monitoring. Two features in this somewhat technocratic manoeuvre of transposing the WFD to a national statute are of interest here.

In Finland, two environmental permitting procedures regulate waters and/or their quality: the Environmental Protection Act and the Water Act.[53] The former implements the Industrial Emissions Directive (IED) and covers water pollution, but the latter is of sovereign origin, controlling hydromorphological changes, i.e. water construction endeavours and other undertakings affecting waters and water bodies.[54] Though previously, the Water Act regulated water pollution too, nowadays, all pollution regulation is centralised in the Environmental Protection Agency (EPA). Both permitting systems are coupled with water management in a clause that advises that the permit decision shall *indicate how account has been taken of the river basin management plan* under the Act on Water Resources Management.[55] In other words, the Finnish legislature refers to the RBMPs and their content in general, not to the 'good status objective' or achievement of it. It is not specified what in the RBMPs or their content should be considered or how that examination ought to be performed. Nonetheless, the implementation emphasises overall water resources management and shuns any reference to environmental quality standards or other normative aspects within the management process.[56] It is worth noting that neither the rulings from the CJEU nor from domestic courts have resulted in amending the legislation.

52 Act on the Organization of River Basin Management and the Marine Strategy 1299/2004, legally non-binding English translation available at <https://finlex.fi/en/laki/kaannokset/2004/en20041299> (accessed 10 April 2021). The act was originally issued for the needs of the WFD in 2004. Ten years later, the same statute was used for implementating the Marine Strategy Directive, Directive 2008/56/EC of 17 June 2008 establishing a framework for community action in the field of marine environmental policy (Marine Strategy Framework Directive) [2008] OJ L 164.

53 Water Act 587/2011, legally non-binding English translation available at <http://www.finlex.fi/en/laki/kaannokset/2011/en20110587.pdf> (accessed 10 April 2021); Vihervuori (n 51) para 1042.

54 Directive 2010/75/EU of 24 November 2010 on industrial emissions (integrated pollution prevention and control) [2010] OJ L 334/17.

55 Water Act 3:6, italics here. Similar clause is in 51 § of the Finnish EPA. The obligation is cross-linked to the RBM Act 28 §.

56 Not that it would have not been known at the time of implementation that the 'good status objective' could also be interpreted otherwise – research had already then elaborated various possibilities on the matter, e.g. William Howarth, 'Accommodation without Resolution? Emission Controls and Environmental Quality Objectives in the Proposed EC Water Framework Directive' (1999) Environmental Law Review 1(1) <https://doi.org/10.1177/146145299900100103>, 21.

During the legislative process, strong stances were taken to oppose any legal effects of the RBMPs between or on individuals, and the Constitutional Law Committee concurred with these stances.[57] As an outcome, the obligation is only to take the RBMPs into account in decision-making. This obscure phrase of lesser normative weight is a prime example of flexibility in environmental law and the legislator's conventional solution when it wants to leave room for the judiciary in their work, but naturally, it does not constitute a legal provision on which authorisations could be based.[58] The open-ended phrasing has worked accordingly when the formulation has been concretised in the courts. Six years after the RBM Act was issued, the Supreme Administrative Court of Finland (SAC) first rejected an administrative authorisation because the detrimental impacts would cause waters already in moderate condition to deteriorate further.[59] Later, the SAC coupled the permit duration with the upcoming RBMP revisions so that the permit revision would occur after the new RBMPs were issued, and the most up-to-date information could be used when considering it.[60] Finally, in the landmark Finnpulp ruling in 2019, the SAC took a clear stance, declaring that due to the loyalty principle and the principle of indirect effect in EU law, the norms established in the Weser ruling – the good status objective and the non-deterioration principle – are indeed also in force in Finland in matters dealing with the EPA.[61] The SAC rather elegantly identified three distinct matters that must be considered in such cases: first, the permit conditions; second, the precautionary principle; and third, the norms established in the Weser ruling. As argued elsewhere, '[n]one of these attenuate each other, nor does passing one threshold equal passing all

57 In the *travaux preparatoires* the Government declared that the WFD has no competence in the area of water protection, HE 120/2004 (Governments Proposal to the Parliament 120/2004) 21; Constitutional Law Committee 45/2004 in relation to the Government's Proposal to the Parliament 120/2004, 3. Finland lacks a separate constitutional law court: the compatibility between the proposed acts and the country's constitution is decided by the Committee for Constitutional Law of the Parliament, conducting the review in advance. Thus no legislative act can proceed without its clearance.

58 Douglas Fisher, *Legal Reasoning in Environmental Law: A Study of Structure, Form and Language* (Edward Elgar Publishing Ltd 2013) 480, 23–44; Aulis Aarnio, *The Rational as Reasonable: A Treatise on Legal Justification* (Reidel cop. 1987) XIX, 276 s, 89ff. The Commission paid due attention to this also when reporting on Finland's implementation; Commission, 'Commission Staff Working Document Member State Finland, Report from the Commission to the European Parliament and the Council on the Implementation of the Water Framework Directive (2000/60/EC) River Basin Management Plans (Implementation SWD Finland)' SWD (2012) 379 final, 6.

59 The SAC 20.8.2010 t. 1869 (KHO 20.8.2010 t. 1869).

60 The SAC 2015:102 (KHO 2015:102 ECLI:FI:KHO:2015:102). See also, e.g. The SAC 2016:36 (KHO 2016:36 ECLI:FI:KHO:2016:36). In line with Paloniitty and Kotamäki (n 12) 17, 25–6, this solution is an example of a 'legal mechanism' the court employs to advance reciprocality and adaptivity.

61 The SAC 2019:166 (KHO 2019:166 ECLI:FI:KHO:2019:166); the case is dissected in Paloniitty and Kotamäki (n 12) 19–22.

three. But if an impact breaches the WFD's non-deterioration principle, that impact counts as "significant pollution" in the EPA's regime.'[62]

In all the cases, the SAC has *de facto* referred to the environmental objectives in the RBMPs: what has been 'taken into account' is the achievement of the good status objective and, later, also the non-deterioration principle. The case law proves how the environmental objectives have steadily gained more impetus: the Constitutional Law Committee's standing that the RBMPs should not interfere with individuals' legal position was finally overturned in the Finnpulp ruling.[63] However, prior to the Finnpulp case, the normativity of the environmental objectives was neither secure nor certain. The development of the Finnish case law shows how the SAC has found sophisticated solutions beyond the legally binding–non-binding discourse, gradually nudging the legal system towards accepting the significance of the norms established in the Weser ruling.[64] The scope of review of the administrative courts enables the role of said obligation or even emphasises it, as do the mechanisms for acquiring scientific knowledge in Finnish administrative courts.[65]

With this basic knowledge of the journey the WFD has encountered in Finland, future prospects are considered. Besides analysing the challenges, I shall also investigate potential solutions for the regulation of adaptive water management.

Framing Water in Three Accounts

The socio-ecological foundation explained in Chapter 3 calls for flexibility and learning; attaching it to anything fixed risks creating discrepancy. The challenge lingers, then, and forcing adaptive management into the box of legal formalism might save the lawyer's day but is an abysmal match for a constantly evolving system. Whether this fixed ingredient exists at the normative level (as legal norms) or at the factual level (as fixed environmental quality standards or objectives) is actually irrelevant, even though both are present in the current reading of the WFD. What is relevant is that the adaptive socio-ecological system deserves better than being unwillingly married with anything too detailed or precise.

In what follows, the formalism imposed in the Weser ruling is explained. After that, I explain variations that look beyond the 'rules and their exemptions'

62 Paloniitty and Kotamäki (n 12) 20.

63 Regarding water construction, regulated in the Water Act, a similar stance was taken earlier in the *Sierilä* case (the SAC 2017:87; KHO 2017:87 ECLI:FI:KHO:2017:87); Sara Kymenvaara and others, 'Variations on the Same Theme: Environmental Objectives of the Water Framework Directive in Environmental Permitting in the Nordic Countries' (2019) RECIEL 28(2) <https://doi.org/10.1111/reel.12273>, 203.

64 The SAC 2015:102 (KHO 2015:102).

65 More on both at text to n 186ff.

pattern present in the ruling.[66] The variations study the legal and administrative underpinnings with which the current WFD could better serve the needs of adaptive water management. As noted in Chapter 3, adaptive law is compatible with the rule of law as long as judicial review is available.[67] Thus, after the variations, judicial review in Finland is explored to consider whether they could be properly reviewed, satisfying the fundamental requirement.

Acknowledge the Inconsistency, Retain Action

As is the case with the Environmental Impact Assessment, the non-action opportunity also needs to be acknowledged. This variation consists of admitting that the Finnish environmental legal system is already as adaptive and resilient as one could reasonably desire. This is for two reasons: the flexibility-producing mechanisms already present in environmental law and the Finnish judicial review, including the broad scope of review, extensively interpreted principle of judicial investigation, and opportunity to have recourse to scientific experts within the court chambers.[68] In this understanding, these characteristics outweigh the potential setbacks established by the Weser ruling.

Turn to Formalism: The Weser Ruling

The Weser ruling was the CJEU's answer to the question of whether the environmental objectives laid down in the WFD are legally binding with regard to individual undertakings or not. The intrinsic nature of adaptive management did not hinder the turn to legal formalism in the CJEU's assessment of the WFD, nor did the WFD's openly expressed desires for an integrative and holistic approach. In the Weser ruling, the CJEU had its chance to have a say on the normativity of the established management system. Concurrently, the CJEU, retaining within the limits of its discretion, resolved the most suitable mode of regulation for a holistic water management system. Underlining the importance of the ruling, the Weser case was adjudged in the Grand Chamber, which only deals with the most important matters nowadays.[69]

The preliminary reference that prompted the CJEU's stance contained skilfully established question-setting that focused solely on the normativity of

66 Of similar attempt in the Dutch context, see Marleen van Rijswick and Imelda U Tappeiner, 'Developing an institutional legal framework for sustainable regional water management in times of climate change' in Michael Kidd and others (ed), *Water and the Law: Towards Sustainability* (EE 2014) 274.

67 Text to n 196 ff in ch 3.

68 As described at text to n 186 ff.

69 HFMW van Rijswick and Chris W Backes, 'Ground Breaking Landmark Case on Environmental Quality Standards?' (2015) JEEPL 12(3-4) <https://doi.org/10.1163/18760104-01201006>, 366.

individual undertakings. The request gave the CJEU a free hand to deliberate how the 'good status' objective and the non-deterioration principle ought to be interpreted and how they relate to individual undertakings and authorising them.[70] The referring court insisted especially on the meaning and significance of the status classifications – understandably so, considering the confusing manner in which the EU-wide comparability of national status classifications is secured in the intercalibration mechanism: the status of a water body is determined by various parameters indicative of quality status. The value of these quality parameters is transformed into a ratio expressed as a numerical value. A consequence of this numerical formula is that the quality of a single parameter can deteriorate without lowering the water quality status overall.[71] The referring court wished to know which aspect of this process is decisive in defining the acquisition of the good status objective.

Unlike previous scholarly literature, the CJEU did not employ a distinction between objectives of best effort and objectives of result in its reasoning but referred to two distinct but intrinsically linked obligations taken into the WFD: *the obligation to prevent deterioration* and *the obligation to enhance*.[72] The CJEU continued to understand that the obligations came into being because of deliberate choices of the EU legislator, and hence protecting their normativity best served the legislator's intention. Thus the Member States must refuse to authorise projects that might undermine the attainment of said objectives, providing no exemption is granted according to Article 4(7).[73] The second aspect in which the CJEU deviated from scholarly ponderings was its focus on the non-deterioration principle.[74] The CJEU established the principle as an independent key objective of the WFD. To achieve such an interpretation, the CJEU dismissed the 'status class' theory – emphasising the classifications, good status being one of them – as one with merely instrumental value and opted for the 'status quo' version instead.[75] Thus instead of understanding the status quo as a situation that prevailed at the time the WFD was issued, the CJEU understood the status quo to refer to the highest water quality achieved at any point in time.[76] Hence the quality of a water body is relegated from the desired objective whenever deterioration occurs and, consequently, deterioration of water bodies becomes accessible only when derogation is granted.

70 The Weser Case, the request.

71 WFD, Annex V, ss 1.3. and 1.4.1. and text to n 22 ff.

72 The Weser Case, para 39.

73 The Weser Case, paras 22, 50–51.

74 The non-deterioration principle has been noted but often not further elaborated since it has usually been interpreted as applying only between statuses or to the most severe cases, such as agricultural runoff. See for example Van Kempen (n 17) 527–8; Keessen and others (n 17) 210–12.

75 The Weser case, para 52 and, in more detail, Opinion of AG Jääskinen, para 90.

76 The Weser case, para 55.

In giving full normative clout to the environmental objectives and the non-deterioration principle, the CJEU imposed traditional, formalistic legal logic on a water management regime that could – nay, ought – to be holistic, integrated, and even adaptive. In the CJEU's reading, they are legal norms in the strictest sense and should be interpreted as such.[77] The WFD in its current state includes now-clear rules, and as with any rule, there is also the possibility of exemptions. The CJEU did not hesitate to refer to the scope of derogation, but being reminded of them does not make acquiring one any easier.

From Good Status Objective to the Non-Deterioration Principle

In preliminary references, the CJEU is bound to answer the presented questions.[78] However, the CJEU can rephrase them when necessary, but its discretion does not extend beyond the scope of the WFD(s) in question.[79] Regarding the narrow line between factual and normative questions in the Weser ruling, the Advocate General took a clear stance on the matter, stating that answering the posed questions required analysis of the WFD's scientific side since the status classifications were established in a scientific manner.[80] However, the scope of the CJEU's authority led to two interlinked consequences: the CJEU applied formalistic logic and, while doing so, dismissed the fundamental question that adaptive water management presents for the legal sphere.[81] Even if dreadful, the consequences are understandable: the CJEU cannot rewrite the whole of the WFD, only interpret the legislation at hand.

The benefit of the CJEU's resolution is that even when the underlying philosophy of adaptive management might not be accommodated by the ruling, the scientific and legal questions are now more clearly distinguished than before. The relevant scientific analysis relates to the environmental objectives of the WFD; the legal analysis focuses on weighing and balancing interests in relation to planned projects and whether they fall within the scope of derogation. Before the ruling, this was not the case: for years, the normative and the factual were commingled. This was so because, in the WFD, the status analyses include normative assessments: the normative begins to form while the

77 Van Rijswick and Keessen (n 9) 51, 58.

78 Naturally, while doing so, the CJEU can take a stance on broader issues, as was done in the Weser ruling; Van Rijswick and Keessen (n 9) 57–8.

79 In the Weser ruling, the original questions were rephrased, combining the first and the fourth, and the second and the third – this allowed the CJEU to first adjudge the question on the 'good status objective' and then on the 'non-deterioration objective'; the Weser case paras 29 and 52.

80 Opinion of AG Jääskinen, para 5.

81 This is not to be read as a critique of the CJEU's actions: the CJEU has limits to its power and is bound to its tradition. The manner in which the CJEU employed its discretion in the Weser ruling is to be found adequate and reasonable: the consequences listed can at the most serve as a points of departure for the legislature in its evaluation and development of the WFD (taking place in 2019).

necessary scientific information is gathered.[82] Before the Weser ruling, the roles of fact-provider and decision-maker were not as distinct as one might desire, a fundamental issue that is now more settled, though, of course, not fundamentally. Nonetheless, the regulatory system is now more integrated than before: instead of finding the obligations separate, they ought to be read together, finding a holistic interpretation in them as well. 'Unexpected and unwanted' consequences loom if one attempts to single out parts of the WFD and neglect others.[83] As emphasised by AG Jääskinen, the WFD is to be considered as an overall venture where all the means serve the same end.[84]

There remain many challenges for socio-ecological water management in the post-Weserian era.[85] The WFD has long been criticised for how its use of ecology does not secure the ecologically best outcomes or how the outcome is not ecologically reasonable. The CJEU distanced itself from the status class theory that would have made the status definitions decisive, an act that might appear a sensible reaction to the critique: by doing so, the CJEU detached the WFD from being explicitly bound to certain fixed standards. The reasons behind this were partly historical, relating to the long traditions and established notions of water law. As AG Jääskinen has stated, the concept of deterioration is a well-established concept of water law, having a general rather than a technical or detailed scope.[86] In other words, the CJEU attempted to distance itself from the much-criticised technicalities and examine adaptive management regulation from a broader perspective.[87] But did the CJEU rid itself of the thinking, or did it only move the fixed borders elsewhere? Its aim might be in accordance with adaptive management theory, but the trouble lingers because the parameters defining the acquisition of the non-deterioration principle are equally as detailed and technical as those defining the good status objective. One might conclude that the CJEU shifted the concept of deterioration from

82 Tiina Paloniitty, 'Taking Aims Seriously – How Legal Ecology Affects Judicial Decision-Making' (2015) JHRE 6(1) <https://doi.org/10.4337/jhre.2015.01.03>, 59–62.

83 Van Rijswick and Keessen (n 9) 60; Van Rijswick and Backes (n 69) 366, 374.

84 Van Rijswick and Keessen (n 9) 60 and Opinion of AG Jääskinen para 6, this ultimate goal being water protection.

85 Durner has a more ardent view, when he holds that these contemporary developments, originating from the courts, especially the non-deterioration principle and normativity of good status objective, push the EU water law beyond the threshold of enforceability ('Die derzeitige zulassungsbezogene Handhabung des "Verschlechterungsverbots" und des "Verbesserungsgebots" durch die Rechtsprechung führen das Wasserrecht an oder vielleicht sogar über die Schwelle der Nichtvollziehbarkeit'), W Durner, 'Das "Verschlechterungsverbot" und das "Verbesserungsgebot" im Wasserwirtschaftsrecht' (2019) Natur und Rect 41 <https://doi.org/10.1007/s10357-018-3458-3>, 8.

86 Opinion of AG Jääskinen, para 99.

87 As also confirmed by Van Rijswick and Keessen (n 9) 58.

the general status classifications to a more detailed level, that of quality elements in the meaning of Annex V of the WFD.[88]

Thus, even though the CJEU managed to fiddle away the problem of fixed status analyses, the problem itself remains unresolved. The link between deterioration and the detailed and meticulous annexes is still present: whether deterioration occurs or not is evaluated within the framework of the WFD, and the evaluation is performed with quality parameters within river basin districts. Interpreting the CJEU's ruling on this matter is not straightforward. Van Rijswick and Backes have hesitantly taken the stance that minor detrimental changes are excluded from the scope of the non-deterioration principle since the status of a quality element must fall by one class until deterioration can be detected (if the question is of quality elements already in the category of good), so some deterioration could be present within the elements before they fall by one class – even though the CJEU openly expressed dislike towards coupling deterioration with status classifications and emphasised the broad understanding of said principle.[89] That stance would favour the conclusion that even minor detrimental impacts ought to be forbidden.

In any case, a link between deterioration and the WFD's technical details prevails if it is to be interpreted that deterioration can be detected only with the tools made available in the WFD and its annexes. It might be that the link is imperative. The WFD's integrated and holistic, catchment-oriented approach necessitates measuring the utterly complex system, and measurement most often makes use of indicators in order to grasp the system's performance.[90] One is left to wonder if the WFD, in order to fulfil its main imperative of enhanced water quality, must measure the development and, by doing so, must let go of an excessive desire for flexibility and adaptivity.[91]

As is often the case, the CJEU continued discussing the WFD in subsequent rulings. Less than a year after the Weser case, the CJEU decided on the Schwarze Sulm case (C-346/14).[92] The essence of the case dealt with the derogation regime and the definition of 'overriding public interest' in Article

88 The Weser Case paras 69 and 70.

89 Van Rijswick and Backes (n 69) 373–4; the Weser case paras 69 and 70; text to n 118 ff. The discussion before the CJEU covered minor detrimental changes on the one hand and *erheblich* ones on the other. The latter was tranlated as 'serious' in the English version but 'significant' or 'considerable' might be more accurate; Van Rijswick and Backes (n 69) 373 fn 15. Also JR Starke and HFMW van Rijswick, 'Exemptions of the EU Water Framework Directive Deterioration Ban: Comparing Implementation Approaches in Lower Saxony and The Netherlands' (2021) Sustainability 13(2) <https://doi.org/10.3390/su13020930>, 6.

90 Nikolaos Voulvoulis, Karl Dominic Arpon, and Theodoros Giakoumis, 'The EU Water Framework Directive: From Great Expectations to Problems with Implementation' (2017) Sci Total Environ 575 <https://doi.org/10.1016/j.scitotenv.2016.09.228>, 360.

91 This is elaborated further at text to n 127 ff.

92 Case C-346/14 *Commission v Austria* [2016] OJ C361 (The Schwarze Sulm Case); Johanna Söderasp and Maria Pettersson, 'Before and After the Weser Case: Legal Application of the Water Framework

4(7)(c) in a planned Austrian hydropower plant, proposed in a Schwarze Sulm stream of 'high' quality as defined according to the WFD's classifications.[93] The CJEU reaffirmed the stances taken in the Weser ruling – recapitulating its key points by stating that 'it is impossible to consider a project and the implementation of management plans separately' – acknowledging that the norms established there affect, also and especially, undertakings that physically modify the waterways and water bodies.[94] Thus the case to resolve was whether enhancing the supply of renewable energy sources was adequate public interest to allow the relegation of a water body from high to good status[95] – and whether such a claim is adequately linked to the proposal in question and its prospective environmental consequences in a specific manner. The Commission considered that the defendant referred to the climate change argument in a rather abstract and undefined manner not linked closely enough to the Schwarze Sulm hydropower plant. [96]

The CJEU, however, shied away from these deliberations. Unlike in the Weser ruling, where it found its place to be one of giving detailed and normatively binding guidance to the Member States, here the CJEU argued for a margin of discretion to be granted to them. Whether the undertaking under scrutiny falls under the scope of overriding public interest is at the discretion of the Member States, not the CJEU.[97] One might find the CJEU to have an equivocal self-understanding: at first, it assumes the power of defining the concepts to itself, and then it passes it on to the Member States. Since the CJEU first gave strict norms and then allowed the Member States to adjudge on their exceptions, it has effectively been overruling its own decisions. However, it is more likely that the CJEU differentiated between procedural and substantial scopes of review. In the Weser ruling, the question was mainly on the substantive content of the WFD (or that is the interpretation the CJEU wished to give to the environmental objectives); in the Schwarze Sulm ruling, the question was instead about the correct level of administration for the decision-making.

Directive Environmental Objectives in Sweden' (2019) JEL 31(2) <https://doi.org/10.1093/jel/eqz003>, 271–2.

93 Part of the proceedings was to take a stance on whether the river was of 'high' or 'good' status: in an RBMP from 2007 it was the former, in a decision from 2013, the latter. The CJEU relied on the 2007 assessments, paras 31, 47–8.

94 The Schwarze Sulm case, para 56.

95 This was the defendant's point of view, especially after its claim that the waterbody was not in 'high' but in 'good' status failed to convince the CJEU, the Schwarze Sulm case, para 61.

96 The Schwarze Sulm case, para 67.

97 The Schwarze Sulm case, paras 70–1; also Frederik H Kistenkas and Irene M Bouwma, 'Barriers for the Ecosystem Services Concept in European Water and Nature Conservation Law' (2018) Ecosystem Services 29 <https://doi.org/10.1016/j.ecoser.2017.02.013>, 223–7. On the consequences to advancing renewable energy, Sander van Hees, 'Large-Scale Water-Related Innovative Renewable Energy Projects and the Water Framework Directive: Legal Issues and Solutions' (2017) JEEPL 14(3–4) <https://doi.org/10.1163/18760104-01403004>, 331–2.

The CJEU did not consider itself entitled to evaluate the closer content of the derogation regime, as in its reading that power is left to the Member States. The CJEU only examined whether the weighing and balancing that the derogation regime includes was conducted – since it was, and since the competent authority had adequately analysed the consequences of the planned undertaking, taking into account all the factors featured in Article 4(7), the Member State was not in default of its obligations.[98] The CJEU did state that renewable energy may allow for a derogation, but the door has been left open for further claims on other environmental gains.[99]

Derogation Regime as the Epitome of Formalism

So, in the CJEU's opinion, assessing the exception criteria belongs to the Member States' jurisdiction. There are certain considerations that must be fulfilled while deciding upon the authorisations – first and foremost, the conditions under which a permanent derogation can be granted are listed in Article 4(7). It is noteworthy that this exception clause applies only to new endeavours causing a decline in water quality.[100] Thus, if an existing activity is replaced with a new one and the detrimental effects remain equal or lessen, no exemption is needed.[101] This fundamental aspect of the derogation regime sets the stage for a mechanism that could be called 'replacement measures' – an attunement of more common compensatory measures – applied when a novel undertaking in a particular river basin district buys out existing establishments with detrimental effects, in order to ensure that water quality either improves or remains in status quo.[102] Another variation could be called 'measures of balance': development causing detrimental effects is coupled with activities that improve the water in said river basin district, causing the overall level of the assessed quality elements not to degrade.[103]

In the Weser ruling, the CJEU *obiter dicta* drafted guidelines for the reasoning on the exemption decision-making.[104] First, even though no weighing and

98 The Schwarze Sulm case, paras 74, 80–2.

99 Kistenkas and Bouwma (n 97) 2.

100 For an illustrative chart on the location of exemptions in the WFD's system see Figure 1 in Starke and Van Rijswick (n 89).

101 Common Implementation Strategy for the Water Framework Directive (2000/60/EC), Guidance Document No. 20, Guidance Document on Exemptions to the Environmental Objectives (Office for Official Publications of the European Communities 2009) 24.

102 Cf. Van Rijswick and Backes (n 69) 372, who rule out possibility for compensatory measures in the post-Weserian EU water law.

103 The options of the latter one have been probed in the context of Finland in Laura Leino and Antti Belinskij, 'Vesienhoidollinen kompensaatio hankkeiden toteuttamisen edellytyksenä' (2018) Ympäristöpolitiikan ja-oikeuden vuosikirja (Itä-Suomen yliopisto) 117.

104 It is debatable whether the CJEU's preliminary reference can have *obiter dicta* at all. One comprehensive analysis of the CJEU's role in law-making initiates an 'alternative model' to this much

balancing take place in determining whether the environmental objectives in Article 4 have been met, a decision on whether a derogation should be granted is partly based on a weighing-up of interests. The CJEU considered this when emphasising that the non-deterioration principle includes no weighing and balancing of interests whatsoever, unlike the derogation regime, which does. The relevant interests are, on the one hand, the attainment or maintenance of the WFD's water status objectives and the fulfilment of the non-deterioration principle, and on the other hand, the significance of the undertaking requiring exemption. 'Serious impairment' (or, better, considerable impairment) in the quality of the water body could possibly be accepted when the interests favouring the endeavour are sufficiently significant.[105] It may well be debated whether these notions are of any genuine help to the decision-maker, be it the government accepting the RBMPs as its administrative decision or environmental authorities deciding upon individual undertakings – however, these are the sole instructions the CJEU found necessary to deliver on this occasion.[106]

When deciding upon derogations, the non-deterioration principle and the good status objective are usually treated differently: according to Article 4(7), a derogation can be granted if the proposed undertaking causes detrimental effects due to 'new modifications to the physical characteristic of a surface water body' or when the status of a surface water body is projected to relegate from high to good because of an endeavour that is deemed sustainable. Thus, a novel undertaking may be granted an exemption to cause effects resulting in a fall from good status only if the relegation is not caused by emissions but by direct physical alterations of the water body. Detrimental effects caused by the emission-pollution mechanism can be given exemptions only when statuses above good are in question, providing that the undertaking is pronounced sustainable.[107]

This difference in the treatment of the non-deterioration principle and the good status objective has another, perhaps only academic aspect: the question of whether the non-deterioration principle and the good status objective also bind those waters not listed as water bodies according to the WFD's classifications. The evaluative work is ongoing and the portion of waters incorporated in the RBMPs increases in each river basin planning period. However, the WFD's Annex II allows for two manners in which the characterisation of water

discussed theme; Marc Jacob, *Precedents and Case-Based Reasoning in the European Court of Justice: Unfinished Business* (Cambridge University Press 2014).

105 The Weser case, para 68; Starke and Van Rijswick (n 89) 3–4.

106 In the pressing situation the Weser ruling created, it is likely that some Member State requests another preliminary ruling regarding Article 4(7) in the near future. Be that the case, the ruling will take another two or more years to resolve and as such most likely it would be adjudged in close proximity with the WFD's review in 2019.

107 The WFD art 4(7).

bodies can take place, system A and system B.[108] Finland opted for system B but interpreted it in a manner in which a vast amount of smaller water bodies are excluded from the classification. After the first RBMP round, the coverage was 86 per cent for lakes, 90 per cent for rivers, and all-inclusive only in the case of coastal waters. The Commission considers this a serious setback in implementation, and the country has promised to rescale its thresholds to obtain better equivalence between systems A and B.[109] However, since the environmental objectives bind the Member States irrespective of the phase of the WFD's implementation, the most reasonable interpretation might be that both norms cover all waters even when the Member State in question has not yet managed to evaluate all waters in its territory.[110] Naturally, the question remains as to how the presumed deterioration is to be detected if a large number of smaller water bodies is not assessed and evaluated according to the WFD's requirements.

Apart from these two general notions, there are four more qualifications to be fulfilled if derogation is desired. The exemption from the rules is to be treated as a last resort (all other means to avoid the decline of quality must have been employed), the reasoning behind the planned modifications must be detailed in the RBMPs, and the conditions – such as technical feasibility or disproportionate cost – obstruct using an option that would be environmentally significantly better.[111] The fourth condition is the most complex one. According to Article 4(7)(c), reasons such as human health, safety, or sustainable development might outweigh the attainment of the non-deterioration principle or the good status objective: the article establishes a weighing and balancing mechanism in the exception regime. The good status objective is defined with detailed scientific analysis where no balancing act is present, but after the norm has been set, some weighing and balancing is allowed when deciding upon whether a norm or its exemption is applied. Weighing and balancing here is not a general assessment of the undertaking's pros and cons with no strings attached but a considerably more restricted activity between the attainment of the environmental objectives in Art. 4(1) (inclusive of the non-deterioration principle) and benefits for human health, safety, or sustainable development. Only 'an overriding public interest' makes this weighing and balancing unnecessary. That being the case, the condition of Art. 4(7)(c) pertains to the public interest only, and all other requirements can be omitted.

108 The WFD Annex II, 1.2.

109 In system A, lakes and rivers with 10 km^2 catchment ought to be covered, when in system B, à la Finland, the threshold is 200 km^2, even though the WFD obliges that if system B is opted for, 'the same level of protection' should be secured. In its evaluation, the Commission hesitated whether and how the excluded, small waterbodies are proteced; Commission, Implementation SWD Finland, 4, 9.

110 See Case Nomarchiaki; text to n 33.

111 The WFD Art 4(7)(a)–(b), (d); Starke and Van Rijswick (n 89) 2–4.

Article 4(7) operates with vague concepts, all familiar from elsewhere in environmental law, particularly nature conservation law: health and safety, public interest, and sustainability, but the article offers no further advice on interpretation.[112] Since the case law on the WFD has yet to develop its own guidelines, some analogical aid can be sought from the case law of nature directives, especially the Habitats Directive, a pivotal piece of EU nature conservation legislation utilising similar concepts, the derogation regime of which loosely resembles the one created in the WFD. The significance of the planned project to economic development and employment has been taken into account in a harbour case in Hamburg, Germany.[113] Also, elsewhere, the severe employment situation and harsh economic conditions have been decisive when ruling in favour of an undertaking.[114] In Rotterdam, the Netherlands, a major harbour was again granted an exemption due to its importance to the EU transport network.[115] When deciding upon an artificial lake development in notoriously dry southern Europe, securing the water supply for local and regional water consumption, agriculture, and industry have been determining factors, providing again that other feasible solutions have been absent.[116]

All these stances call for significant national or regional beneficial consequences, and the social factor, e.g. enhancing employment or the overall economic situation, has been included in the considerations. The balancing act is thus more about securing socio-economical sustainability and has little to do with understanding the social part of adaptive socio-ecological management.

112 Starke and Van Rijswick (n 89) 3–4. Ecological quality standards, now admittedly part of the WFD, have long been present in nature conservation law. Analogies on their scopes of derogation are examined also in, e.g. Van Rijswick and Backes (n 69) 376–7; Kistenkas and Bouwma (n 97).

113 Commission Opinion of 6.12.2011 delivered upon request of Germany pursuant to Art. 6(4) sub par. 2 of Council Directive 92/43/EEC of 21 May 1992 on the conservation of natural habitats and of wild fauna and flora, concerning the deepening and widening of the ship fairway Unter- and Außenelbe (river Elbe) to the port of Hamburg (Germany), 6.12.2011 C(2011) 9090 final. This analogy was first referred to in Antti Belinskij and Tiina Paloniitty, 'Poikkeaminen vesienhoidon ympäristötavoitteista uuden hankkeen takia' (2015) Ympäristöpolitiikan ja-oikeuden vuosikirja 8 (Itä-Suomen yliopisto) 271, 289.

114 Opinion of the Commission of 24/04/2003 Delivered upon request of Germany according to Art. 6 (4) sub par. 2 of Council Directive 92/43/EEC of 21 May 1992 on the conservation of natural habitats as well as wild animals and plants, concerning the approval of an operational master plan ('Rahmenbetriebsplan') of the Prosper Haniel Colliery operated by Deutsche Steinkohle AG (DSK), for the period 2001–2019, 24.4.2003.

115 Opinion of the Commission delivered pursuant to Article 6.4 § 2 of Council Directive 92/43/EEC of 21 May 1992 on the conservation of the natural habitats and of wild fauna and flora (Habitats Directive), concerning the 'Request by the Netherlands for advice and exchange of information with the European Commission within the framework of the Birds and Habitats Directives,' in relation to the 'Project Mainport Rotterdam' Development Plan, 24.4.2003.

116 Opinion of the Commission pursuant to Article 6.4 § 2 of Council Directive 92/43/EEC of 21 May 1992 on the conservation of natural habitats and of wild fauna and flora, concerning the 'Request by the Kingdom of Spain in relation to the La Breña II reservoir project.' C(2004)1797, 7.5.2004 (only proposed opinion is made available).

Relying on the Commission's authority is the polar opposite of local or regional decision-making over natural resources but simultaneously illustrates well the risks of excessive formalism: the 'hardest cases' are inevitably solved at the highest instance available after being taken further and further up the ladders of legal review.

The preceding interpretations of the Habitats Directive deem that the qualifications for a derogation might appear strict in the wording of Article 4(7) of the WFD but meeting the conditions is not impossible. In any case, the planned projects must have *significant* benefits before derogation could be granted, which excludes the common but small projects from its scope.[117]

The Post-Weserian WFD in the Finnish Legal System

As is known, the WFD has been realised differently across the Member States.[118] In Finland, the scope of derogation is regulated in a vague and abstract manner, presumably since legislators did not realise the importance of the articles they needed to implement: if the environmental objectives are only 'to be taken into account,' the scope of derogation is internalised in the clause, and further law drafting is unnecessary.[119] Due to the looming risk of infringement, Article 4(7) nonetheless has its equivalent in Finnish water management regulation, which follows the WFD's example by and large. The RBM Act 23 § regulates the scope of derogation and its substantial prerequisites – both similar to those in the WFD – and the procedure by which the derogation is granted.[120]

Of these three features, the procedural solutions are the only ones fully sovereign to a Member State and, simultaneously, most entwined with the Member State's administrative-legal system.[121] The RBM Act 23.3 § describes the process vaguely, consisting only of an obligation to give an account in the RBMP of the impact the undertaking has on the water body and its status alongside a description of how the substantive conditions will be fulfilled. Apart from these notions, the closer procedural aspects are left unregulated. Remembering the single-minded Finnish implementation, focusing on overall management and the RBMPs instead of the normativity of the objectives, this

117 Examples of this can be found from Sweden, where aquaculture is among the 'common and small' undertakings not falling within the scope of derogation. MMÖD cases M 8374-15, M 2620-16, M 8882-15, M 8673-15, available in Swedish at <http://www.markochmiljooverdomstolen.se/Avgoranden-fran-Mark--och-miljooverdomstolen/2017/>.

118 Starke and Van Rijswick (n 89) 4; Durner (n 85) 9; Söderasp and Pettersson (n 92) 288.

119 As the Commission noted, omitting clear reference to the environmental objectives leaves room for interpretation of how they are to be treated in the national law; see text to n 105 and Implementation SWD Finland, SWD (2012) 379 final 4, 9; Leino and Belinskij (n 103) 123.

120 Belinskij and Paloniitty (n 113) 288–92; Antti Belinskij and others, 'Vesienhoidon ympäristötavoitteista poikkeaminen –perusteet ja menettely' (Publications of the government's analysis, assessment and research activities 42/2018) 22–5.

121 Söderasp and Pettersson (n 92) 288.

is not surprising: the emphasis here is on the RBMPs, in the need for them to be up-to-date and consistent with the actual situation of the waters. The statuses have only an informative or additional role in the attempt to give a full account of the detrimental impacts. As peculiar as it may seem, in this regard, Finnish implementation is in line with what the CJEU later found decisive in the WFD: the status classifications only have an indirect impact.[122]

Since neither the statute itself nor the lower-level decrees regulate the procedural questions any more closely, some speculation can be allowed.[123] What would be the most suitable authority to adjudge the derogation, and when should that decision-making occur to ascertain a flexible and continuous adjudication of potential undertakings? This condition is established according to the general qualifications of adaptive water management as an attempt not to stray any further from its requirements than is necessary. According to Article 4(7), the reasoning justifying the use of exemptions must be taken into the RBMPs, but the exemptions themselves can be decided upon elsewhere and another time. This is clearly expressed in the Finnish implementing legislation, but the obligation in Art. 4(7)(b) can also be deemed a responsibility to report the exemptions in the RBMPs, not as a responsibility to make the decision concurrently with the approval of the RBMPs.

The RBMPs are compiled every sixth year, approved by the government, and then reported to the Commission. Suitable authorities for the decision-making are either authorities that gather and compile the RBMPs or the government responsible for accepting them. To ensure that the formal decision-maker still has a decision to make, the latter might be a better-justified option – the con is that when dealing with such a detailed and individualised plan as the RBMP, the expertise needed to compile the draft proposal might exceed its formal role. The generality of the derogation conditions and the fact that only major undertakings fall within the derogation regime would favour the government as the decision-maker.[124] In any case, amending the legislation according to either solution should not be a major task.[125]

The procedural aspects aside, the substantive features of the scope of derogation constitute a prominent challenge to the nation's societal activities. As noted above, the conditions to grant an exemption are sweeping but demand gravity: significant public interest, human health and safety, and sustainable development, all appearing in different combinations. In Finland, a country rich in shallow surface waters, even small undertakings influence the water quality, emphasising the problem of combining the prohibition of deterioration, the

122 Belinskij and Paloniitty (n 113) 288.

123 Belinskij and Paloniitty (n 113) 292–9.

124 This would not be the only time when environmental legislation would empower the Government as decision-maker of the most significant questions. Ibid 298.

125 The fact that Finland has yet to revise its legislation apparently diverging from the post-Weserian WFD would constitute as a strong counter argument against this stance.

strict conditions for derogation, and the practical, everyday need to authorise undertakings that do not pass the threshold of significance. Thus the path of formalism reached a gridlock, and a new way must be found.[126] The choice here is to turn to the management practice.

Focus on the Management

Embedding legal formalism in the WFD was the CJEU's solution, and since it emphasised the WFD's importance, it simultaneously emphasised its management aspects. The often scientifically derided management practice is now of even more pressing importance. Could its details offer us new insights for a less legalistic reading of adaptive management and law?

Quality With Quality Elements

The Weser ruling put the concept of quality elements in the spotlight. The first step in understanding the scope of this action is to acknowledge the difference between quality elements and quality parameters, neither of which are defined in Article 2 of the WFD that otherwise contains the definitions. When the CJEU in the Weser case ruled in favour of the status quo theory and disregarded the decisive role of the status classes, it shifted the focus from the quality parameters to the quality elements.[127] Though not obvious on the surface, this decision might give some leeway for a less legalistic reading of the Weser ruling.

The WFD's Annex V acknowledges four categories of quality elements: biological, chemical, physiochemical, and hydromorphological, the last three of which are to be supportive of the first. (Also, the chemical and physiochemical elements are often considered as one.) This emphasis on an ecological approach is among the reasons that implementing the WFD has been challenging since it differs so greatly from traditional water management practice.[128] Each typological area – rivers, lakes, transitional waters, coastal waters, and artificial or heavily modified surface waters – has a different set of quality elements for each status category, resulting in long lists described as 'normative elements' in Annex V 1.2. In this Annex, the table of biological quality elements includes 'composition and abundance of aquatic fauna' or 'of benthic invertebrate fauna,' or 'composition, abundance, and age structure of fish

126 To a certain extent this is an exaggeration, as definite stances tend to be. Nonetheless, the recent Finnish case law underlines the challenges major (yet not 'significant') developments with too uncertain long-term impacts face; Paloniitty and Kotamäki (n 12) 19–22 and text at n 59.

127 The Weser case paras 69 and 70 and text to n 87 of the significance of the differentiation when interpreting the non-deterioration principle.

128 Voulvoulis, Arpom, and Giakoumis (n 90) 362, disagreeing with Hering and others (n 7) on the point of whether the focus on ecological status is meant to establish a more integrated management practice.

fauna.' Hydromorphological elements consist of such factors as river continuity, depth variation, connection to groundwater bodies, and quantity and dynamics of water flow, to name a few from different typological categories. Chemical and physiochemical elements refer to salinity, nutrients, and thermal or oxygenation conditions.

Each of these quality elements is monitored with the help of quality parameters. The aim of the monitoring system is to 'provide a coherent and comprehensive overview' of the ecological and chemical statuses of each river basin; the Member States are obliged to monitor features indicative of this.[129] The indicators are at the discretion of the Member States. The selection is contained in Annex V 1.3. An intercalibration process establishes comparability between the status class evaluations of the Member States, that is to say, the output of the process.[130] The limits between the status classes are determined in the intercalibration process, again with the help of the quality parameters, enhancing their importance in the definition of the statuses. In the process, the quality parameters are transformed into a ratio expressed as a numerical value.[131] A consequence of this numerical formula is that the quality of a single parameter can deteriorate without lowering the water quality status overall.[132] The concepts of status class theory and status quo theory were built on this mechanism: deliberations on which aspects are significant and what is the role of deterioration in the process.

The overall aim of the system is to observe the 'structure and functioning' of ecosystems that would be compatible with the adaptive management paradigm.[133] Unfortunately, this mechanism does not accomplish its aim. As the CJEU noted, the status class apparatus limits the discretion left to the Member States.[134] That is why the statuses have no independent significance, only instrumental. The CJEU was thus unwilling to give the status definitions a decisive role. Interestingly, opting out of this status class theory made the quality elements elementary: the CJEU clearly stated that when defining whether the non-deterioration principle has been violated, *quality elements* are decisive.[135] Hence the infringement of the non-deterioration principle is

129 The WFD, Annex V 1.3.

130 As emphasised by Voulvoulis, Arpom, and Giakoumis (n 90) 363.

131 See text to n 22 ff and n 70 ff.

132 The WFD, Annex V, 1.3. and 1.4.1. Much of the criticism the WFD has gained is rooted on aspects of this mechanism.

133 Art. 2(21) of the WFD, the Weser case, para 60.

134 The Weser case, para 61 and Opinion of AG Jääskinen, para 99.

135 According to the ruling,

> there is deterioration as soon as the status of at least one of the quality elements, within the meaning of Annex V to the directive, falls by one class, even if that fall does not result in a fall in classification of the body of surface water as a whole.
>
> The Weser Case, point 2.

coupled with the relegation of at least one quality element. The CJEU justified its stance by finding that an opposite interpretation would not encourage Member States to maintain water quality within classes – the interpretation it adopted was the most certain way of retaining all the practical effects of the obligation of non-deterioration.[136] The CJEU reasoned that the classification system is an instrument with a broad scope. The classes have been established as an overall control on the detailed and technical work that Member States must undertake in determining the quality of the water bodies.[137] This impacts the enforcement of the Weser ruling. Consistent enforcement of the ruling in the Member States would have been even more challenging had the infringement of the non-deterioration principle been coupled with the parameters indicative of the quality elements. When the deterioration of quality elements is given the leading role, implementation retains some flexibility that counts as a step towards adaptive socio-ecological management. When the quality elements are as broad as they are – dealing with fish fauna or flora or salinity or river continuity in general – and not with the parameters emblematic of them, the Member States are able to maintain some discretion at the enforcement level.[138]

The CJEU opted not to take a stance on whether *the obligation of result* or *best effort* is the correct interpretation of the WFD's environmental objectives but instead resorted to the *obligation to enhance* and *obligation to prevent deterioration*.[139] Even though the normativity of the environmental objectives is now clear, interpretations favouring the procedural aspects of the WFD are still available, and this long-debated theme has also gained support after the issuance of the Weser ruling. Various aspects of the WFD's development can be taken as favouring its procedural features instead of objectives. The classification system itself can be deciphered as an indicator of whether management actions are needed, shifting focus to the measures listed in the PoMs

In this regard, the CJEU's stance was in line with that of the Commission but contradicted the viewpoint of the German Federal Government, giving the CJEU a chance to educate the latter on the wording of art 4(1)(a)(i): ibid, paras 68–9.

136 The Weser case, paras 62 and 66.

137 Ibid, para 61 and Opinion of AG Jääskinen, paras 98–9, stating that

> [I]t is also undeniable that determination of limit values between the classes results in the adoption of extremely wide ranges. The classes are thus merely an instrument which restricts or limits the Member States' very detailed action consisting in determining the quality elements which reflect the actual status of a specific body of water.

138 For example, in Finland the quality elements from Annex V of the WFD are taken to the 9 § of the Decree on Water Resources Management 1040/2006, legally non-binding English translation available at <https://www.finlex.fi/fi/laki/kaannokset/2006/20061040> (accessed 10 April 2021), as they are the three categories of quality elements listed in the section and closer details can be found in the Annex 1 of the Decree.

139 The Weser case para 39; Keessen (n 17); Tiina Paloniitty, 'The Weser Case: Case C-461/13 BUND V GERMANY' (2016) JEL 28(1) <https://doi.org/10.1093/jel/eqv032>, 153–4.

instead of the achievement of certain statuses. The CJEU did clarify that the status classifications are to be given only instrumental value, which might support the claim.[140] In this understanding, the reference conditions employed in the intercalibration process are not to be taken as templates for measures in the PoMs but only facilitators of the assessment and classification assignments. The ecological status is more of an indicator rather than the final outcome.[141] Even when they might conflict initially, this reading of the WFD fits surprisingly well with the norms given in the Weser ruling. Individual authorisation procedures and the management done with the PoMs and RBMPs must be kept apart: authorisations of individual undertakings are bound to the ongoing management work conducted with the WFD's mechanisms, but the mechanisms themselves remain intact. Among these mechanisms are also the temporal aspects of management, explained immediately in the next subsection.

In its post-Weserian form, the WFD consists of two entities: (A) the internal and (B) the external part (Figure 4.1). The internal part covers the water management practice: the RBMPs, PoMs, and constantly ongoing work in which status classifications and assessments are used as tools to fulfil the requirements set in the WFD for the management. The external entity covers all activities (in the Figure boxes 1., 2., etc.) that might have detrimental effects on the environment: all undertakings requiring authorisations, other types of environmental planning (e.g. land-use planning and building) – the list is indefinite since the activity is identified only by its harmful impacts on waters, not by the administrative-legal instrument it is governed by (if it is at all). This detrimental effect is determined according to the non-deterioration principle as understood in the Weser ruling: if the quality elements face harmful consequences, the activity can be allowed only exceptionally. Due to the holistic and integrated nature of the WFD, the external part (B) is borderless. Its scope is as broad as the obligation to prevent deterioration extends. The arrows in Figure 4.1 illustrate the non-deterioration principle in action.

As explained when discussing formalism, the derogation regime, according to Art. 4(7) of the WFD is the most obvious realm of exception in the WFD.[142] However, the internal life of the WFD, the adaptive cycles, may offer another one in the form of replacement measures. In order to understand their logic, the temporal and spatial aspects of the management are examined next.

140 The Weser case, para 52 and, in more detail, Opinion of AG Jääskinen, para 90 and text to n 66ff.

141 Voulvoulis, Arpom, and Giakoumis (n 90) 362–3, referring to the CIS from 2005 and also newer Commission's reporting on the WFD, European Communities (2005) 'Common implementation strategy for the Water Framework Directive (2000/60/EC). Guidance Document No. 13, Overall Approach to the Classification of Ecological Status and Ecological Potential' and European Commission (2016) 'Introduction to the New EU Water Framework Directive', available at <http://ec.europa.eu/environment/water/water-framework/info/intro_ en.htm>.

142 Text to n 69.

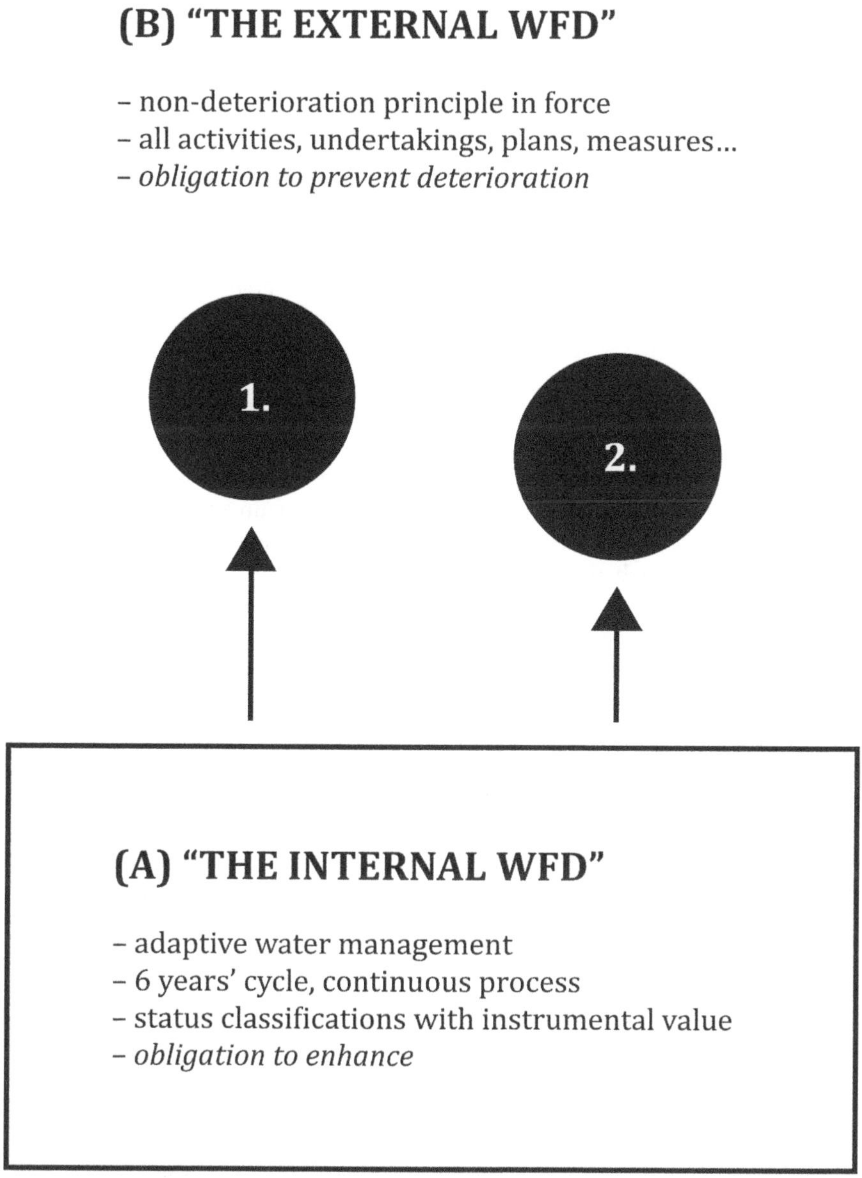

Figure 4.1 The External and Internal WFD. Figure by Marko Myllyaho. Source: Tiina Paloniitty, *(In)Compatibility Between Adaptive Management and Law: Regulating Agricultural Runoff in the EU* (Juvenes Print 2017, XIII + 250p).

THE TEMPORALITIES

One way to examine diversity within water management praxis is to differentiate between factors of time and space. At a more general level, adaptive management can be comprehended as a two-phase process that unravels these two aspects. The first phase refers to the timeframe in which the management cycles are practised, and the second phase refers to the geographical scale of the management experiment; in the case of the WFD, the cycle is six years, and the scale is river basins and water bodies within them. If keeping in line with the adaptive management paradigm, management decision-making ought to be a process consisting of iterative and deliberate phases, both succeeding each other during the desired timespan. The process is enclosed by the factor of space.[143] The deliberative phase includes framing the management issue; setting the scene with the key components of stakeholder participation, desired objectives of the management action, estimated alternatives, and models used. In the iterative phase, said components are linked together in a sequential decision-making manner – the ingredients are seen to constitute an ongoing cycle in which the inherent learning occurs. The inherent uncertainty is primarily present in the first phase; the second is more about time. The timespan is seen as linear, during which the management actions, monitoring, and assessment triangles unfold.[144]

A lesson from the temporal aspect is that even though management begins at the beginning – at the management actions – that needs not necessarily be the case. The cycles can just as reasonably begin from the feedback or assessment and continue from there. Time is regarded as linear, but the mere existence of time does not constrain the order of appearance of the factors.[145] This has been the case with the WFD, which began with the feedback phase: it was evaluated that the existing water regulation did not sufficiently protect the waters in the EU's territory, and further efforts were desired.[146] The factor of time diversifies adaptive management experiments, increasing the number of options available, and elucidates the looming risk of trial-and-error management.[147] Using concurrent interventions on various management sites is considered a more reasonable alternative as they create space for full exploitation of randomisation, replication, and control; generating rather broad and abstract hypotheses

143 Byron K Williams, 'Adaptive Management of Natural Resources – Framework and Issues' (2011) J Environ Manage 92(5) <https://doi.org/10.1016/j.jenvman.2010.10.041>, 1346.

144 Since the triangles are multiple, the result is a sequent of them, continuing in time and eventually (hopefully) affecting space. The feedback feature, affecting the future triangles, sustains this hope; Williams (ibid) 1348–9, Fig. 3.

145 Williams (n 143) 1350.

146 Discussion is truncated to the preambles of the WFD, see e.g. (2), (3), (9), (16), and (19).

147 Williams (n 143) 1350.

in which all the experiments in various sites can affect is another, more solid option.[148]

However, the most relevant aspect is the simple fact that the ecological system changes during the timespan of the management. One might assume this to be crystal clear in a field emphasising uncertainty, chance, and learning, but, interestingly, the assumption of stable ecosystems prevails: there is a bias towards seeing the changes in the ecosystem resulting from management actions, not from the inherent characteristics of the ecosystem in question. The structural features that characterise the managed ecosystem can nonetheless change. The challenge is thus twofold: monitoring tries to trace the changes that the management spawns, but simultaneously the monitored structure alters by itself, even radically. Evaluating which of the resource's modifications are due to this 'natural' (even though anthropogenic) evolution and which are due to management actions is often difficult. Time can be on the managers' side, though, if the limited timespans during which the underlying structures are relatively stable can be distinguished and analysed.[149]

The temporal aspects of the WFD's management endeavours may have caused misunderstandings in the works concentrating on the normative aspects of the instrument.[150] According to the WFD, the RBMPs are compiled and accepted by the Member States and reported to the Commission every sixth year. That is the timeframe by which the obligation to enhance and obligation to prevent deterioration are evaluated. Nonetheless, surveillance and operational monitoring programmes, regulated in Annex V, ensure that assessment is conducted more often. Surveillance monitoring aims to observe the long-term changes in the natural conditions of water bodies and track the results of widespread anthropogenic activities while also gathering information for the most efficient monitoring system for the upcoming planning periods. Operational monitoring is reserved for those water bodies that are at risk of failing the achievement of the environmental objectives.[151]

The surveillance consists of evaluating chosen quality parameters indicative of the change and able to produce reliable, long-term data. They should be chosen so that the seasonal variations can be differentiated from the anthropogenic impact.[152] As noted above, decisions regarding the quality parameters are at the discretion of the Member States, and the intercalibration procedure

148 Ibid.

149 Williams (n 143) 1351.

150 Voulvoulis, Arpom, and Giakoumis (n 90) 363, referring to Duncan Liefferink, Mark Wiering, and Yukina Uitenboogaart, 'The EU Water Framework Directive: A Multi-Dimensional Analysis of Implementation and Domestic Impact' (2011) Land Use Policy 28(4) <https://doi.org/10.1016/j.landusepol.2010.12.006>, 712.

151 The WFD Annex V 1.3.

152 The WFD Annex V 1.3.1.

is to secure the compatibility of the outcomes.[153] The surveillance periods are listed separately for each quality element. The shortest time span is for the hydrological flux in the rivers, where the monitoring ought to be continuous – regarding lakes, monthly observation suffices, as it also does when it comes to the occurrence of priority substances in any type of water body. For all the other quality elements, the emblematic chance is monitored either every three or six months or three or six years.[154] The longest time frames are for hydromorphological elements such as continuity (of rivers) and morphology (of all typological categories).

The data gathered in these monitoring processes is then taken to the RBMPs. The RBMPs are check-in points at which the objectives are compared with the actual situation of individual water bodies every six years. When the Weser ruling established that the environmental objectives were legally binding, this checking point appeared challenging: how should the Member States co-ordinate the individual permitting procedures, occurring at a steady pace, with the RBMPs being accepted and reported so rarely.[155] The Advocate General emphasised how considering 'a project and the implementation of a management plan separately' would be impossible.[156] In the structure of the WFD, the environmental objectives are defined in Article 4 (coupled with Annex V), the measures with which those aims are to be met are regulated in Article 11, and Article 12 guides the compilation of the RBMPs, with reference to further details in Annex VII. The two pages constituting Annex VII list at a general level (general only here and in comparison with the otherwise detailed approach characteristic of the WFD) the information or elements that must be reported in an RBMP. Much of what is taken into the RBMP is a summary of the data gathered according to the other articles and annexes. The fact that monitoring is conducted continually during a planning period and then summarised in the RBMP augments the RBMP's role as a reporting tool.

Thus, the WFD, in the form of the non-deterioration principle, has legally binding consequences even outside the management regime. The RBMPs themselves can be seen as tools securing the fulfilment of the objective to enhance, as the RBMPs outline the pursued activities. It would be in line with this understanding to list in the RBMPs those undertakings that have gained derogation according to Article 4(7) of the WFD. Perhaps a fuller account of the cases could also be given in order to blueprint the threshold between acceptances and refusals. As noted, coupling temporal aspects with spatial ones

153 Text to n 21 ff.

154 The WFD Annex V 1.3.4.

155 The CJEU bound the individual measures, whichever way they are decided upon, with the non-deterioration principle. Arguments on subsidiarity or the Member States' freedom to choose implementation mechanisms would have supported another conclusion; Van Rijswick and Backes (n 69) 370; Paloniitty (n 139) 158.

156 The Weser case Opinion of AG Jääskinen para 78.

may offer benefits for the adaptivity of the management.[157] Whether this is so in the case of the WFD is examined after considering the spatiality perspective.

The Perpetual Trials of Spatiality

The whole EU's territory is composed of river basin districts, and it is for the Member States to decide – solely or jointly with their neighbouring countries – how the watersheds are divided among the districts.[158] Due to the manner in which the management is organised, spatiality is of utmost importance in the WFD's regime: the smaller the river basin districts are, the sooner the recipient capacity of the waters becomes fulfilled, and the obligation to enhance or obligation to prevent deterioration are breached.[159]

The problem that said structure creates has been conceptualised as a discrepancy between large-scale and smaller-scale adaptive management projects.[160] The details of this challenge have been explained by describing how in the first phase, the watersheds are turned into bodies of water serving the classification and analysis purpose of the WFD. The body of water is where the environmental objectives must be achieved. Thus, an individual watershed can consist of multiple bodies of water, even to the extent that a river basin is understood as a compilation of *separate* bodies of water.[161] Dividing the watersheds into bodies of water in the WFD serves the management purpose of definition and differentiation, but in particular, it aids the intercalibration procedure. Because intercalibration exists for the comparability between different waters and types of water in the EU, this has prompted doubts that adaptive water management in the form it has taken in the WFD does not suit large-scale management at all.[162] The Member States are not completely free when they choose the size of their water bodies: if they attempt to do so, the Commission second-guesses their choice, as was done in the case of Finland.[163]

In the WFD, the chosen management alternative is thus that of simultaneously having multiple management sites, being managed at the same time in a similar manner.[164] Were the bodies of water larger, the Member States would face fewer challenges in achieving the normative environmental objectives of

157 Williams (n 143) 1346.

158 The WFD Art. 2(13), 2(15), art. 3(1)–(4) and art. 5.

159 Implementation SWD Finland, SWD (2012) 379 final 4, 9.

160 Henrik Josefsson, 'Assessing Aquatic Spaces of Regulation: Key Issues and Solutions' (2015) Nordisk miljörättslig tidskrift 2014(3) 23, 25.

161 Josefsson Ibid 26 (emphasis here). From the ecological viewpoint the practice might be somewhat questionable: the problem of narrowing down the ecological system as a whole and oversimplifying the scientific understanding of them prevails; Josefsson and Baaner (n 21) 463.

162 Josefsson 'Assessing Aquatic Spaces of Regulation: Key Issues and Solutions' (n 160) 25.

163 Implementation SWD Finland, SWD (2012) 379 final 4, 9.

164 Williams (n 143) 1350.

the WFD. Thus the system created in the WFD is centrally governed, for better or for worse, and the geographical realities are even decisive in the employment of the WFD and in the accomplishment of the environmental objectives. This is because the WFD's concepts are stringent and predetermined: the definition of 'body of water' is not spatially convertible since the river basins are divided into various water bodies, each lying next to another, making extensions impossible. Also, neighbouring water bodies can have completely different quality parameters in use, leaving management incoherent. The WFD leaves some aspects to the discretion of the Member States – e.g. decisions upon the emblematic parameters – but the link between spatiality and substance is not among them. Bearing in mind the underpinning aim of a holistic socio-ecological system management, this result is counterproductive. Adding to the predicament, individual water bodies are managed according to their similarities to and differences from other water bodies in the same typological category, not according to their individual features.[165] The detrimental side to this practice is that when individual water bodies are co-ordinated with other, seemingly similar ones in other locations, co-ordination within the river basin district of the water body is secondary. The assumption in the WFD is that the qualifications of the reference body of water are like those in the referring body of water in the regions, i.e. their desirables and undesirables are akin.[166]

However, this interpretation has also been contested in claims that intercalibration never sought to compare anything but management outcomes, and no more should be read into it.[167] If this is taken to be the case, the spatial aspect narrows down to the question of size and its connectedness to reaching the environmental objectives. The size of the body of water is at the Member States' discretion, and even though that discretion is not fully free, it is still significant. The spatial features of the WFD encourage the Member States to have the largest water bodies possible and to be cautious when deciding upon the quality parameters.

If the environmental objectives are understood as the WFD's substantive content, the differentiation of watersheds into bodies of water would be the procedural counterpart – however, this traditional dichotomy serves the reality of water management poorly. Directives, as part of EU law, leave the means to the (collectively decided) end at the Member States' discretion, but this latitude does not extend to their procedural obligations.[168] Thus, those obligations in

165 Josefsson (n 160) 26–7.

166 Josefsson (n 160) 26–7. The challenges this causes for large-scale undertakings are many; Ibid 29.

167 Voulvoulis, Arpom, and Giakoumis (n 90) 363. Accepting this understanding would favour a stance that the WFD is still a water management endeavour even though the Weser ruling drew attention to the normativity of the objectives and the CJEU elucidated that the WFD is not only about management – the management procedural aspects of the WFD did not drown in the Weser.

168 Josefsson (n 160) 26.

the directives that are comprehended as procedural must be implemented as such without further discretion by the implementing Member State. This traditional differentiating is challenging in water management due to the strong link between substantial aims and certain procedures. The reality, especially after the Weser ruling, is that the measures taken in the PoMs are at the discretion of the Member States but how the water management is conducted and how its objectives are to be comprehended is not – measures in the PoMs are at the Member State's discretion, management practice, procedure, and substance are not. The subsidiarity principle appears in the Member State's right to decide upon the derogations according to Article 4(7), as was also emphasised in the CJEU's Schwarze Sulm ruling,[169] and also in the manner in which the Member State can freely choose which measures it allows as water pollutants, and which not.

On a more general level, the problems of large-scale water management are at least three-fold. First is the above-mentioned change in the managed resource over time, creating a system in flux. The second aspect is monitoring, which requires means and time. Since monitoring needs to be tightly linked with objectives (as the WFD well illustrates) and conducted with care to ascertain the learning, it is almost inevitably expensive, especially due to the temporal aspects: to discern the cumulative knowledge, monitoring ought to extend across all political and economic currents.[170] The third aspect is the creation of learning institutions: for long-term management to succeed, institutions are even more fundamental.[171] Adjusting them to the needs of adaptive management has been estimated to be the greatest obstacle to the management's ability to thrive.[172] The manner in which river basin management is conducted in the Finnish implementation illustrates these institutional risks well: when the RBMPs are compiled, monitoring and management planning are not necessarily always dealt with in the same administrative units or considered sides of the same coin. The procedural parts relating to the administrative structure of the Member State are left entirely at the Member State's discretion, but they can easily obstruct the best manner to conduct water management. A question worth pondering is whether the WFD, in its renewed form, should include guidelines or advice on how the administration of management practices best facilitates successful long-term management.

169 Text to n 89 ff.

170 That is not to claim that monitoring ought to be professional work to be qualified: monitoring can just as well be conducted by a group of amateurs collecting data or carefully selected experts producing refined analysis, Byron K Williams and Eleanor D Brown, 'Adaptive Management: From More Talk to Real Action' (2014) Environ Manage 53(2) <https://doi.org/10.1007/s00267-013-0205-7>, 474.

171 This question is dealt in detail on a general level at text to n 138 in ch 3.

172 Williams and Brown (n 170) 474.

The spatial aspect of the WFD serves to illustrate how the procedural and substantial requirements overlap and how the traditional dichotomy does not offer the best possible conceptual advice for water management. In the WFD's context, procedural and substantial requirements become entangled with much else. It might be beneficial to accept that, regarding water management, substance consists of both the environmental objectives and management practice. Procedure (in the meaning of being at the discretion of a Member State) are the measures with which the Member States reach the desired outcomes, not the mechanisms by which they conduct management. However, those mechanisms also contain points of discretion with which individual Member States can tailor the substance according to their needs.

In addition to studying temporal and spatial aspects separately, they can also be read together. In doing so, the question condenses to 'replacement measures': whether the deterioration allowed for could be replaced by quality-enhancing measures in the same spatial entity.

REPLACEMENT MEASURES

As previously mentioned, the scope of derogation establishes some leeway from the non-deterioration principle; replacement measures offer another path.[173] The derogation regime covers 'the external Directive,' whereas the replacement measure regime works within the WFD's system.[174] In the replacement measures, the temporal and spatial aspects combine: permanent environmental damage allowed at one site is justified and compensated for by improving measures elsewhere. Compensatory measures have been used in environmental regulation elsewhere, but the replacement measures here are not like those: the ratio does not compensate for the damage caused elsewhere but exists to allow for such a balance of measures in the PoMs that the managed area stays within the normative borders.[175]

In cases when new emissions replace old ones, Article 4(7) does not operate.[176] Replacement measures deliberately cause that situation; hence they would be an alternative option available for those undertakings excluded from

173 See text to n 97.

174 As explained in Figure 1, text to n 132 ff. What is presented here is tentative, not part of either national nor EU legislation at the moment.

175 If something, replacement measures remind the 'in-kind' version of compensatory measures – however, since the 'compensation for the damage' is done in/by the same waterbody, not elsewhere, further connotations with compensatory mechanisms might only be diverting and thus the choice of wording here; Brian J Preston, 'Biodiversity Offsets: Adequacy and Efficacy in Theory and Practice' (2016) Environmental and Planning Law Journal 33(2) 93. Leino and Belinskij (n 103) have discussed the details of the tentative practice in the WFD in Finland, nutrient-loading being the justification of their examination.

176 Text to n 98.

the narrow scope of derogation: in other words, new undertakings that, without replacement measures, would increase the total emission load in the water body might be authorised if the replacement measures were enacted. The possibility of replacement activities would be scrutinised in the administrative authorisation of the undertaking causing detrimental effects. Were deterioration predicted and were the undertaking not worthy of derogation, the practitioner would have the opportunity to suggest water management measures to replace the detrimental effect of their planned undertaking. Detrimental undertakings and replacement measures would be jointly considered to ascertain an outcome where no deterioration would occur to the water body when evaluated at the level of quality elements, as obliged by the Weser ruling.[177] Decisions would be made at the same instance that it is opted to decide upon the derogations, and the appeal route would follow the standard path.

In the case law of the Habitats Directive, the CJEU has disapproved of compensatory measures as justifications for the planned undertaking.[178] Even though analogical interpretation may be reasonable elsewhere, the Habitats Directive and the WFD differ here due to the manner in which water management is to be conducted. The WFD's environmental objectives, especially the obligation to enhance, ensure that the threshold of unwanted adverse effects on the waters is already set, and due to the non-deterioration principle, they cannot be circumvented. However, the case might be very different if it was interpreted that measures taken to replace the planned project's detrimental influence were feasible and ought, in any case, to be part of the PoMs due to the binding nature of the *obligation to enhance*. The WFD in its post-Weserian form would allow for either interpretation. Ultimately, the temporal aspects of water management à la the WFD are of lesser significance in the notion of replacement measures. Even though certain quality elements are monitored only sporadically, harming them is also prohibited in the meantime due to the continuous nature of the non-deterioration principle. The question of when to resolve the issue of replacement measures could be determined similarly with the derogations, whichever procedure the Member States opt for. Spatially speaking, the most obvious challenge lies in the smallness of the evaluated areas. In order to have a 'playground' of any significance, the evaluated water area ought to be larger than the smallest water bodies can now be or are.[179]

Regarding individual undertakings, the WFD, in its post-Weserian form, seems to allow for three different categories. The planned projects can be separated into undertakings that are estimated to cause:

177 Text to n 123 ff.

178 Case C-521/12 *T.C. Briels and Others v Minister van Infrastructuur en Milieu* [2014] ECLI:EU:C:2014:330, paras 29 and 32.

179 Especially so in the Finnish context, texts at n 186, but prospectively also elsewhere in the EU. If the replacement measures were to be taken further, the WFD's Annex II on characterisations of water body types might be in need of amending to enable large enough water bodies.

(A) detrimental effects, which *cannot* be discerned when assessed at the quality elements' level; or
(B) detrimental effects, which *can* be discerned when evaluated at the quality elements' level. Such undertaking can either
 (B1) be significant enough to be eligible for derogation according to the WFD's Article 4(7); or
 (B2) be authorised if adequate replacement measures can be enacted
(C) detrimental effects, which *can* be distinguished when evaluated at the quality elements' level and which cannot be mended with replacement measures. The undertaking does not fall into the scope of derogation. Such an undertaking cannot be authorised.

In other words, if the planned project belongs to Group (A) the non-deterioration principle is not evoked at all, and the planned project can be taken further. If the project falls into Group (B), its position is dependent on whether it can gain an exemption, i.e. whether it is significant enough for such, or whether the concept of replacement measures can be materialised.[180] Undertakings in Group (C) do not have any prospect to gain authorisation: in those planned undertakings, the normative rule created in the Weser ruling curbs the activity and binding water quality standards, predicted more than a decade ago, are present.[181]

Across the EU, agricultural runoff produces the 'background pollution' obstructing the fulfilment of the WFD's objective. Water pollution from diffuse sources could increase in significance and visibility if the concept of replacement measures was accepted. When no further deterioration is allowed, current and ongoing pollution becomes important: diminishing it offers opportunities for new undertakings with water impacts. From this point of view, the post-Weserian interpretation of the WFD may have amended the instrument into a more honestly holistic and adaptive management tool: even in cases when agricultural water pollution would not require any administrative authorisation, it would be incorporated in the discretion over new permits because of its influence on the water quality on-site. Thus, indirectly, agricultural runoff would be incorporated into the administrative authorisations. The scientific critique of the WFD has included the consideration that reaching good status is not economically feasible or even probable – the latter because of internal accumulation of nutrients, a reality of waters surrounded by intense agriculture

180 The scope of derogation according to Article 4(7) is more closely examined at text to n 97.

181 As put by Howarth already in 2006: 'Not before time perhaps, the ecological impacts of development projects upon waters will need to be fully evaluated against precise criteria and justified before they are allowed to proceed,' William Howarth, 'The Progression Towards Ecological Quality Standards' (2006) JEL 18(1) <https://doi.org/10.1093/jel/eqi049>, 24 and fn 86.

for a long period of time.[182] However, if good status is accepted as a management aim and the non-deterioration principle taken as the normative objective influencing matters beyond the WFD's management purposes, the discussion on the 'non-WFD entity' is only about whether the overall consequences are detrimental or not.[183]

The presentation thus far has discussed the (in)compatibility between adaptive management and law as realised in the WFD. Instead of bringing the analysis to its conclusion here, one more step is taken. Following the argument first presented by Lees – that the judiciary ought to be considered as an actor within the decision-making process – the role of courts and judicial review is included in the analysis.[184] As noted at the end of Chapter 3, the jurisprudential literature encourages the act; after all, advancing adaptive management was found appropriate as long as adequate judicial review is secured.[185] Thence, the judicial review of our sample Member State, Finland, is examined. The inquiry is conducted with the sole purpose of finding out whether the judiciary could, even theoretically, review the decisions made during the management practice. For such examination, Finland suits fine: after all, in global comparison, the Finnish environmental judicial review is intense, and the courts have broad scrutiny. Would judicial review in Finland allow for re-evaluation of the choices made in water management, thus reassuring the concerned observer that adaptive management and law can be reconciled?

Water Management in Judicial Review in Finland

In the EPA and Water Act, matters that this volume focuses on, the Finnish administrative courts conduct inquisitorial investigation, have a broad scope of review, and enjoy the room to manoeuvre that the reformatory process produces.[186] The administrative courts have wide discretion in their adjudication:

182 Turo Hjerppe and others, 'Probabilistic Evaluation of Ecological and Economic Objectives of River Basin Management Reveals a Potential Flaw in the Goal Setting of the EU Water Framework Directive' (2017) Environmental Management 59(4) <https://doi.org/10.1007/s00267-016-0806-z>, 591–2.

183 Figure 1, text to n 132 ff.

184 Emma Lees, 'Allocation of Decision-Making Power under the Habitats Directive' (2016) JEL 28(2) <https://doi.org/10.1093/jel/eqw002>, 191–3.

185 Text to n 207 in ch 3 and Ebbesson (n 13) 414.

186 Vihervuori (n 51) para 1333. More thoroughly than here, Finnish environmental judicial review from the viewpoint of science and its uncertainties is explained in Tiina Paloniitty and Sinikka Kangasmaa, 'Securing Scientific Understanding: Expert Judges in Finnish Environmental Administrative Judicial Review' (2018) European Energy and Environmental Law Review 27(4) 125–139, and in Tiina Paloniitty and Hanna Nieminen-Finne, 'The EU Nature Conservation Law in Finnish judicial review: various avenues, coalescing case law?' in Mariolina Eliantonio, Emma Lees, and Tiina Paloniitty (eds), *EU Environmental Principles and Scientific Uncertainty Before National Courts: The Case of the Habitats Directive* (Hart 2022, upcoming).

within the boundaries of the appeal, the courts have the right to examine the case at hand almost as broadly as they deem necessary.[187] Here, this process is glanced over in an attempt to clarify how Finnish administrative courts acquire and exploit the scientific knowledge required in their review. Is the review thorough enough to enable an adequate review of the WFD's water management system? Even though Finnish environmental regulation is substantially ordinary by European standards, the Finnish option of having in-house scientific and technical expertise in the court chamber, in the form of expert judges, is, globally speaking, unusual.[188]

Holistic Reading of 'Legality' Review

In general, Finnish administrative courts are akin to the general courts: their task is to review the first-instance administrative authorisations, and they are not part of the administration itself. The review is understood as a legality review (that is to say, the review is not about the expediency or opportunity of the underlying decision). The scope of the legality to be reviewed is understood broadly and holistically, without established boundaries between the legal and scientific considerations.[189] As a result, the scope of review extends to all the relevant components of the first-instance authorisation being appealed. The examination is investigative and inquisitorial, and the only restriction originates from the appeal(s): the courts cannot exceed the request or demand.[190] However, it is worth bearing in mind that the breadth of review is contingent on the substantive legislation: consideration in cases dealing with the EPA is often more limited than in cases dealing with the Water Act, even though the post-Weserian norms are equally binding in both pieces of legislation.[191] The general guideline of restraint in dealing with straightforward policy issues or

187 Paloniitty and Kangasmaa (ibid) 129; also the court's territorial jurisdiction must be considered *ex officio*.

188 Though not unique, the Finnish system was originally a Swedish one, described in Jan Darpö, 'Environmental justice through environmental courts? Lessons learned from the Swedish experience' in Jonas Ebbesson and Phoebe Okowa (eds), *Environmental Law and Justice in Context* (CUP 2009) 211–27. Also India has similar in-house expert judges these days, Gitanjali Nain Gill, *Environmental Justice in India: The National Green Tribunal* (Routledge 2017) 148 ff.

189 Pekka Vihervuori, 'Totuudesta hallintolainkäytössä' in *Juhlajulkaisu Pekka Hallberg 1944–12/6–2004* (Suomalainen lakimiesyhdistys 2004) 46. Variations on the readings of 'legality' review are manyfold, see e.g. Mariolina Eliantonio and Tiina Paloniitty, 'Scientific Knowledge in Environmental Judicial Review: Safeguarding Effective Judicial Protection in the EU Member States?' (2018) EEELR 27(4) 108.

190 Jukka Mattila, 'Oikeudenmukainen oikeudenkäynti hallintotuomioistuimessa' in *Korkein hallinto-oikeus 90 vuotta* (Otavan Kirjapaino 2008) 278, 284.

191 The Water Act 3:4 allows for balancing of interests whereas the EPA 48 § revolves around the concept of pollution.

exercise of executive power is also retained, though drawing the line in environmental matters may be an onerous task.[192]

Traditionally, the Finnish solution lies between the models adopted in the USA and in Germany, but closer to the latter.[193] The logic behind the country's reading of *trias politica* is, in general, such that since the SAC deals with only the most difficult cases – especially after 2018 when leave to appeal was required in most matters categorised as environmental – the legal interpretation is by default disputed.[194] The country has found it desirable that, when deciding upon such matters, the intensity of review is not unnecessarily constrained, and the court is granted latitude in its consideration. To further enable its independent decision-making, in the reformatory process, the courts can also amend the permit and its conditions.[195] This allows them to shape the case rather – but not completely – freely, and its benefits are seen, for example, in the evolution of the case law during the WFD era.[196]

Procedure and Practice Enabling Holistic Review

Also, other details in Finnish judicial review support a thorough examination of the cases. Alongside the scope of review and interpretation of legality, the principle of judicial investigation is interpreted comprehensively, also serving the need to gather scientific knowledge to equip the decision-making. The process is inquisitorial and investigative: according to the Administrative Judicial Procedure Act, the appellate authority must make sure that the matter is examined thoroughly and, if the case requires, ask for further clarification from the first-instance administrative authority or the parties. The appellate authority must, on its own initiative, investigate the matter to the extent that impartiality, fairness, or the nature of the case necessitate.[197] Interestingly, the Finnish type of inquisitorial procedure may encourage appeals from private parties or environmental non-governmental organisations, furthering the aspects taken into account.[198]

192 Olli Mäenpää, 'Judiciary v. Executive: Judicial Review and the Exercise of Executive Power' (2017) JFT 2–4 <https://doi.org/10.1007/978-3-030-31539-9_9>, 248, 250.

193 Olli Mäenpää, 'Tarkoituksenmukaisuus – vallanjaon rajapyykki?' in Samuli Hurri, *Demokraattisen oikeuden ehdot* (Tutkijaliitto 2008) 137, 145.

194 Though only from 2018 as a leave has been required to take the matter to the SAC.

195 Olli Mäenpää, *Hallintoprosessioikeus* (2nd edition, WSOYpro 2007) 89, 502.

196 Text to n 50.

197 Administrative Judicial Procedure Act (laki oikeudenkäynnistä hallintoasioissa 808/2019), legally non-binding English translation available at <https://www.finlex.fi/fi/laki/kaannokset/2019/20190808> (accessed 10 April 2021), 37 and 39 §; Mäenpää (n 195) 355–9; Mäenpää (n 192) 252.

198 The expert judge system has been found to secure the access to justice requirements and also comply with the adversary principle; Hanna Nieminen-Finne, *Asiantuntija tuomarina: Tekniikan ja luonnontieteiden alan hallinto-oikeustuomarit ympäristönsuojeluasioissa* (Suomalainen Lakimiesyhdistys

The in-house expert judges are the single most important feature of the procedural possibilities. 'Expert judges' refer to judges with a scientific or technical background; they do not hold legal qualifications, and in court, their position is equal to the court's lawyer judges.[199] In the matters discussed here, expert judges are part of the court's panel in both the administrative court and the SAC.[200] The SAC's expert members work part-time, usually holding university professorships as their chief occupation. Temporarily appointed expert members provide diverse and up-to-date expertise to the SAC, and when the expert members work only part-time, the pool from which they are chosen is broad, enabling more leeway in finding the expert who best fulfils the requirements of the pending case.[201]

Thus, the courts are to perform rather inclusive procedures in order to examine and discern the matter as thoroughly as necessary. Since the judiciary is trusted to deliberate without many external constraints, comprehensive use of scientific understanding and access to scientific and technical knowledge is secured when that knowledge and the ability to interpret it are readily available in the courts themselves. The substantial and procedural features are also a two-way street: as Tegner Anker and others have speculated, '[t]he court's attitude towards a restricted or a full review may be partly dependent on their knowledge of the substantive issues.' Thus the very presence of in-house expert judges can influence the court's interpretation of its own scope of review.[202] Even with this concise description, the holistic review conducted in Finland looks promising for our prime interest, the judicial review of decisions dealing with our science-intense regulatory instrument. Can the Finnish system deliver what is required, judicial review so thorough that adaptive management becomes acceptable from the legal perspective?

The Continuum of Normativity: From Judgements to Judgments

As argued in Chapter 3, socio-ecological natural resources management encompasses axiological decisions, and this does not necessarily pose a problem

2020), 127–54, 241–5; Helle Tegner Anker and others, 'The Role of Courts in Environmental Law – A Nordic Comparative Study' (2009) Nordic Environmental Law Journal 9, 11, 16.

199 With the one exception that only a lawyer can be a panel chair.

200 In the SAC, the experts are called 'expert members', Kari Kuusiniemi, 'Domstolarna och experterna: Hur trygga sakkunskapen i miljömål?' in Lena Gipperth and Charlotta Zetterberg (eds), *Miljörättsliga perspektiv och tankevanor* (Iustus Förlag AB 2013) 319, 321. Matters dealing with the EPA and Water Act are centralised to one administrative court that employs full-time expert judges.

201 Pertti Vakkilainen, 'Asiantuntijajäsenen rooli korkeimmassa hallinto-oikeudessa' in *Korkein hallinto-oikeus 90 vuotta* (Otavan Kirjapaino 2008) 453, 457, 461.

202 Tegner Anker and others (n 198) 17.

as long as the judicial review of matters relevant to the management can be arranged.[203] Judicial review in Finland allows for a thorough examination of most environmental cases. Scientific expertise is readily available: the object of enquiry, the 'legality' of the authority's decision, is interpreted as allowing its exploitation. However, when it comes to water management à la the WFD, especially the version inclusive of the normative non-deterioration principle, even that might not be a watertight system. This is primarily because of the *continuum of normativity* that this and the previous chapter have elaborated. To conclude the work, pieces of the puzzle are put together here, articulating the continuum.

As noted earlier, compiling the RBMPs is detailed work in the hands of environmental authorities, resulting in plans being finally accepted at the highest political level.[204] Determining status classification is the chief reason for the work, but the same analysis is used to determine whether the forbidden deterioration occurs. The evaluation process is conducted using meticulous scientific analysis as directed in the WFD's annexes and the ensuing guidelines, while evolution in the European and national courts has generated the normativity of the good status objective and non-deterioration principle.[205] Put otherwise, defining the meaning of these legal norms in the WFD regime depends on the evaluations and assessments performed as administrative work, even when this might read like the usual patterns of environmental management. However, the more detailed mechanisms of the WFD management practice can result in adequate judicial review being easier said than done. Water management, according to the WFD, operates with mathematical models, these inferential tools being utilised so extensively through the management process that the WFD exemplifies an instrument of regulatory strategy models. Due to its inferential essence, decisions made during the modelling process are axiological, and the modelling outcome is evaluative.[206] Models are employed in identification, design, implementation, and evaluation – all essential parts of the iterative cycles of river basin management.[207] Models are so crucial to the practice that it has been suggested that in order to secure timely public participation, the public ought to be heard before the models are even chosen.[208] When both modelling

203 Text to n 207 in ch 3 and Ebbesson (n 13) 414.

204 Text to n 50.

205 Text to n 24. The direct effect of the EU law, in principle, makes such confirmations redundant but in practice the SAC's stance is required for the CJEU case law to have domestic importance.

206 Fisher, Pascual, and Wagner (n 12) 273, 279–82.

207 Jens Christian Refsgaard and others, 'Uncertainty in the Environmental Modelling Process–A Framework and Guidance' (2007) Environ Model Softw 22(11) <https://doi.org/ 10.1016/j.envsoft.2007.02.004>, 1546; Paloniitty and Kotamäki (n 12) 5–6.

208 Olli Malve and others, 'Participatory Operations Model for Cost-Efficient Monitoring and Modeling of River Basins – A Systematic Approach' (2016) Sci Total Environ 540 <https://doi.org/10.1016/j.scitotenv.2015.06.105>, 83, 85; Hjerppe and others (n 182) 591–2.

and environmental administrative-legal decision-making revolve around the uncertainties of prospective developments, they can be comprehended as the scientific and legal mechanisms of uncertainty management.[209] Here, decisions taken during modelling – or before it, for the choice of the most appropriate model already necessitates normative judgement – establish the first step in the continuum of normativity. The administrative-judicial decisions are the ensuing parts. As a result, in the continuum, (1) gathering information, (2) analysing it with scientific models, (3) administrative decision-making drawing on those analyses, and (4) reviewing the authorisations in courts all entail axiological decisions.[210]

In such a setting, separating acts of science from acts of law becomes very difficult, even in a conformist evaluation. This scientific-administrative-legal reality is very much compatible with the adaptive management paradigm but can the crucial normative decisions be reviewed in court? As argued above, the answer ought to be in the affirmative. Do administrative courts have grounds to review the content and process of this RBMP practice, heavily relying on models, the outcome of which is already normative? Up until now, the answer has been no: when reviewing matters dealing with the WFD, the emphasis of the courts' action (European and Finnish) has been on the normative weight of the principles enshrined in the Articles of the WFD. The role of the RBMPs themselves has not altered in these rulings: the RBMPs are sources of information on manners and mechanisms to define the closer content of the two principles. Both the European and Finnish landmark rulings, the Finnpulp and the Weser case, shared this point of departure. The scientific knowledge in them is not to be contested in the administrative appeal procedure, as it is so detailed, site-specific, and elaborate. As argued elsewhere when discussing the extent of judicial review in Finland (currently corroborating a fact/norm dichotomy),

> [i]f the focus is on the axiological decisions shaping the legitimacy of the proposed project, should the line rather not be drawn at the decision over parameters, choice of competing models, or some other point of the modeller's inferential process?[211]

In sum, if we pay full attention to the manners and mechanisms of the scientists' work within European water management, the picture of the compatibility between adaptive management and law becomes more nuanced. If the established benchmark is judicial review of normative administrative decisions, water management, as it is practised in the WFD, does not comply, not even in the legal context in which the judiciary otherwise examines cases broadly

209 Paloniitty and Kotamäki (n 12).
210 Ibid 2.
211 Ibid 24, 22–6.

and intensively and has even opened up the court chambers to expert judges.[212] The accountability of decisions made during management eludes administrative-legal scrutiny. Unfortunately, for the compatibility of adaptive management and law, the dichotomy of facts and norms is upheld, and the challenge posed by the continuum of normativity is yet to be resolved.

At the beginning of this chapter, it was proposed that the original Finnish implementation could offer insights to find better congruence between adaptive management and law. At this point, the gridlock seems as unresolvable as ever. Even when the management outcome – advanced knowledge of the status of the waters – has secured a firm place in the normative ranks, decisions made *during* management are most likely not reviewable in the courts but remain outside the scope of judicial review. A way forward could be paved if the water quality assessments, management decisions, and judicial review were better integrated, and if the legal found a way to be more welcoming to modern ways of producing knowledge of the environment. As explained in the following chapter, the ontological differences between these two realms are vast, but this does not mean that (better) compatibility is unachievable. Even though 'focusing on the management' faces difficulties when attempted with the current WFD, it does not need to mean that future versions of it would automatically lead to the same results. In what follows, the challenges revealed in this chapter are approached from a jurisprudential angle as a theoretical legal challenge. Chapter 5 revolves around scientific knowledge, 'facts,' the ontological differences between the scientific and legal realms, adjudication, and the role of transparent decision-making as a prospective solution. Thereafter, in Chapter 6, it is time for the concluding analysis bringing together the various instruments and findings the five chapters contain.

Bibliography

Aarnio A, *The Rational as Reasonable: A Treatise on Legal Justification* (Reidel cop. 1987).

Baaner L, 'Programmes of Measures Under the Water Framework Directive – A Comparative Case Study' (2011) 1 Nordisk miljörättslig tidsskrift 31 <https://ssrn.com/abstract=1813662>.

Belinskij A and others, 'Vesienhoidon ympäristötavoitteista poikkeaminen –perusteet ja menettely' (Publications of the Govenrment's Analysis, Assessment and Research Activities 42/2018).

Belinskij A and Paloniitty T, 'Poikkeaminen vesienhoidon ympäristötavoitteista uuden hankkeen takia' (2015) 8 Ympäristöpolitiikan ja -oikeuden vuosikirja (Itä-Suomen yliopisto).

212 The ibid SAC cases dealing with modelling and waters were systematically searched. None of the found reviewed models were utilised in the impact assessment of individual developments, nor the models utilised during the management process. Ibid 22.

Birk S and others, 'Intercalibrating Classifications of Ecological Status: Europe's Quest for Common Management Objectives for Aquatic Ecosystems' (2013) 454 Sci Total Environ 490 <https://doi.org/10.1016/j.scitotenv.2013.03.037>.

Darpö J, 'Environmental Justice Through Environmental Courts? Lessons Learned from the Swedish Experience' in Ebbesson J and Okowa P (eds), *Environmental Law and Justice in Context* (CUP 2009).

Durner W, 'Das "Verschlechterungsverbot" und das "Verbesserungsgebot" im Wasserwirtschaftsrecht' (2019) 41 Natur und Rect 1 <https://doi.org/10.1007/s10357-018-3458-3>.

Ebbesson J, 'The Rule of Law in Governance of Complex Socio-Ecological Changes' (2010) 20(3) Global Environ Change 414 <https://doi.org/10.1016/j.gloenvcha.2009.10.009>.

Eliantonio M and Paloniitty T, 'Scientific Knowledge in Environmental Judicial Review: Safeguarding Effective Judicial Protection in the EU Member States?' (2018) 27(4) EEELR 108.

Fisher D, *Legal Reasoning in Environmental Law: A Study of Structure, Form and Language* (Edward Elgar Publishing Ltd. 2013).

Fisher E, Pascual P and Wagner W, 'Understanding Environmental Models in Their Legal and Regulatory Context' (2010) 22(2) JEL 251 <https://doi.org/10.1093/jel/eqq012>.

Folke C and others, 'Adaptive Governance of Social-Ecological Systems' (2005) 30(1) Annual Review of Environment & Resources 441 <https://doi.org/10.1146/annurev.energy.30.050504.144511>.

Gawel E, 'Cost Recovery for Water Services in the EU' (2015) 50(1) Intereconomics 40 <https://doi.org/10.1007/s10272-015-0523-5>.

Gill GN, *Environmental Justice in India: The National Green Tribunal* (Routledge 2017).

Hering D and others, 'The European Water Framework Directive at the Age of 10: A Critical Review of the Achievements with Recommendations for the Future' (2010) 408(19) Sci Total Environ 4007 <https://doi.org/10.1016/j.scitotenv.2010.05.031>.

Hjerppe T and others, 'Probabilistic Evaluation of Ecological and Economic Objectives of River Basin Management Reveals a Potential Flaw in the Goal Setting of the EU Water Framework Directive' (2017) 59(4) Environmental Management 584 <https://doi.org/10.1007/s00267-016-0806-z>.

Holling CS (ed), *Adaptive Environmental Assessment and Management* (Wiley-Interscience 1978).

Hollo EJ, Vihervuori P and Kuusiniemi K, 'Environmental Law and Administrative Courts in Finland' (2010) 51(3) J. Ct. Innovation 51.

Howarth W, 'Accommodation without Resolution? Emission Controls and Environmental Quality Objectives in the Proposed EC Water Framework Directive' (1999) 1(1) Environmental Law Review 6 <https://doi.org/10.1177/146145299900100103>.

———'The Progression Towards Ecological Quality Standards' (2006) 18(1) JEL 3 <https://doi.org/10.1093/jel/eqi049>.

———'Aspirations and Realities under the Water Framework Directive: Proceduralisation, Participation and Practicalities' (2009) 21(3) JEL 391 <https://doi.org/10.1093/jel/eqp019>.

Jacob M, *Precedents and Case-based Reasoning in the European Court of Justice: Unfinished Business* (Cambridge University Press 2014).

Janssen MA, 'Changing the Rules of the Game: Lessons from Immunology and Linguistics for Self-Organization of Institutions' in Janssen MA (ed), *Complexity and Ecosystem Management: The Theory and Practice of Multi-Agent Systems* (Edward Elgar 2002).

Josefsson H, 'Assessing Aquatic Spaces of Regulation: Key Issues and Solutions' (2015a) 2014(3) Nordisk miljörättslig tidskrift 23.

———'Ecological Status as a Legal Construct – Determining its Legal and Ecological Meaning' (2015b) 27(2) JEL 231 <https://doi.org/10.1093/jel/eqv009>.

———and Baaner L, 'The Water Framework Directive – A Directive for the Twenty-First Century?' (2011) 23(3) JEL 463 <https://doi.org/10.1093/jel/eqr018>.

Kallis G and Butler D, 'The EU Water Framework Directive: Measures and Implications' (2001) 3 Water Policy 125 <https://doi.org/10.1016/S1366-7017(01)00007-1>.

Karkkainen BC, 'Adaptive Ecosystem Management and Regulatory Penalty Defaults: Toward a Bounded Pragmatism' (2002a) 87 Minnesota Law Review 943 <https://scholarship.law.umn.edu/mlr/760>.

———'Collaborative Ecosystem Governance: Scale, Complexity, and Dynamism' (2002b) 21 Virginia Environmental Law Journal 189.

Keessen AM and others, 'European River Basin Districts: Are they Swimming in the Same Implementation Pool?' (2010) 22(2) JEL 197 <https://doi.org/10.1093/jel/eqq003>.

Kistenkas FH and Bouwma IM, 'Barriers for the Ecosystem Services Concept in European Water and Nature Conservation Law' (2018) 29 Ecosystem Services <https://doi.org/10.1016/j.ecoser.2017.02.013>.

Korkea-aho E, 'Watering Down the Court of Justice? The Dynamics between Network Implementation and Article 258 TFEU Litigation' (2014) 20 ELJ 649 <https://doi.org/10.1111/eulj.12076>.

Kuusiniemi K, 'Domstolarna och experterna: Hur trygga sakkunskapen i miljömål?' in Gipperth L and Zetterberg C (eds), *Miljörättsliga perspektiv och tankevanor* (Iustus Förlag AB 2013).

Kymenvaara S and others, 'Variations on the Same Theme: Environmental Objectives of the Water Framework Directive in Environmental Permitting in the Nordic Countries' (2019) 28(2) RECIEL 197 <https://doi.org/10.1111/reel.12273>.

Lee M, 'Law and Governance of Water Protection Policy' in Scott J (ed), *Environmental Protection: European Law and Governance* (OUP 2009).

Lees E, 'Allocation of Decision-Making Power Under the Habitats Directive' (2016) 28(2) JEL 191 <https://doi.org/10.1093/jel/eqw002>.

Leino L and Belinskij A, 'Vesienhoidollinen kompensaatio hankkeiden toteuttamisen edellytyksenä' (2018) Ympäristöpolitiikan ja -oikeuden vuosikirja XI (Itä-Suomen yliopisto) 117–167.

Liefferink D, Wiering M and Uitenboogaart Y, 'The EU Water Framework Directive: A Multi-Dimensional Analysis of Implementation and Domestic Impact' (2011) 28(4) Land Use Policy 712 <https://doi.org/10.1016/j.landusepol.2010.12.006>.

Lindhout PE and van Rijswick HFMW, 'The effectiveness of the principle of recovery of the costs of water services jeopardized by the European Court of Justice - Annotations on the judgment in C-525/12' (2015) 12(1) JEEPL 80 <https://doi.org/10.1163/18760104-01201006>.

Mäenpää O, *Hallintoprosessioikeus* (2nd edn, WSOYpro 2007).

———'Tarkoituksenmukaisuus – vallanjaon rajapyykki?' in Hurri S, *Demokraattisen oikeuden ehdot* (Tutkijaliitto 2008).

———'Judiciary v. Executive: Judicial Review and the Exercise of Executive Power' (2017) 2–4 JFT 242 <https://doi.org/10.1007/978-3-030-31539-9_9>.

Malve O and others, 'Participatory Operations Model for Cost-Efficient Monitoring and Modeling of River Basins – A Systematic Approach' (2016) 540 Sci Total Environ 79 <https://doi.org/10.1016/j.scitotenv.2015.06.105>.

Mattila J, 'Oikeudenmukainen oikeudenkäynti hallintotuomioistuimessa' in Aalto E, Vihervuori P, Jääskinen N and Arolainen T (eds), *Korkein hallinto-oikeus 90 vuotta* (Otavan Kirjapaino 2008).

Moss B, 'The Water Framework Directive: Total Environment or Political Compromise?' (2008) 400(1) Sci Total Environ 32 <https://doi.org/0.1016/j.scitotenv.2008.04.029>.

Nieminen-Finne H, *Asiantuntija tuomarina: Tekniikan ja luonnontieteiden alan hallinto-oikeustuomarit ympäristönsuojeluasioissa* (Suomalainen Lakimiesyhdistys 2020).

Olsson P, Folke C and Berkes F, 'Adaptive Comanagement for Building Resilience in Social–Ecological Systems' (2004) 34(1) Environ Manage 75 <https://doi.org/10.1007/s00267-003-0101-7>.

Paloniitty T, 'Taking Aims Seriously – How Legal Ecology Affects Judicial Decision-Making' (2015) 6(1) JHRE 55 <https://doi.org/10.4337/jhre.2015.01.03>.

———'The Weser Case: Case C-461/13 BUND V GERMANY' (2016) 28(1) JEL 151 <https://doi.org/10.1093/jel/eqv032>.

———and Kangasmaa S, 'Securing Scientific Understanding: Expert Judges in Finnish Environmental Administrative Judicial Review' (2018) 27(4) European Energy and Environmental Law Review 125.

———and Kotamäki N, 'Scientific and Legal Mechanisms for Addressing Model Uncertainties: Negotiating the Right Balance in Finnish Judicial Review?' (2021) 2 JEL <https://doi.org/10.1093/jel/eqab001>.

———and Nieminen-Finne H, 'The EU Nature Conservation Law in Finnish Judicial Review: Various Avenues, Coalescing Case Law?' in Eliantonio M, Lees E and Paloniitty T (eds), *EU Environmental Principles and Scientific Uncertainty Before National Courts: The Case of the Habitats Directive* (Hart 2022, upcoming).

Preston BJ, 'Biodiversity Offsets: Adequacy and Efficacy in Theory and Practice' (2016) 33(2) Environmental and Planning Law Journal 93.

———'The Judicial Development of the Precautionary Principle' (2018) 35 EPLJ 123.

Quevauviller P and others, 'Science-Policy Integration Needs in Support of the Implementation of the EU Water Framework Directive' (2005) 8(3) Environ Sci & Policy 203 <https://doi.org/10.1016/j.envsci.2005.02.003>.

Refsgaard JC and others, 'Uncertainty in the Environmental Modelling Process–A Framework and Guidance' (2007) 22(11) Environ Model Softw 1543 <https://doi.org/10.1016/j.envsoft.2007.02.004>.

Scott J, 'In Legal Limbo: Post-Legislative Guidance as a Challenge for European Administrative Law' (2011) 48 CML Rev 329.

Senden L, 'Soft Post-Legislative Rulemaking: A Time for More Stringent Control' (2013) 19 ELJ 57 <https://doi.org/10.1111/eulj.12013>.

Söderasp J and Pettersson M, 'Before and after the Weser Case: Legal Application of the Water Framework Directive Environmental Objectives in Sweden' (2019) 31(2) JEL 265 <https://doi.org/10.1093/jel/eqz003>.

Starke JR and van Rijswick HFMW, 'Exemptions of the EU Water Framework Directive Deterioration Ban: Comparing Implementation Approaches in Lower Saxony and The Netherlands' (2021) 13(2) Sustainability 930 <https://doi.org/10.3390/su13020930>.

Tegner Anker H and others, 'The Role of Courts in Environmental Law – A Nordic Comparative Study' (2009) 9 Nordic Environmental Law Journal.

Tripolszky S, 'Water Services and Why a Broad Definition Under the WFD is Needed to Ensure the Polluter Pays Principle' (2012) 2 elni Review 59.

Vakkilainen P, 'Asiantuntijajäsenen rooli korkeimmassa hallinto-oikeudessa' in *Korkein hallinto-oikeus 90 vuotta* (Otavan Kirjapaino 2008).

van Hees S, 'Large-Scale Water-Related Innovative Renewable Energy Projects and the Water Framework Directive: Legal Issues and Solutions' (2017) 14(3–4) JEEPL 315 <https://doi.org/10.1163/18760104-01403004>.

van Kempen JJH, 'Countering the Obscurity of Obligations in European Environmental Law: An Analysis of Article 4 of the European Water Framework Directive' (2012) 24(3) JEL 499 <https://doi.org/10.1093/jel/eqs020>.

van Rijswick HFMW and Backes CW, 'Ground Breaking Landmark Case on Environmental Quality Standards?' (2015) 12(3–4) JEEPL 363 <https://doi.org/10.1163/18760104-01201006>.

van Rijswick M and Keessen A, 'The EU Approach for Intergrated Water Resource Management: Transposing the EU Water Framework Directive Within a National Context – Key Insights from Experience' in Allan A, Hendry S and Rieu-Clarke A (eds), *Routledge Handbook of Water Law and Policy* (Routledge 2017).

van Rijswick M and Tappeiner IU, 'Developing an Institutional Legal Framework for Sustainable Regional Water Management in Times of Climate Change' in Kidd M and others (ed), *Water and the Law: Towards Sustainability* (EE 2014).

Vihervuori P, 'Totuudesta hallintolainkäytössä' in Nuolimaa R, Vihervuori P and Klemettinen H (eds), *Juhlajulkaisu Pekka Hallberg 1944 –12/6 – 2004* (Suomalainen lakimiesyhdistys 2004).

———*Environmental Law in Finland* (2nd edn, Wolters Kluwer Law International 2021).

Voulvoulis N, Arpon KD and Giakoumis T, 'The EU Water Framework Directive: From Great Expectations to Problems with Implementation' (2017) 575 Sci Total Environ 358 <https://doi.org/10.1016/j.scitotenv.2016.09.228>.

Walters CJ, *Adaptive Management of Renewable Resources* (Blackburn Press 1986).

Williams BK, 'Adaptive Management of Natural Resources – Framework and Issues' (2011a) 92(5) J Environ Manage 1346 <https://doi.org/10.1016/j.jenvman.2010.10.041>.

——— 'Passive and Active Adaptive Management: Approaches and an Example' (2011b) 92(5) Journal of Environmental Management 1371 <https://doi.org/10.1016/j.jenvman.2010.10.039>.

——— and Brown ED, 'Adaptive Management: From More Talk to Real Action' (2014) 53(2) Environ Manage 465 <https://doi.org/10.1007/s00267-013-0205-7>.

ECJ Case Law

Case C-33/05 *Commission v Belgium* [2005] ECLI:EU:C:2006:48.

Case C-67/05 *Commission v Germany* [2005] ECLI:EU:C:2005:791.

Case C-85/05 *Commission v Italy* [2006] ECLI:EU:C:2006:33.

Case C-118/05 *Commission v Portugal* [2006] ECLI:EU:C:2006:35.

Case C-32/05 *Commission v Luxembourg* [2006] ECLI:EU:C:2006:749.

Case C-85/07 *Commission v Italy* [2007] ECLI:EU:C:2007:822.

Case C-264/07 *Commission v Greece* [2008] ECLI:EU:C:2008:69.

Case C-561/07 *Commission v Spain* [2009] ECLI:EU:C:2009:363.
Case C-351/09 *Commission v Malta* [2010] ECLI:EU:C:2010:815.
Case C-43/10 *Nomarchiaki Aftodioikisi Aitoloakarnanias and Others* [2012] ECLI:EU:C:2012:560.
Case C-233/11 *Commission v Portugal* [2012] ECLI:EU:C:2012:379.
Case C-297/11 *Commission v Greece* [2012] ECLI:EU:C:2012:228.
Case C366/11 *Commission v Belgium* [2012] ECLI:EU:C:2012:316.
Case C-403/11 *Commission v Spain* [2012] ECLI:EU:C:2012:612.
Case C-190/14 *Commission v Denmark* [2014] ECLI:EU:C:2014:2341.
Case C-525/12 *Commission v Germany* [2014] ECLI:EU:C:2014:2202.
Case C-521/12 *T.C. Briels and Others v Minister van Infrastructuur en Milieu* [2014] ECLI:EU:C:2014:330.
Case C–346/14 *Commission v Austria* [2016] OJ C361 (The *Schwarze Sulm* Case).
Case C-648/13 *Commission v Poland* [2016] ECLI:EU:C:2016:490.

Opinions by the Advocate General

Case C-43/10 *Nomarchiaki Aftodioikisi Aitoloakarnanias and Others* [2012] Opinion of Advocate General Kokott ECLI:EU:C:2011:651.
Case 525/12 *Commission v Germany* [2014] Opinion of Advocate General Jääskinen ECLI:EU:C:2014:449.

Finnish Jurisprudence (Supreme Administrative Court)

SAC 20.8.2010 t. 1869 (KHO 20.8.2010 t. 1869).
SAC 2015:102 (KHO 2015:102 ECLI:FI:KHO:2015:102).
SAC 2016:36 (KHO 2016:36 ECLI:FI:KHO:2016:36).
SAC 2019:166 (KHO 2019:166 ECLI:FI:KHO:2019:166).
SAC 2017:87 (KHO 2017:87 ECLI:FI:KHO:2017:87).
The SAC 2015:102 (KHO 2015:102).

Swedish Jurisprudence (Mark Och Miljööverdomstolen, Land and Environment Court of Appeal)

M 8374–15.
M 2620–16.
M 8882–15.
M 8673–15.
All Cases Available in Swedish <http://www.markochmiljooverdomstolen.se/Avgoranden-fran-Mark--och-miljooverdomstolen/2017/>.

Secondary EU Legislation

Directive 2000/60/EC of 23 October 2000 Establishing a Framework for Community Action in the Field of Water Policy [2000] OJ L327/1.

Directive 2008/56/EC of 17 June 2008 Establishing a Framework for Community Action in the Field of Marine Environmental Policy (Marine Strategy Framework Directive) [2008] OJ L 164.

Directive 2010/75/EU of 24 November 2010 on Industrial Emissions (Integrated Pollution Prevention and Control) [2010] OJ L 334/17.

European Commission.

Opinions

Commission Opinion of 6.12.2011 delivered upon request of Germany pursuant to Art. 6(4) sub par. 2 of Council Directive 92/43/EEC of 21 May 1992 on the conservation of natural habitats and of wild fauna and flora, concerning the deepening and widening of the ship fairway Unter- and Außenelbe (river Elbe) to the port of Hamburg (Germany), 6.12.2011 C(2011) 9090 final.

Opinion of the Commission of 24/04/2003 Delivered upon request of Germany according to Art. 6 (4) Sub Par. 2 of Council Directive 92/43/EEC of 21 May 1992 on the conservation of the natural habitats as well as the wild animals and plants, concerning the approval of an operational master plan ('Rahmenbetriebsplan') of the Prosper Haniel Colliery operated by Deutsche Steinkohle AG (DSK), for the period 2001–2019, 24.4.2003.

Opinion of the Commission delivered pursuant to Article 6.4 § 2 of Council Directive 92/43/EEC of 21 May 1992 on the conservation of the natural habitats and of wild fauna and flora (Habitats Directive), concerning the "Request by the Netherlands for advice and exchange of information with the European Commission within the framework of the Birds and Habitats Directives", in relation to the "Project Mainport Rotterdam" Development Plan, 24.4.2003.

Opinion of the Commission pursuant to Article 6.4 § 2 of Council Directive 92/43/EEC of 21 May 1992 on the conservation of natural habitats and of wild fauna and flora, concerning the "Request by the Kingdom of Spain in relation to the La Breña II reservoir project." C(2004)1797, 7.5.2004 (only proposed opinion is made available).

Communications, Reports, Decisions and Staff Working Documents

Commission, 'Commission Staff Working Document Membes State Finland, Report from the Commission to the European Parliament and the Council on the Implementation of the Water Framework Directive (2000/60/EC) River Basin Management Plans (Implementation SWD Finland)' SWD (2012) 379 final.

Common Implementation Strategies

European Communities (2005) 'Common Implementation Strategy for the Water Framework Directive (2000/60/EC). Guidance Document No. 13, Overall Approach to the Classification of Ecological Status and Ecological Potential'.

Common Implementation Strategy for the Water Framework Directive (2000/60/EC), Guidance Document No. 20, Guidance Document on Exemptions to the Environmental Objectives (Office for Official Publications of the European Communities 2009).

Other EU Sources

European Commission (2016) 'Introduction to the New EU Water Framework Directive', <http://ec.europa.eu/environment/water/water-framework/info/intro_ en.htm>.

Commission, WFD Guidance Documents, <https://ec.europa.eu/environment/water/water-framework/facts_figures/guidance_docs_en.htm>.

Finnish Legislation

Water Act (vesilaki) 587/2011, leGally Non-Binding English Translation <http://www.finlex.fi/en/laki/kaannokset/2011/en20110587.pdf>.

Act on the Organization of River Basin Management and the Marine Strategy 1299/2004, Legally Non-Binding English Translation<https://finlex.fi/en/laki/kaannokset/2004/en20041299>.

Administrative Judicial Procedure Act (laki oikeudenkäynnistä hallintoasioissa 808/2019), Legally Non-Binding English Translation <https://www.finlex.fi/fi/laki/kaannokset/2019/20190808>.

Decree on Water Resources Management (Valtioneuvoston asetus vesienhoidon järjestämisestä) 1040/2006, Legally Non-Binding English Translation <http://www.finlex.fi/en/laki/ kaannokset/2006/en20061040.pdf>.

Preparatory Documents

Governments Proposal to the Parliament on River Basin Management 120/2004 (Hallituksen esitys Eduskunnalle laiksi vesienhoidon järjestämisestä, laiksi ympäristönsuojelulain muuttamisesta ja laiksi vesilain muuttamisesta sekä maasta toiseen ulottuvien vesistöjen sekä kansainvälisten järvien suojelusta ja käytöstä tehdyn vuoden 1992 yleissopimuksen vesivaroja ja terveyttä koskevan pöytäkirjan hyväksymisestä ja laiksi sen lainsäädännön alaan kuuluvien määräysten voimaansaattamisesta 120/2004).

Constitutional Law Committee 45/2004 in Relation to the Government's Proposal to the Parliament 120/2004 (PeVL 45/2004 vp – HE 120/2004).

Other Sources

Maanmittauslaitos, 'Suomi 57 000–168 000 järven maa' (12 July 2019) <https://www.maanmittauslaitos.fi/ajankohtaista/suomi-57-000-168-000-jarven-maa>.

Chapter 5

Adaptivity and Law in Jurisprudential Analysis

Introduction

As the two preceding chapters have shown, adaptive natural resources management as a field of science has presented almost unbearable challenges to modern environmental law, in theory and in practice. The more fundamental considerations underlying this regulatory and adjudicatory challenge are presented in this chapter. Here, the natural resources paradigm is examined as a jurisprudential challenge and, from the viewpoint of the judicial decision-maker, examines the established notions of the fact and norm premise. The chapter also studies 'facts' in the context of risk regulation research, where similar questions have been addressed and also solved in past decades. The following explains the changes that ecology forces upon such a distinction; the challenge was described in the preceding chapters as the continuum of normativity. Furthermore, a critique is presented of transparency as a panacea to these challenges; the applicability of straightforward *in dubio pro natura* argumentation is also given critical consideration. The scrutiny is concluded with some epistemological considerations that tentatively offer solace in the face of otherwise bleak results. Finally, the chapter sums up by explaining the critique of scientism at the root of the scientific endeavour of the whole volume.

There Is No There There: Facts, Regulation, and Adaptive Management

Thus, as the first step, context is provided with lessons from the law and regulation of risk, for many of the underpinning questions have already long been scrutinised there – applying adaptive management or the concept of resilience are not the only solutions to the uncertainty that haunts environmental regulation and adjudication. Uncertainty can also be perceived as a source of risk to be evaluated and regulated. Risk regulation is an alternative to the adaptive management paradigm since, in the former, uncertainty is not cherished but taken for granted in proceeding with the regulation, whereas if adaptive management is to be regulated according to its own rationale, then uncertainty ought to be

DOI: 10.4324/9781003197829-5

acclaimed and enabled even after regulatory intervention. Regardless of their differing ontologies, risk regulation might offer a helping hand in understanding uncertainty in adaptive management.

Facts, Uncertainty, and Risks

Even though there is no unanimous definition of the concept of risk, the definitions used in research can be categorised to mean either a situation in which something valued by humans is endangered and the end result is uncertain or a situation where an uncertain consequence of an event might endanger something deemed valuable. Thus, the ontology of risk is independent of our perception or knowledge.[1] However, uncertainty or likelihood are not parts of the concept of the risk itself but merely dimensions associated with the construct. Here these most commonly used notions of risk differ from the understanding of uncertainty in adaptive management: there, uncertainty is an inherent part of the cycle that the concept is to represent. Even though these two definitions are most common in risk research, others have been suggested, tentatively, of greater use to the environmental regulator vexed with adaptive management. In one proposal, the uncertainty and severity of the consequences are coupled: 'Risk refers to uncertainty about and severity of the events and consequences (or outcomes) of an activity with respect to something that humans value.'[2] This definition might serve the present enquiry better – unsurprisingly, perhaps, when noted that the definition covers the ontological and epistemological aspects but leaves the normative judgement to the evaluator or to the regulator. When uncertainty and severity are considered as sides of a two-dimensional apparatus, the adjudicator or legislator is required to consider both. Interestingly, in the last-mentioned definition, risk is dependent on the evaluator and, as such, is an explication of the evaluator. If risk was comprehended as a two-dimensional couple, the 'human impact' would be present, similar to the understanding of the adaptive management paradigm. Subjectivity does not, however, make scientific scrutiny redundant; it only allows for personal or social attributes. Importantly, such attributes are group-dependent: the more the group of the evaluator suffers from the consequences

1 Terje Aven and Ortwin Renn, 'On Risk Defined as an Event Where the Outcome is Uncertain' (2009) Journal of Risk Research 12(1) <https://doi.org/10.1080/13669870802488883>, 1–2; Ortwin Renn, 'Three Decades of Risk Research: Accomplishments and New Challenges' (1998) Journal of Risk Research 1 <https://doi.org/10.1080/136698798377321>, 50. Even though risk is not consistently defined, the feature of differentiating between reality and possibility prevails in all comprehensions; Ibid, 50.

2 Aven and Renn (n 1) 8–9. As they clarify, the definition does not include, e.g. a component of multiplication that would have brought the normativity along.

of the event or the less familiar the evaluator is with the situation, the more highly the risk is evaluated.[3]

The perceived risk is biased in multiple ways. People tend to regard spontaneously incurred risks as more likely, as they do with risks they can anchor to already-existing knowledge. Also, stories of individuals, and the harms or incidents they face, make probabilities seem more likely than if they occur as frequencies – not to mention the extent to which people go in order to avoid cognitive dissonance.[4] Interestingly, regarding the legislature's or adjudicator's task in environmental matters, when perceived risk is analysed with the help of psychometric modelling, activities seen as immoral or unnatural tampering with nature create a higher notion of risk.[5] Even when risk assessment is not regarded as a purely subjective activity, national and cultural habits affect the assessment: the evaluated risk is conditioned by values.[6] Due to this and the fact that the phenomena being evaluated have become increasingly complex, factors such as moral considerations or political or social concerns have been incorporated into the research arrangements – even to the extent of pursuing a 'constructionist' approach.[7] It has been comprehended that even when the research data is free of subjectivity, the risk assessment founded on said data is not: risk assessment consists of scientific but also non-scientific aspects.[8] The development results partly from the increased amount of risk analyses conducted: routine risk assessment might lure the actors into a false sense of security when the limitations of the research methods and the faults they produce are not fully acknowledged.[9]

Eventually thus, risk research seems to have chosen a path akin to adaptive management. Structured risk research began from a technical analysis, later strongly criticised by social scientists as dismissive of the values inevitably

3 Aven and Renn (n 1) 8–9. Aven and Renn strongly emphasise that this does not result in risk being 'socially construct[ed]' or something else post-modern would prefer: risk is still related to the objective world and its phenomena – ignorance or unlikeliness of a danger does not result in it becoming non-existent. 'Risk is then not a state of the world, but the events/consequences that are associated with the risk – are states of the world.' Ibid, 10.

4 Renn (n 1) 58.

5 Lennart Sjöberg, 'Perceived Risk and Tampering with Nature' (2000) Journal of Risk Research 3(4) <https://doi.org/10.1080/13669870050132568>, 353–5.

6 Asa Boholm, 'Comparative Studies of Risk Perception: A Review of Twenty Years of Research' (1998) Journal of Risk Research 1(2) <https://doi.org/10.1080/136698798377231>, 135–6; Renn (n 1) 53. For comparisons in risk research, this results in serious methodological problems; ibid Boholm 136.

7 Andrew Stirling, 'Risk at a Turning Point?' (1998) Journal of Risk Research 1(3) <https://doi.org/10.1080/136698798377204> 98–8; Boholm (n 6) 139; Sjöberg (n 5) 355.

8 Jacqueline Peel, *Science and Risk Regulation in International Law* (Cambridge University Press 2010) 377–78.

9 Renn (n 1) 49. Further integration of risk assessment and management with the sciences underpinning the evaluation is offered as a solution – sciences including three of natural, technical, and social ones; ibid.

present in any risk evaluation. Those value analyses and their implications were then accounted for, the third stage of research turning to institutional and procedural considerations, regarding processes as enhancers of risk distribution decisions.[10] The routine manner in which risk assessments are conducted might have influenced the misguided understanding or vice versa – ultimately, the assumptions that risk evaluation is value-free, neutral, and objective have required correcting.[11] However, in remembering the similarities with adaptive management, anyone familiar with the Water Frame Directive (WFD) should not be surprised by this turn to proceduralisation in risk research. The WFD is, alas, the prime example of the increased emphasis on proceduralisation in natural resources management.[12] Regulating risk establishes a system, researchable with a system-theory-based approach, in which the risks regulated form 'risk regimes.' The benefits of systemic analysis are plentiful, including the comprehensive and disaggregated view that can be presented.[13] Risk regimes can thus increase the knowledge of the gaps of risks regulated and be an effective tool for the legislator, but as with any systematic analysis, it cannot answer the question of why certain risks are less regulated than others, being blind to the question of value choice behind the decision – and the legitimacy of that decision. However, the different stages of risk research require a different approach from the regulator. As far as participatory rights or mediation go, the role of proceduralisation is surely acknowledged, forming one answer to the call of the third stage of risk research, the institutional considerations.[14]

These institutional considerations can also be comprehended as a lack of understanding of the legal's role in technical risk assessment, as can be seen in how the question of subjectivity is conceptualised as part of the science/democracy dichotomy prevailing in much risk regulation scholarship. Subjectivity in risk research demands attention, regardless of the extent to which constructivism is shattered or cherished: to regulate risk in a legitimate manner, the question of subjectivity must be addressed. Legally speaking, the question can be framed as one of administrative constitutional law, producing clarification over technological risk evaluation and the debates over it, illustrating the incompatibility between risk research and the legal. The discourse over the challenges of technological risk assessment is bifurcated, being either rational-instrumental

10 Renn (n 1) 53, 62–3.

11 E Fisher, 'Drowning by Numbers: Standard Setting in Risk Regulation and the Pursuit of Accountable Public Administration' (2000) Oxford Journal of Legal Studies 20(1) <https://doi.org/10.1093/ojls/20.1.109>, 110.

12 As we have learned, the original transposition of WFD in Finland exemplifies the phenomenon excellently; text to n 50 in ch 4.

13 Christopher Hood, Henry Rothstein, and Robert Baldwin, *The Government of Risk: Understanding Risk Regulation Regimes* (Oxford University Press 2001) 10, 16.

14 This is not to allude that when it comes to adaptive management the two realms would suffice. That is, however, the extent to where the legal has thus far ventured.

or deliberative-constitutive – both discourses trapped by the legal's requirement over the certainty of the facts employed in decision-making.[15] The role of law in regulating technological risk is not instrumental, as commonly comprehended, but independent to the extent that different legal cultures (as discourses of entwined legal concepts) play significant roles in the complexity. When it comes to regulating environmental or health risks, the assumption is the opposite from what it is in the other, more accusatory or arbitrary fields of law: when it comes to regulating environmental threats, 'regulation should occur except if it can be proved that it should not'.[16] Due to borrowing concepts from the arbitrary spheres of law, the rational-instrumental understanding of risk assessment is explicitly emphasised. To correctly meet the demands of environmental decision-making, the concept of the 'burden of proof' is thus inadequate – the discourse ought to be re-oriented to better meet the needs of environmental administrative decision-making. The Finnish judicial review examined earlier supports the notion: there, too, the judicial discretion is a broader, more holistic endeavour.[17]

These notions from risk regulation studies illustrate clearly why securing common ground between adaptive management, and the legal is such a challenge. Adversarial fields of law concentrate on the burden of proof in order to find the culprit, while environmental risk regulation focuses on the definition and evaluation of threats that are or are not likely. To best ascertain the correct implementation of the scientific work when regulating adaptive management, the onus of the legal's actions ought to be on 'playing along,' facilitating the actions of the managers and scientists, and while doing so, ensuring that the conditions for the rule of law are fulfilled. With risk regulation, the legal has long ignored the questions and challenges of scientific knowledge; an attitude also present regarding the regulation of adaptive management. This should only give us more reason to address the issue of facts, adaptive management, and its regulation. In risk regulation, one path forward was found in tackling the science/democracy dichotomy, exposing its irrelevance and acknowledging that administrative decision-making of environmental matters is both. This outcome emphasises the role of the administrators, clearing space for accusations of undemocratic and excessive use of public power. However, as Fisher

15 That being the infamous 'burden of proof'; Elizabeth Fisher, *Risk Regulation and Administrative Constitutionalism* (Hart Publishing 2007) 290, 5.

16 The dichotomy between science and democracy is thus an oversimplification, proven by the legal's role in administrating risk; Fisher (n 15) 39, 44, 46.

17 Text to n 186 in ch 4. Also Mikael Hildén, 'Opportunities and challenges in providing and using scientific knowledge in environmental appeal cases in Finland' in Kari Kuusiniemi, Outi Suviranta, and Veli-Pekka Viljanen (eds), *Juhlajulkaisu Pekka Vihervuori 1950–25/8–2020* (SLY 2020) fn 14 and text to it.

states, 'governing is an inherently normative enterprise'; attempts to whitewash it as something else are doomed to fail.[18]

If easy answers to the legitimacy crises of risk regulation have slid out of reach, what about the regulation of adaptive management? In what follows, concepts of the fact and norm premise are examined in an attempt to resolve whether they carry any explanatory force in the regulation of adaptive management. First, facts in judicial decision-making are examined, and thereafter the changes that ecology as a field of science has wrought on the administrative-legal system. From there, the examination continues to the daunting task of separating decisions on facts and values from administrative-legal decision-making à la the WFD and, possibly, beyond the regime of water governance.

Fact Premise or Premise Facts?

Legal scholarship, obsessed as it is with norms, appears to have left facts to their own business, and environmental legal scholarship, whether animated by policy analysis or a more abstract, principle-oriented approach, has shared the same tendency.[19] Judicial decision-making in environmental matters is most often forward-looking, be it about limiting threats or evaluating the acceptable amount of pollution or other environmental harm in authorisations. At the earliest stages in the administrative permitting process, the decision-maker attempts to evaluate the undertaking's consequences and defines permit provisions under which the evaluated consequences would most likely be tolerable – or legitimate.[20] At times this process can even include educated guesses about events occurring in the distant future and founding the normative evaluation on those guesses. If this process is to be described with the fact/norm dichotomy, the facts in such cases are without historical relevance: they are estimates, assessments of tentative future impacts. Due to the forward-looking decision-making, the tasks of the legislature and the judiciary in environmental matters have much in common: neither is able to justify their decisions on historical facts but must resort to forecasting the future course of events.

Regardless of the dearth of historical facts, facts also constitute one half of environmental judicial decision-making, the other being norms. As with any dichotomy, the strict division between the fact and norm premise has proven to be troublesome.[21] The forward-looking nature of environmental

18 Fisher (n 15) 246, 290, 247–8, 252

19 Richard Posner, *The Problems of Jurisprudence* (Harvard University Press 1990) 216.

20 Brian J Preston, 'Contemporary Issues in Environmental Impact Assessment' (2020) EPLJ 37 423, 423.

21 As discussed at text to n 176 ff in ch 3.

adjudication further challenges the dichotomy of facts and norms, further complicated still by the relative rarity of the phenomenon, explaining why the fact premise has gained relatively limited attention in general jurisprudence.[22] Some established notions can, nonetheless, prove useful for contemporary environmental adjudication too; Keeton's classic concept of *premise facts* being such.[23] Premise facts refer to a rare type of fact, convened in common law decision-making, surmised during the adjudication and, either explicitly or implicitly, used as premises when deciding upon the normative question.[24] The verb is relevant here: premise facts are not found or decided upon but presumed, assumed. Often premise facts are hidden in how the adjudicator does not rule the case; premise facts are presuppositions, alleged notions that influence the direction of the ruling.[25] In particular, allegations that are not verbalised in the reasoning might imply that the adjudicators' own views and biases influenced the resolution.[26]

The discourse over premise fact includes features specific to common law, premise facts being fruits of the abundant discourse over legislative facts and adjudicative facts, developed in the analysis of administrative fact-finding.[27] In this dichotomy, premise facts are legislative facts presupposed during adjudication. The precise category cannot be deduced from the fact itself but from how the fact is used.[28] Relevant to the examination here is that the premise facts can be defined as the results of interpretation or anticipations instead of descriptions of previous turns of events.[29] Premise facts are 'exogenous generalisations,' deriving from extra-judicial considerations and rarely if ever, founded on historical, empirical facts.[30] In adjudication, the question is whether the information underpinning the ruling is sufficient or which normative implications

22 It is not insinuated that there would not be adjudication with historical facts in environmental law – not all environmental decision-making is forward-looking. Those environmental atrocities that are criminalised are decided upon with historical facts, as are cases where enforcing administrative compulsion is allowed.

23 Robert E Keeton, 'Legislative Facts and Similar Things: Deciding Disputed Premise Facts' (1988) Minn L Rev 73(1) <https://scholarship.law.umn.edu/mlr/2241>, 13, 32.

24 Todd S Aagaard, 'Factual Premises of Statutory Interpretation' (2009) Geo Wash L Rev 77(2) <https://ssrn.com/abstract=1126730>, 398; Keeton (ibid) 8, 66. The former finds it plausible that the legislator's reliance upon premise facts is subconscious activity.

25 Keeton (n 23) 286 fn 100; Aagaard (ibid) 385–6.

26 Aagaard (n 24) 398, where Aagaard takes a stronger stance on the matter, discussing the latent disadvantage the situation has for the impartiality of the adjudication.

27 Allison Orr Larsen, 'Confronting Supreme Court Fact Finding' (2012) Virginia Law Review <https://scholarship.law.wm.edu/facpubs/1284>, 1256 fn 5; Kenneth Culp Davis, 'Approach to Problems of Evidence in the Administrative Process' (1942) Harv. L. Rev. 55(3) <https://doi.org/10.2307/1335092>.

28 Aagaard (n 24) 382 fn 83, 383 fn 86.

29 Keeton (n 23) 11, 16, 20. The relation between premise facts, assumptions, and presupposition as a part of the decision-making process; Aagaard (n 24) 282 fn 87 and the references therein.

30 Aagaard (n 24) 386; Keeton (n 23) 11, 16, 20.

ought to be derived from the evaluations of the prospective environmental impacts of the planned project. The adjudicator needs to both assess future events while constrained by inadequate knowledge and interpret the normative consequences of such presumptions. What makes adjudication relating to adaptive water management interesting in premise facts is that in the gathering of said presumptions, technical or scientific knowledge becomes more significant than in the standard decision-making with historical facts.[31] Due to the lack of historical references, the ordinary rules of evidence, of its acceptance or reasoning, do not apply to premise facts.[32] The only restrictions are that when adjudicating with premise facts, one ought to follow the same guidelines of transparency and clarity as are required with the norm premise.[33]

In the US, the decisions on premise facts in higher instances of the court take the preliminary position that the overall ruling possesses.[34] Since premise facts are not facts in the traditional sense but assumptions, this can result in a situation where the inherent flexibility turns against it: after a certain assumption is given a preliminary position, the lower instances cannot build their reasoning on the latest scientific knowledge but need to refer to an underlying scientific inquiry later found faulty.[35] Though legal systems vary in details like this, there can also be risk elsewhere that the inherent uncertainty of scientific data or the underpinning presuppositions of the adjudicator are effectively effaced – or emphasised – in later decisions.[36] Nonetheless, not only facts but also the concept of facts are contested, and premise facts are interesting intellectual tools to understand their circumstances.[37] One lesson to be learned is that when it comes to environmental adjudication, jumping hastily to the norms and their interpretative challenges might be unwise, so much does the forward-looking nature of the activity influence the terrain surrounding and underpinning the normative discretion. Also, traditional accounts of judicial action can accommodate assessments and estimates as the factual premise.

31 Keeton (n 23) 20–1; Aagaard (n 24) 401.
32 Keeton (n 23) 44; Allison Orr Larsen, 'Factual Precedents' (2013) U Pa L Rev 162(1) 59, 71–2.
33 Stance of Keeton (n 23) 34.
34 Keeton (n 23) 26; Larsen (n 32) 59. According to Larsen, even factual preliminary rulings are possible – in such cases the lower instances would not refer to the evidence of the case at hand but to the stance the higher instance has taken on such facts. Larsen is critical of such possibilities irrespective of where the knowledge relied upon in the higher court is produced or published.
35 Stephanie Tai, 'Uncertainty About Uncertainty: The Impact of Judicial Decisions on Assessing Scientific Uncertainty' (2008) U Pa J Const L 11(3) <https://ssrn.com/abstract=1265153>, 698.
36 David Michaels and Celeste A Monforton, 'Scientific Evidence in the Regulatory System: Manufacturing Uncertainty and the Demise of the Formal Regulatory System' (2005) J L & Pol'y 13(1) <https://ssrn.com/abstract=707136>, 34.
37 Keeton (n 23) 44–5; Larsen (n 32) 71–2.

Reconciling Different Ontologies of Ecology and Law?

After these more general aspects of facts in environmental adjudication, ecology comes to the fore. Environmental regulation, as a field of science, is an offspring of ecology, the science of relations between organisms that occur in ecosystems. On top of being forward-looking, the questions raised by ecology further complicate environmental decision-making because the theoretical foundation of ecology has until recently been more empirical than conjectural. That is to say, the answers ecology may provide differ in important respects from the answers supplied by pure – and less applied – fields of science.[38] To contextualise the issue in what follows, a closer look is taken at how scientific knowledge can be assessed and evaluated in everyday environmental adjudication. Then, the focus is shifted to more rudimentary features, the differences between scientific and legal inquiry and question-setting, and the influence of these differences on judicial decision-making.

Assessing Scientific Knowledge

There are four ways in which the judiciary exploits scientific knowledge in environmental matters. These methods are not mutually exclusive but can be used concurrently and often are.[39] The object of analysis is the merits review conducted in Australia, which attempts to establish whether the decision under review is 'the correct or preferable one,' thus extending beyond the scope of review in our example state, Finland.[40] The results are referred to as prime examples of how scientific knowledge could be exploited in judicial review (though if being accurate, whether merits review resembles judicial review or replaces the original decision is a contested question).[41] Arguments have been presented against the strict differentiation between the two, even going to the extent of claiming merits review 'as judicial review in disguise,' formally located in the executive branch but employing the methods and values of the judiciary.[42] The obscurity is of only limited relevance here: it is sufficient that merits review has a normative goal in its attempt to enhance the quality of the administrative decision-making in question. Fairness, transparency, and openness ought to be promoted, granting the makers of merits review broad authority to examine all

38 Olli Malve, *Water Quality Prediction for River Basin Management* (Teknillinen korkeakoulu, Vesitalouden ja vesirakennuksen laboratorio, ed, Teknillinen korkeakoulu 2007) <http://lib.tkk.fi/Diss/2007/isbn9789512287505> (accessed 10 April 2021).

39 Patrick Ky, 'Qualifications, Weight of Opinion, Peer Review, and Methodology: A Framework for Understanding the Evaluation of Science in Merits Review' (2012) Journal of Environmental Law 24(2) 207, 221.

40 Where these considerations are left outside of the 'legality' review, text to n 186 in ch 4.

41 Ky (n 39) 214; Fisher (n 15) 126; Peter Cane, 'Merits Review and Judicial Review – The AAT as Trojan Horse' (2000) Fed L Rev 28(2) <https://doi.org/10.22145/flr.28.2.4>, 223.

42 Cane (ibid) 225.

features of the reviewed decisions, an activity that is undertaken in a 'judicialised' manner, i.e. with resemblance to the work of the judiciary, weakening the dichotomy between considerations of legality and 'rightness' of the decision. Merits review examines the latter type of questions.[43]

So there are at least four ways in which scientific knowledge has been evaluated in court: the qualifications, weight of opinion, peer-review, and methodology approaches; the correctness of the scientific data being examined differently in each. In the qualifications approach, the decisive factor is the professional status of the scientist(s) offering the information – with the weight of opinion approach, the focus lies on the number of scientists behind a certain option: the greater the number, the more valid the solution.[44] In the peer-review approach, the focus is on the (quality of the) forum in which the decisive scientific paper is published, whether the journal is peer-reviewed or not.[45] Lastly, in the methodology approach, the centre of attention is the methodology used to gain the scientific data. Since the scientific method is understood to decrease the amount of uncertainty of the results, a decent method equals a more reliable outcome, but naturally, employing the last-mentioned requires the adjudicator to be able to adjudge various scientific methods.[46]

This analysis highlights the diversity of the issue, how both the problem itself – using scientific knowledge in court – and the available solutions vary. Categorising the court practice offers insight into how adjudicators justify their discretion in employing some pieces of scientific information instead of others. The scrutiny is, however, external and, as such, descriptive. The question can, however, also be examined from another, more fundamental and potentially also more internal point of view: the differences between scientific and legal question-setting and decision-making. These epistemological differences are explained next in order to enhance our understanding of the underlying tension in all administrative-legal decisions based on ecology.

From Legal and Scientific Causalities...

Wahlberg, whose thinking is focused on below, examines the problems that the legal confronts when trying to draw on scientific knowledge.[47] If the concepts

43 Cane (n 41) 221; Gabriel Fleming, 'Administrative Review and the Normative Goal – Is Anybody out There' (2000) Fed L Rev 28(1) <https://doi.org/10.22145/flr.28.1.3>, 63, 82. The indeterminacy of the aims is not left unnoted; ibid Fleming 81.

44 Ky (n 39) 221, 226.

45 Ky (n 39) 241. The peer review approach is naturally a variation on the weight of the opinion approach, the former being somewhat narrower that the latter in its reliance on the quality of a journal, not to a broader scientific community; ibid Ky 242.

46 Ky (n 39) 230–2.

47 Lena Wahlberg, *Legal Questions and Scientific Answers: Ontological Differences and Epistemic Gaps in the Assessment of Causal Relations* (Lund University 2010); cf. Tarlock, 'Is There a There There in

of causality that the legislature and the judiciary hold differ from each other, the legal and the scientific also hold divergent views: legally relevant relations pertain between legally relevant causes and legally relevant effects regardless of whether these are scientifically relevant.[48] What makes matters so difficult is that the legal ask different questions from those posed by the relevant scientists in the course of their studies, resulting in a conceptual and disciplinary gap. At worst, the result is that the findings needed might not even exist in the terms in which they are sought.[49] The same applies to adaptive management and its regulation: the questions found relevant by the scientists (and also managers) might not be relevant to the legislator attempting to regulate the management.

The manner in which scientific information could help in forming legally relevant causation can be divided into two steps. First, an association should be established between scientific entities that are instantiated by a certain legally interesting behaviour and the damage in question.[50] For example, an action – e.g. the use of pesticides – might have been taken into the sphere of regulation since the behaviour is generally associated with harmful effects – regardless of whether those effects have taken place in a specific case.[51] Secondly, a legally relevant relation should be established between instances of these scientific kinds. In this case, specific behaviours and specific forms of damage are placed under scrutiny.[52] Bearing in mind that several actions and forms of damage that may be of interest to legal scholars remain uninspiring for scientists, achieving the first step is not as straightforward as it sounds. The phrase 'scientific entities' poses another challenge: the way behaviour is isolated and defined in scientific research does not automatically equate with the behaviours of interest to the legal. Legally relevant causality is commonly established as answers to two questions, one retrospective and the other prospective: 'Did this action cause this consequence?' or 'What are the consequences of this action?'[53] In environmental decision-making, the prospective evaluation is more common.[54]

Despite their obvious differences in the temporal aspect, both questions focus on the question of legally relevant causality regarding specific human behaviours or environmental effects. Scientific causality and legally relevant

Environmental Law?' (2004) Journal of Land Use and Environmental Law 19(2) <https://www.jstor.org/stable/42842841>, 253.

48 Wahlberg (n 47) 27. Here 'the legal' is understood broadly, including the legislature, the judiciary, and the administrative authorities. This point is by no means privilege of environmental law only: legally relevant causation or a legally relevant standard of proof differs from scientific causation in various occasions; Wahlberg (ibid) 15 fn 8, 130.

49 Wahlberg (n 47) 16.

50 Wahlberg (n 47) 157.

51 Wahlberg (n 47) 69–70.

52 Wahlberg (n 47) 157, 167ff.

53 The regulations thus produced is either respectively or prospectively evaluated one; Wahlberg (n 47) 71, 155.

54 Wahlberg (n 47) 155–7.

causality are not indistinguishable. In retrospective questions, their dissimilarity is often described by accounting for the extent of legally relevant causality – how much of the scientific aspect is included in said causality.[55] The question of legally relevant causality is one of the relations between the action in question and other actions *and* the relation of both to the consequence in question. Traditionally, causality is comprehended as the so-called 'but-for test,' which 'requires that the effect would not have occurred *but for* the alleged cause.' As can be noted from the definition, the but-for test is best suited to retrospective questions, being of limited value in environmental regulation.[56] The but-for test demonstrates those causalities often comprehended as 'traditional' legal causalities. Another more suited to environmental regulation is the so-called 'NESS test,' which focuses on assessing whether the activity in question has been 'a necessary element in sufficient sets of human behaviour.'[57] In environmental regulation, the inevitability of the presupposed consequences is relevant. If the consequence is a fundamental part of the activity, the need for regulation (or the chance to employ scientific knowledge as facts of the case in adjudication) is naturally more urgent than when the effect is only indirect. The scrutinised causalities in various situations differ, as does the employability of the scientific information available.[58]

The NESS test is thus superior when searching for legally relevant causalities. Naturally, this depends on whether one can ask retrospective or prospective questions and also on the inevitability of the consequence, i.e. the probability of the effect. The causalities employed thus vary according to the question asked. As often anticipated, scientific knowledge increases as time proceeds – or as should be phrased in the case of adaptive management that time enhances scientists' learning opportunities. Even when different types of rules would have similar general aims, the manner in which different rules can benefit from increased knowledge varies.[59] If causalities in the available scien-

55 Wahlberg (n 47) 84–5.

56 Adding to the impracticality, employing the test requires that all the factors influencing the consequence under scrutiny can be detailed. After establishing them one can evaluate which one has been indispensable for the existence of the consequence; Wahlberg (n 47) 87.

57 Ibid, 87–8. It has even been concluded that the 'NESS test' is not only a test for causality but causality *an sich*. The two tests are naturally interlinked: if the circumstances are simple enough, the NESS test dismantles into the simpler 'but for test'; Richard W Wright, 'Causation in Tort Law' (1985) Calif Law Rev 73(6) <https://doi.org/10.2307/3480373>, 1802.

58 In other words, the differences between the but-for test and the NESS test cause differences in the causalities that are required or accepted as justifications of legal or regulative action; Wahlberg (n 47) 196–7.

59 E.g. the precautionary principle relies on the notion of estimated causes and the BAT's, assessment of which employs prospective questions and benefits from the increased knowledge only at the time when granted permits are re-evaluated, whereas in cases of strict liability in tort law the actor is liable of the harm they have caused irrespective of the state of their knowledge; Wahlberg (n 47) 71, 191–3.

tific information are weak, prospective questions serve better environmental regulation drafting. However, when asking the prospective question, both the activity and its likely consequences must be clearly detailed, and the estimated benefits of the regulation must be reasonable in relation to the regulation costs. Implementing a cost-benefit analysis often leads to a situation in which activities remain unregulated: under uncertainty of consequences and causality, the benefits of regulation are undermined in relation to the costs.[60] There are situations, though, where neither of the questions properly fits. If the prospective question results in excessive costs and undermined benefits, and the retrospective one is unsuitable due to uncertainties in causalities, the activity slides out of the reach of the regulator. It is likely that these considerations underlie the prolonged and pertinent lack of regulation of agricultural runoff.

...To Persistent Ontological Differences

Scientific inquiry understands causality in various manners, all derived from these two models. Causality is most often proven by examining the factors of interest in relative isolation, fending off the other prospective causes and by doing so, attempting to prove the significance of the examined activity. One can also group the relative factors in an attempt to even out the effects of other potentially relevant factors. These methods of isolation and grouping, often also used concurrently, enable results from the scientific enquiry in the first place but at the same time restrict the causalities known to science.[61] Ecology gains its results by analysing scientific entities at a macrolevel. These are less homogenous than the subjects of more traditional fields of science occurring at the microlevel, e.g. chemistry or physics. The way in which these different fields of science produce laws is illustrative: the laws of biology (if they exist) are more probabilistic than accurate, general, and exceptionless. In ecological studies, the scrutinised group cannot be isolated as it is in more traditional, less applied fields of science. This results in the lack of said general and exceptionless laws and, also, uncertainty over whether the results of ecology are as reliable as the results of microlevel research.[62]

Even though the differentiation between microlevels and macrolevels of scientific inquiry is a generalisation, it has had its consequences in the establishment of legally relevant causality: the results of macrolevel studies are not regarded as accurate enough to be used for the needs of adjudication.[63] This

60 To counteract the problem, it has been suggested that unlikely but preventable consequences would be included in the regulative cost–benefit analysis; Wahlberg (n 47) 194–5.

61 Wahlberg (n 47) 137.

62 Wahlberg (n 47) 108–9. The same is discussed at text to n 186 in ch 4 in the context of water resources management.

63 Kristin S Shrader-Frechette and Earl D McCoy, *Method in Ecology: Strategies for Conservation* (Cambridge University Press 1993) 330, 5. The simple fact that studies in microlevel science are less

exemplifies how the questions of the legal and the scientific differ from each other, hampering the implementation of the latter's results to the benefit of the former. Legally relevant causality is about finding answers to either question mentioned above – to examine causality in its natural surroundings. Scientific causality is acquired by isolating features or grouping them in a certain manner – the fact that the causalities thus found do not necessarily function similarly in the natural environment is of interest only to applied studies. Due to the difference in their causalities, the scientific cannot always present answers that the legal would desire.[64] And the legal cannot answer the needs of the scientific, as is seen throughout this volume in the legal's inadequate response to the challenge that adaptive natural resources management poses. As Wahlberg puts it,

> ontological differences between law and science will systematically hamper efforts to establish the relations sought when retrospective and prospective questions are raised.[65]

In sum, the differentiation between scientifically and legally pertinent questions and answers is at the root of both the challenge of regulating adaptive management and of reviewing the conducted management in courts. The environmental issue is deciphered at macrolevel ecology, to which the legal is more or less blind. This might serve to explain why the regulation of complex ecological systems, like adaptive management, is at the stage of judicial review narrowed down to ecological quality standards: fixed norms like the ones coined in the Weser ruling resemble the results of the microlevel scientific inquiry traditionally more familiar to the legal.[66] Thus the examination shifts to the level of the WFD, where attempts to resolve the irresolvable may have created more problems than answers.

The WFD in Courts: The Limited Effect of Transparency

The WFD is a useful heuristic device when it draws upon ecological knowledge in particular and aims to establish an integrated, holistic, and adaptive legal instrument – in which abstract, overall aims appear compatible with each other but have encountered many issues at the enforcement level. These dynamics have been described in the previous chapter.[67] Here, I examine the relations

sensitive to environmental variations than the macrolevel ones can also serve to explain the situation; Wahlberg (n 47) 108 fn 221.

64 Wahlberg (n 47) 101.

65 Wahlberg (n 47) 101, 182.

66 Text to n 39 in ch 4.

67 Text to n 66 in ch 4. This section is a critical reading of the author's earlier examination on the challenge the WFD poses for judicial review; Tiina Paloniitty, 'Taking Aims Seriously – How Legal

between ecology and law as manifested in judicial review; as such, the following elaborates on thoughts from the end of Chapter 4.[68]

The understanding of judicial decision-making has long been about facts and norms: *sein* and *sollen*, meaning *is* and *ought*, as distinct domains. Adjudication is understood to act like a logical syllogism – a nearly automatic pattern in which the factual and normative follow each other until a conclusion is reached – even though that understanding has been criticised repeatedly.[69] Understandably, the criticism has stimulated a quest for a more nuanced perception of judicial decision-making.[70] Still, all the various ways of trying to grasp the problem have glossed over the meaning of the concepts of norms and facts while trying to explain how they interact – and in a rather persistent manner, trying to assure the reader that at the end of the day norms are superior to facts: what is normative is defined by the norms; facts are only *used* in the process, as grist to the mill. The types of facts relevant to legal decision-making can be analysed and divided, but even then, facts are conceived of as something that law refers to – at most, the 'facts referred to in law have certain characteristics imposed by law.'[71] The scientist might be of great utility to the decision-maker, but still, the roles of fact provider and decision-maker remain distinct.[72]

The WFD challenges this fundamental logic. On top of the questions of environmental models discussed earlier, the officials classifying the status and evaluating the waters, as mandated by the WFD, have a very clear understanding that their actions are, by their very nature, normative.[73] The normative and factual elements have been intentionally commingled in the management practice. Even though the Weser ruling clarified the roles of the scientific and the judiciary, the underlying tension has not been fully removed.[74] In assessing whether the non-deterioration principle has been infringed or not, one must pay full attention to the concepts of quality elements and water bodies as they

Ecology Affects Judicial Decision-Making' (2015) JHRE 6(1) <https://doi.org/10.4337/jhre.2015.01.03>, 55–74.

68 Text to n 186 in ch 4.

69 Aulis Aarnio, *The Rational as Reasonable: A Treatise on Legal Justification* (Reidel cop. 1987) 120–1; Douglas Fisher, *Legal Reasoning in Environmental Law: A Study of Structure, Form, and Language* (Edward Elgar Publishing Ltd. 2013) 480, 13. All start by describing the syllogism and continue to criticise it by analysing either other logical processes or argumentation models commonly employed in adjudication.

70 Eveline T Feteris, 'Dialogical Theory of Legal Discussions: Pragma-Dialectical Analysis and Evaluation of Legal Argumentation' (2000) Artificial Intelligence and Law 8(2) <https://doi.org/10.1023/A:1008344203269>, 115.

71 Jerzy Wróblewski, *Meaning and Truth in Judicial Decision* (Juridica 1979) 132.

72 Hans Kelsen, *Reine Rechtslehre: Einleitung in die rechtswissenschaftliche Problematik* (Scientia 1985) 35, 37–8; Wróblewski (n 71) 132.

73 Text to n 204 in ch 4; Jussi Kauppila, 'Pintaveden normatiivinen tila' (2000) Edilex, <http://www.edilex.fi/lakikirjasto/8600.pdf;>.

74 Text to n 66 in ch 4.

are defined in the WFD and its annexes. In the WFD, scientific information is not merely used as a tool to define which norms should apply or how those norms should apply; thus, the normative is partly formed while the necessary scientific information is gathered. From the viewpoint of adaptive management, this is merely sensible: since the management is socio-ecological and inclusive of all possible considerations, it is only rational that the decisions are also normative. The same applies more specifically in the WFD: if the societal values are already taken into account in the scientific modelling, as suggested, the management decisions are holistic, inclusive of all available factors.[75] If finding this cumbersome, the legal seems to be the only troubled party.

As repeatedly seen thus far, the manner in which science is utilised in the WFD does not fit so well into the theoretical frameworks of judicial decision-making. Also, the overall endeavour in the WFD – managing water quality in the Member States with the help of detailed scientific analysis and exact norms on procedure but leaving the substantial norms themselves rather flexible – has not been completely successful. What the development of the WFD teaches us is that if we, *in effect*, outsource judicial decision-making to the management, the normative becomes, to a certain extent, predetermined by the scientists, leaving the lawyers and judges with somewhat immutable boundaries. A methodological solution to the dilemma has been presented as *legal ecology*: drawing on the writings of Ronald Dworkin and especially of Robert Alexy, the concept of principles as optimisation requirements is adapted to fulfil the execution of the aim-setting sections frequently used in environmental regulation in order to acquire more transparent but still normative decision-making patterns.[76] In legal ecology, value choice – or the choice of aims for which the management strives – was made visible, thus increasing transparency. The value choice made visible refers to the choice between the environmentalist values underlying both environmental sciences and regulation. In short, legal ecology argued for an *in dubio pro natura* approach for a legal system recoiling from such strongly laden positions for courts.

What is presented as legal ecology might be intuitively agreeable: the act of surfacing the value choices, and arguing them openly during the extent of the continuum of normativity, is alluring. However preferable these features would be, the solution results in problems of its own, primarily the risk of juristocracy. Offering juristocracy instead of technocracy is not much of a solution since it risks replacing one unsatisfactory situation with another. Even though legal ecology has its benefits – in enhancing transparency – it should not be taken as a solution to the challenges created by the WFD. If anything,

75 Text to n 204 in ch 4.

76 Paloniitty (n 67). Even though here the approach is critically evaluated it is not insinuated that it would not have its benefits. It offers a mechanism to openly articulate the balancing act between contesting, even conflicting principles, aims or objectives at the grassroots level; ibid 69.

it is yet another critical approach to law.[77] That should be obvious, though, since legal ecology draws upon the works of Staffan Westerlund, who claimed that lack of ecological sustainability should be taken into the discipline of law itself instead of being seen as something non-legal, located outside the sphere of law.[78] Westerlund goes so far as to claim that ecological and legal problems are inherently entwined under the constraints of the rule of law. This entanglement causes a legal *and* ecological dilemma – and for legal science to be proactive, solving the joint dilemma is necessary.[79] Since the old paradigm of positivism does not meet the challenge, Westerlund constructs *rättsekologi* (law and ecology) as an answer, claiming that ecological sustainability must be allowed to define the paradigm in environmental law.[80] Interestingly, from the viewpoint of adaptive management, Westerlund found that the paradigm shift would develop a feedback system to the law itself, and as a result, the law would include systemic resilience familiar with ecosystems and their means of survival.[81] Westerlund's deliberations were the first in which law was comprehended as an ecosystem-like structure, requiring similar resilience to thrive. It also openly cherishes ecological values and requires full adherence to them. But in doing so, these approaches might overtake the problems resulting from such a decision.[82]

77 On the variety of approaches see Deborah Z Cass, 'Navigating the Newstream: Recent Critical Scholarship in International Law' (1996) 65(3-4) Nordic Journal of International Law 341.

78 Staffan Westerlund, 'Rätt och riktigt rättveteskap' (2010) Nordic Environmental Law Journal 1 3, 11, 18. Naturally Westerlund is not alone in his desire for a better relationship between sustainability and law – for an overview of the concept see Klaus Bosselmann, *The Principle of Sustainability: Transforming Law and Governance* (Ashgate 2008); Hans Christian Bugge and Christina Voigt, *Sustainable Development in International and National Law: What Did the Brundtland Report do to Legal Thinking and Legal Development, and Where can we Go from Here?* (The Avosetta series 8, Europa Law Publishing 2008); or Alan Boyle and David Freestone (eds), *International Law and Sustainable Development: Past Achievements and Future Challenges* (Oxford University Press 1999).

79 Westerlund, 'Rätt och riktigt rättveteskap' (n 78) 18.

80 Westerlund, 'Rätt och riktigt rättveteskap' (n 78) 3, 20, 22. For other reactions to the disappointment of positivism, Bebhinn Donnelly and Patrick Bishop, 'Natural Law and Ecocentrism' (2007) Journal of Environmental Law 19(1) <https://doi.org/10.1093/jel/eql039>; Jonathan I Charney, 'Universal International Law' (1993) The American Journal of International Law 87(4) <https://doi.org/10.2307/2203615>; or David Delaney, *Law and Nature* (Cambridge Studies in Law and Society, Cambridge University Press 2003). For Westerlund, 'paradigm' seems to mean an attitude or viewpoint; a background against which legal problems are conceptualised. He promulgated a Kuhnian paradigmatic change.

81 Staffan Westerlund, 'Law and the Biosphere, or the Biosphere and Law? About the Sustainability Paradigm and Law's Problems with That' (Rätt och utveckling - Oikeus ja kehitys XII Rättsvetenskapens dagar Åbo Academis förlag, Åbo 10.-11.12.2009 2010) 17, 27.

82 In the civil law context, that is to say.

Resolution? A Critique of Epistemological Scientism

The challenge that ecology, adaptive management, or water management, as fields of science, pose to legal decision-making appears to evade easy answers. It is apparent that the results of adaptive natural resources management or water management do not easily fit into the box of facts readily employable to the needs of judicial decision-making.[83] The manner in which natural resources management both is (in the EU water governance) and ought to be (according to the adaptive management paradigm) conducted is so far from the concepts and categorisations of judicial decision-making that attempts to squeeze it into the form of logical syllogisms results in either forced solutions or extensive fuzziness. In other words, focusing on norms and principles and their nature, flexibility, or other features offers only limited help to the regulator of adaptive management. Even though the merging of facts and norms is not as prominent now after the Weser ruling than it was before it, the fundamental challenge lingers. In Chapter 4, an attempt was made to focus on the management: after the limits of the formalistic approach were made evident, the scrutiny went forward towards the spatial and temporal aspects of management practice.[84] Even though the attempt might have been favourable from the viewpoint of gaining better compatibility with the adaptive management paradigm, the lack of availability of judicial review became evident.[85] Even in the legal system of Finland, known for its extensive and in-depth judicial review, reviewing management decisions is not likely when the scientific management work is so detailed and local. It seems that this traditional path of examining norms, facts, and judicial review does not bring fruitful results.

Uncertainty is a key component of adaptive management; cherishing uncertainty has also been contested in critiques that challenge prediction and its role in the paradigm. As noted in Chapter 3, adaptive management is mostly about running carefully chosen trials in order to gain knowledge and impact the managed system. In order to decide upon the management options, predictions of the actions' outcomes are necessary. However, prediction does not necessarily have as central a role as is commonly presumed.[86] It is not that this

83 Regarding adaptive management, even the concept of result is a contested one, since the management undertaking ought to be an unending, constantly evolving process. Admittedly, the focus chosen here – the role of the judiciary in accommodating the adaptive management paradigm – can be criticised as unduly narrow, for the legal consists of also other actors than only the judges. The judicial decision-making has been emphasised because of its constraints, making the analysis more nuanced and detailed, and because of its focus on the individual plans and projects, which can be the most challenging to integrate with the adaptive approach. Of the benefits of a detailed, contingent analysis, see ch 1 n 3.

84 Text to n 143 in ch 4.

85 Text to n 186 in ch 4.

86 Text to ns 1 and 59 in ch 3; Roger Bradbury, 'Futures, predictions and other foolishness' in Marco A Janssen (ed), *Complexity and Ecosystem Management: The Theory and Practice of Multi-Agent Systems*

had not been noted earlier: even at the dawn of the adaptive management paradigm, it was pointed out that prediction plays only a subordinate role in scientific enquiry. The protagonist is an explanation, and prediction ought to be used only as a servant of that main goal.[87] When applied to the field of adaptive ecosystem management, this means that prediction ought to have lesser significance in understanding the scientific activity in question.[88] Even when prediction, in general, is overemphasised, its central role in the enquiries upon complex adaptive systems is even more difficult to justify. Regarding simpler systems, modelling them and predicting according to the models has been proven efficient in knowledge gaining. If modelling is successful, the consequence is simple: the future of the studied object follows the future of the model. The everyday practice of environmental management and modelling of the prospective changes follow this path, forming the reality that the legal ought to account for better in order to yield more effective or reasonable governance.

But if the logic is taken further to the most complex systems – to the extreme examples, so to say – and their ability to evolve, grow, or learn is fully considered, modelling becomes far more strenuous. Language unveils the difference: simple systems have *dynamics*, complex systems, *behaviour*.[89] Modelling such complexity is difficult since it does not follow the philosophical-logical trick developed for simpler systems, that is 'good models equals simple models equals predictive models.' Interactions of complex systems are not linear or strong enough for good modelling.[90] Models of such complex systems cannot include prediction: they are more like simplified pictures or explorations of the modelled system. This notion is grounded in the reality that the understanding of science in complex adaptive systems differs from the traditional understanding of science as mechanistic thinking.[91]

(Edward Elgar 2002) 48, 50, in which Bradbury builds a suggested solution to the problem, a draft of a more suitable way to study complex adaptive systems.

87 Bradbury (ibid) 48, with a direct quote of Richard Levins's work on complex systems from the 1970s, the 'extreme influence' of which is examined and analysed in Michael Weisberg, 'Forty Years of "The Strategy": Levins on Model Building and Idealization' (2006) Biology and Philosophy 21(5) <https://doi.org/10.1007/s10539-006-9051-9>, 623. In the context of modelling, models producing imprecise predictions can even be consistently preferable to more precise ones; Alkistis Elliott-Graves, 'The Value of Imprecise Prediction' (2020) Philos Theor Pract Biol 12(4) <https://doi.org/10.3998/ptpbio.16039257.0012.004>, 8, 14.

88 Bradbury (n 86) 48.

89 Bradbury (n 86) 50–2.

90 Arguably, even the divide between an object and its environment can be contested. To meet the needs of scientific enquiry, the model itself ought to be as complex as the reality it wishes to model, becoming more of a replica than a model; John M Anderies, 'The transition from local to global dynamics: a proposed framework for agent-based thinking in social-ecological systems' in Marco A Janssen (ed), *Complexity and Ecosystem Management: The Theory and Practice of Multi-Agent Systems* (Edward Elgar 2002) 13, 14; Bradbury (n 86) 53.

91 Bradbury (n 86) 48, 55–6.

These features do not, however, make science relative, no matter how alluring it might be to jump to that conclusion. The science of complex systems is a three-dimensional system itself consisting of the people involved, the knowledge, and the algorithm with which any scientific method can be invented.[92] A critique of scientism might expound on these considerations. Similar to the science of complex adaptive systems, a critique of scientism emphasises that 'scientifically proven' and 'truth' are not synonyms. In scientistic epistemology, it is presumed that science and science only is the source of knowledge. The underlying assumption of this inexhaustible capability of the scientific method (that is to say, the underlying scientism) is often expressed in claims that science has finally been able to answer certain fundamental questions that earlier belonged to the realms of philosophy or other non-scientific fields of thought.[93] The critique finds this axiom faulty; the proof is sourced from science's inability to handle logical, mathematical, or conceptual knowledge that does not result from empirical inquiry. Also, introspective knowledge is an obvious challenge for scientism, as is everyday knowledge and common sense, none of which is acquired by the scientific method.[94]

Both the critique of epistemological scientism and the understanding of the science of complex systems share the perception of how science does not hold the ultimate truth but expresses approximations of the current knowledge. As put by Bradbury in discussing adaptive management, '[a]ll of science, the whole edifice, is a work in draft, subject to revision and reconsideration.'[95] Were scientism accepted, one ought to hold a view in which science can eventually provide full knowledge of all the questions it takes under its scrutiny. Regarding complex adaptive systems, this would mean that at the end of the day, science would be able to perfectly model the complex adaptive system it is studying. Due to the utmost complexity of these systems, that is unlikely. Also,

92 Bradbury (n 86) 58–9.

93 Even though scientism can be and has been understood in multiple ways, all of them share a view in which the scientific method is the superior method to human knowledge and understanding. Scientism has ontological and epistemological traits, appearing in all possible combinations. According to epistemological scientism, science is the only source of justified belief or knowledge about ourselves and the world. This definition comes with four conditions: first, epistemological scientism does not entail that everything there is to know would already be known; second, as long as science has remained silent on certain issues other presumed sources of knowledge are allowed; third, epistemological scientism does not deny that people would not form beliefs in other ways than via the scientific method; and fourth, all domains of human knowledge can and ought to be surveyed with the scientific method; Jeroen de Ridder, 'Science and Scientism in Popular Science Writing' (2014) Social Epistemology Review and Reply Collective 3(12) 23, 23–5.

94 Thus even though epistemological scientism might look like common sense in the first place, it actually contradicts it; De Ridder (ibid) 27. Scientism is most visible in the works of scientists that study 'the big questions' but widely present also elsewhere; De Ridder (ibid) 28, 38–9 and Austin L Hughes, 'The Folly of Scientism' (2012) The New Atlantis (37) 32, 38 ff noting especially ethics, epistemology, and metaphysics as fields claimed from philosophy by the practitioners of scientism.

95 Bradbury (n 86) 58.

the critique of scientism and the science of complex adaptive systems assess prediction in a similar manner. Prediction has two sides: those ideas that are beyond our purview (extrapolation) and those that are within our purview but on which we have not yet laid our gaze (interpolation). The former is relevant to adaptive management. Prediction is addressed by creating boundaries and classifying the acquired instances into rational models. The aim is to create a model that might work in the same way that the modelled object would at a specified time in the future. Unfortunately, this pattern, inherent in science, is something to be alert to when it is tried on complex adaptive systems since when it comes to complex adaptive systems, a predictable future does not exist.[96] As Bradbury puts it in criticising approaches that presume prediction,

> [t]here is no 'out there,' since the system is in reciprocal interaction with its environment. In fact the boundary is open and *we often choose as system* that which is convenient. The landscape described here is, at once, system and environment.[97]

In other words, when it comes to complex adaptive systems, the future we want 'comes into existence as we cast the light on it.'[98] There is nothing there that we did not predetermine when creating the system. In a system this entwined, predicting the future is impossible. For the legal, this type of trial sounds familiar: legal scholarship can also be perceived as 'a citizen of two worlds,' studying a given field and simultaneously changing the field with the research conducted.[99]

Regarding the regulation of adaptive management, a lesson worth remembering is that scientific enquiries not resulting in predictions are still scientific enquiries. Adaptive management's role is to draft and learn, and only if the legal accustoms its needs to this epistemological reality will it have solid ground under its feet. The results of adaptive management studies are not to be taken as facts or representations of truth but as models mapping out the likely consequences of actions and, as such, already tarnished by the manager's choices:

96 Bradbury (n 86) 51–2.

97 Bradbury (n 86) 60–1, emphasis here.

98 That is why Bradbury suggests a whole new approach, a palimpsest that might better serve the needs of managing adaptive systems; Bradbury (n 86) 61.

99 Ibid Bradbury 61. The term 'dual citizenship' is used by Kaarlo Tuori, *Ratio and Voluntas: The Tension Between Reason and Will in Law* (Routledge 2016), passim. The discourse in legal scholarship has dealt with the difference between the legal and non-legal (sociological) enquiry; credits of the notion are most often given to HLA Hart's *The Concept of Law* (1st edition 1961). The traditional question-setting and dichotomy was stated by Kelsen in 1934: 'Soll Rechtswissenschaft nich in Naturwissenschaft aufgehen, muß das Recht aufs deutlichste von der Natur abgehoben warden,' Kelsen, *Reine Rechtslehre: Einleitung in die rechtswissenschaftliche Problematik* (n 72) 236 s, 2. Regarding regulation of adaptive management, much of the debate seems to miss the point in its nonchalance about facts and knowledge-gathering.

the normative work begins well before the legal has had a say on the matter. The traditional approach to legal studies suits the regulation of adaptive management poorly, so great is the difference between the understanding of normativity's scope in the traditional sense and the reality of regulating complex adaptive systems. Unlike previous critiques, however, this one is not founded on the characteristics of law, language, or society but on where the dividing line between facts and norms is to be drawn – if anywhere.

Bibliography

Aagaard TS, 'Factual Premises of Statutory Interpretation' (2009) 77(2) Geo Wash L Rev 366 <https://ssrn.com/abstract=1126730>.

Aarnio A, *The Rational as Reasonable: A Treatise on Legal Justification* (Reidel cop. 1987).

Anderies JM, 'The Transition from Local to Global Dynamics: A Proposed Framework for Agent-Based Thinking in Social-Ecological Systems' in Janssen MA (ed), *Complexity and Ecosystem Management: The Theory and Practice of Multi-Agent Systems* (Edward Elgar 2002).

Aven T and Renn O, 'On Risk Defined as an Event where the Outcome is Uncertain' (2009) 12(1) Journal of Risk Research 1 <https://doi.org/10.1080/13669870802488883>.

Boholm A, 'Comparative Studies of Risk Perception: A Review of Twenty Years of Research' (1998) 1(2) Journal of Risk Research 135 <https://doi.org/10.1080/136698798377231>.

Bosselmann K, *The Principle of Sustainability: Transforming Law and Governance* (Ashgate 2008).

Boyle A and Freestone D (eds), *International Law and Sustainable Development: Past Achievements and Future Challenges* (Oxford University Press 1999).

Bradbury R, 'Futures, Predictions and Other Foolishness' in Janssen MA (ed), *Complexity and Ecosystem Management: The Theory and Practice of Multi-Agent Systems* (Edward Elgar 2002).

Bugge HC and Voigt C, *Sustainable Development in International and National Law: What did the Brundtland Report do to Legal Thinking and Legal Development, and where can we go from here?* (The Avosetta Series 8, Europa Law Publishing 2008).

Cane P, 'Meris Review and Judicial Review-The AAT as Trojan Horse' (2000) 28(2) Fed L Rev 213 <https://doi.org/10.22145/flr.28.2.4>.

Cass DZ, 'Navigating the Newstream: Recent Critical Scholarship in International Law' (1996) 65(3–4) Nordic Journal of International Law 341.

Charney JI, 'Universal International Law' (1993) 87(4) The American Journal of International Law <https://doi.org/10.2307/2203615>.

Davis KC, 'Approach to Problems of Evidence in the Administrative Process' (1942) 55(3) Harv. L. Rev. 364 <https://doi.org/10.2307/1335092>.

de Ridder J, 'Science and Scientism in Popular Science Writing' (2014) 3(12) Social Epistemology Review and Reply Collective 23.

Delaney D, *Law and Nature* (Cambridge Studies in Law and Society, Cambridge University Press 2003).

Donnelly B and Bishop P, 'Natural Law and Ecocentrism' (2007) 19(1) Journal of Environmental Law <https://doi.org/10.1093/jel/eql039>.

Elliott-Graves A, 'The Value of Imprecise Prediction' (2020) 12(4) Philos Theor Pract Biol 1 <https://doi.org/10.3998/ptpbio.16039257.0012.004>.

Feteris ET, 'Dialogical Theory of Legal Discussions: Pragma-Dialectical Analysis and Evaluation of Legal Argumentation' (2000) 8(2) Artificial Intelligence and Law 115 <https://doi.org/10.1023/A:1008344203269>.

Fisher D, *Legal Reasoning in Environmental Law: A Study of Structure, Form and Language* (Edward Elgar Publishing Ltd. 2013).

Fisher E 'Drowning by Numbers: Standard Setting in Risk Regulation and the Pursuit of Accountable Public Administration' (2000) 20(1) Oxford Journal of Legal Studies 109 <https://doi.org/10.1093/ojls/20.1.109>.

——— *Risk Regulation and Administrative Constitutionalism* (Hart Publishing 2007).

Fleming G, 'Administrative Review and the Normative Goal—Is Anybody out There' (2000) 28(1) Fed L Rev 61 <https://doi.org/10.22145/flr.28.1.3>.

Hart HLA, *The Concept of Law* (1st edn, Clarendon Press OUP 1961).

Hildén M, 'Opportunities and Challenges in Providing and Using Scientific Knowledge in Environmental Appeal Cases in Finland' in Kuusiniemi K, Suviranta O and Viljanen V-P (eds), *Juhlajulkaisu Pekka Vihervuori 1950–25/8–2020* (SLY 2020).

Hood C, Rothstein H and Baldwin R, *The Government of Risk: Understanding Risk Regulation Regimes* (OUP 2001).

Hughes AL, 'The Folly of Scientism' (2012) (37) The New Atlantis 32.

Kauppila J, 'Pintaveden normatiivinen tila' (2000) Edilex <http://www.edilex.fi/lakikirjasto/8600.pdf;>.

Keeton RE, 'Legislative Facts and Similar Things: Deciding Disputed Premise Facts' (1988) 73(1) Minn L Rev 1 <https://scholarship.law.umn.edu/mlr/2241>.

Kelsen H, *Reine Rechtslehre: Einleitung in die rechtswissenschaftliche Problematik* (Scientia 1985).

Ky P, 'Qualifications, Weight of Opinion, Peer Review and Methodology: A Framework for Understanding the Evaluation of Science in Merits Review' (2012) 24(2) Journal of Environmental Law 207.

Larsen AO 'Confronting Supreme Court Fact Finding' (2012) Virginia Law Review 1255 <https://scholarship.law.wm.edu/facpubs/1284>.

——— 'Factual Precedents' (2013) 162(1) U Pa L Rev 59.

Malve O, *Water Quality Prediction for River Basin Management* (Teknillinen korkeakoulu ed, Teknillinen korkeakoulu, Vesitalouden ja vesirakennuksen laboratorio 2007) <http://lib.tkk.fi/Diss/2007/isbn9789512287505>.

Michaels D and Monforton CA, 'Scientific Evidence in the Regulatory System: Manufacturing Uncertainty and the Demise of the Formal Regulatory System' (2005) 13(1) J L & POL'Y 17 <https://ssrn.com/abstract=707136>.

Paloniitty T, 'Taking Aims Seriously – How Legal Ecology Affects Judicial Decision-Making' (2015) 6(1) JHRE 55–74 <https://doi.org/10.4337/jhre.2015.01.03>.

Peel J, *Science and Risk Regulation in International Law* (Cambridge University Press 2010).

Posner R, *The Problems of Jurisprudence* (Harvard University Press 1990).

Preston BJ, 'Contemporary Issues in Environmental Impact Assessment' (2020) 37 EPLJ 423.

Renn O, 'Three Decades of Risk Research: Accomplishments and New Challenges' (1998) 1 Journal of Risk Research 49 <https://doi.org/10.1080/136698798377321>.

Shrader-Frechette KS and McCoy ED, *Method in Ecology: Strategies for Conservation* (Cambridge University Press 1993).

Sjöberg L, 'Perceived Risk and Tampering with Nature' (2000) 3(4) Journal of Risk Research 353 <https://doi.org/10.1080/13669870050132568>.

Stirling A, 'Risk at a Turning Point?' (1998) 1(3) Journal of Risk Research 97 <https://doi.org/10.1080/136698798377204>.

Tai S, 'Uncertainty about Uncertainty: The Impact of Judicial Decisions on Assessing Scientific Uncertainty' (2008) 11(3) U Pa J Const L 671 <https://ssrn.com/abstract=1265153>.

Tarlock AD, 'Is There a There There in Environmental Law?' (2004) 19(2) Journal of Land Use and Environmental Law 214 <https://www.jstor.org/stable/42842841>.

Tuori K, *Ratio and Voluntas: The Tension between Reason and will in Law* (Routledge 2016).

Wahlberg L, *Legal Questions and Scientific Answers: Ontological Differences and Epistemic Gaps in the Assessment of Causal Relations* (Lund University 2010).

Weisberg M, 'Forty Years of 'The Strategy': Levins on Model Building and Idealization' (2006) 21(5) Biology and Philosophy 623 <https://doi.org/10.1007/s10539-006-9051-9>.

Westerlund S, 'Law and the Biosphere, or the Biosphere and Law? About the Sustainability Paradigm and Law's Problems with That' (Rätt och utveckling - Oikeus ja kehitys XII Rättsvetenskapens dagar Åbo Academis förlag, Åbo 10.-11.12.2009 2010a).

——— 'Rätt och riktigt rättveteskap' (2010b) 1 Nordic Environmental Law Journal 3.

Wright RW, 'Causation in Tort Law' (1985) 73(6) Calif Law Rev 1735 <https://doi.org/10.2307/3480373>.

Wróblewski J, *Meaning and Truth in Judicial Decision* (Juridica 1979).

Chapter 6

Conclusions

The Four Faces of a Regulator

Diffuse water pollution continues to pose a challenge to the regulator. The EU has employed various regulative tools to tackle agricultural runoff, the failures and successes of which have been examined in this volume. Recurring themes through the work have been scientific knowledge – its adequacy, accuracy, and availability – the relation between knowledge-gaining processes and judicial decision-making processes, and the correct time and place of decisions with normative clout. The general outcome is that when the deliberate regulative attempts fail, the issue in all its complexity is left for the scientists to untangle in the administrative work of water management. The traditional pattern, in which the passivity of the legislature results in cases to be solved by the courts, is partially dismantled when the courts – not even those with a broad scope of review extending to the substance of the question, rights to remake the first-instance decision, and in-house experts participating in the court panel – cannot examine the normative assessments made by the administrator in the evaluations regarded as scientific.

The epistemological constraints opted for at the beginning of this volume emphasise the strategic choices needed for effective environmental governance. The examples taken under scrutiny in the preceding pages present the Union regulator as a strategist who has decided to proceed on multiple fronts to obtain the optimal outcome. As mentioned, these illustrative buzzwords are to be taken with a – greater or lesser – grain of salt, for they are simplifications of very complex processes resulting in 'the EU regulator.'[1] But if accepted to structure also these concluding thoughts, the EU appears to be four-faced when it comes to agricultural runoff. We have witnessed the works of *the erratic regulator, the naïve regulator, the candid regulator,* and *the ambitious regulator.*

The twists and turns of the Common Agricultural Policy (CAP) exemplify *the erratic regulator,* whose attempts to produce a financial instrument responsive

1 Text to n 25 in ch 1, text to n 6 in ch 4.

DOI: 10.4324/9781003197829-6

to the changes in axiological climate appear susceptible to failure, as proven by the track record of the CAP reforms. Evaluating the success of the CAP is notoriously difficult due to the complexity of the instrument and the manner in which its reforms have been accomplished: changes with significant consequences have been initiated as mere mid-term reviews. It has been far from straightforward to evaluate the outcomes of the reforms, both regarding the instrument in general and in the narrow sense, especially when examining the 'greening' tendencies within the policy. However, it can be concluded that during the decades of the CAP reform, multiple discourses have been present: productivist, neoliberal, and multifunctional stances have all had their say during the negotiations. The tendency toward more diverse justifications for the policy was already present before the (currently) newest reform of 2013, in which the diversity was such that even arguments denouncing the instrument's collective nature were presented. The newest reform was, nevertheless, initiated, making the policy more environmentalist, but its success has been contested. The causes may be institutional, relating to the new parliamentary committee that participated in the reform for the first time, or temporal, relating to the long time the negotiations took – there seems to be a link between the length of the negotiations and the momentum of reform. However, desires that the environmentalist discourse ought to triumph over all others in the development of the CAP are also exaggerated. The multifunctional discourse has resulted in multiple aims being taken into account during the CAP's amendments, and the environmentalist approach is only one among the many. The balancing act between the interests of trade, food security and supply, and the environment is, however, so onerous that the nickname '*the erratic regulator*' is well deserved. Holding high hopes for the outcomes of future reforms – one way or the other – might not be the best strategic choice, as has been demonstrated in the comments on the yet ongoing negotiations for the Green Deal CAP. Having said that, the instrument's ability to surprise bystanders is well established, and predicting failure would be equally unwise.

The second oldest of the instruments examined is the Nitrates Directive (ND), which gained the EU the title of '*the naïve regulator*.' In the ND, the EU regulator decides to ignore (also scientific) realities perceived as too complex and simplifies the problem as one consisting of pollutants and emissions. Instead of setting normative environmental objects for the Member States to reach, the ND deals with farming practices in a tangible and straightforward manner. There is nothing to belittle about the approach: addressing the nutrient runoff dilemma by curbing the amount of pollutants is a sensible approach. However, the level of strictness the legislator has opted for can arguably be a target for the environmentalist's critique, as can the legislator's reluctance to prioritise the multiple goals that the ND wishes to pursue. Nonetheless, the ND has been a good testing ground for EU water regulation: its implementation practice in the Member States has clarified the need and benefits of enhanced site-specificity, and the basic monitoring and reporting mechanisms enacted in it may have paved the way toward more adaptive regulative instruments. The ND's implementation in Finland also makes visible the difference in treatment between environmental pollution stemming from agricultural sources and other culprits of environmental harm: when the implementation of the ND is made stricter, the farmers are compensated for their trouble through a form of investment support. Thus, even though in the ND, the EU regulator is naïve in the sense that it does not embark on an extensive analysis of the ecological, sociological, and/or economic complexity of the dilemma at hand, the interconnectedness of different instruments is acknowledged and utilised.

Of the more contemporary regulatory approaches, the EU Strategy for the Baltic Sea Region (SBSR) serves as an example of *the candid regulator* who strives to invite all around the same table to discuss the themes relevant to governing the common sea. As a prime example of both collaborative and transnational environmental governance, the SBSR addresses more issues than merely the case of agricultural runoff: the macroregional strategies, in general, were instigated by the demands of territorial cohesion, decentralisation, and enhanced stakeholder collaboration, not by the substantial needs of the regions in question. Regarding the case of agricultural runoff, the SBSR thus introduced a novel feature with potentially broader significance: in it, agricultural runoff is not comprehended as a problem to be tackled but a matter on which the affected parties must find ways to better align their efforts. Surprisingly, perhaps, the reasons for this lay in the motif of this volume, the interface between science and law. Another tool of governance in the region, namely the Helsinki Commission (HELCOM), was criticised for overly relying on scientific data that is claimed to justify more and more stringent measures towards the agriculture industry. Regardless of whether this is factually correct – i.e. whether, scientifically speaking, the causalities and significances are actually so – as a governance instrument, HELCOM's approach did not always encourage balanced interaction between the various stakeholders when some parties found that there was an environmentalist bias. The work of the SBSR is considered more balanced. The finding is interesting: even though the SBSR has not committed to a particular stance regarding environmental questions, water quality is, however, its *ratio moderatio* or the shared problem around which the governance activities gather. It is as if the different views on the HELCOM and the SBSR illustrate the fragile terrains of either acknowledging a problem or making conclusions as to who is to blame for it and on what grounds.

Thus, the SBSR has had impetus among the regional governance apparatuses even when it is not allowed to generate new instruments, legislation, or institutions to solidify or enforce the governance. However, assigning more detailed credits to the different governance tools present in the Baltic Sea region is difficult: there are many actors and networks, and stakeholders participate in more than one governance action at a time. Hence, establishing trajectories of which governance tool led to which result is next to impossible. The SBSR, however, plays its facilitating role in the territorial and transnational governance in the Baltic Sea region. The SBSR is to enable collaboration, and from the viewpoint of the EU legislator, any value that is accumulated while doing so is to be considered added value since, because of the three 'no's, the SBSR's enforcement and implementation do not consume the EU's resources. If accountability is desired, an interactionist one must suffice: when a multifaceted issue is at stake, establishing a balancing tool amongst the conflicting interests is a worthy action in itself. Collaborative governance, the SBSR included, can be cumbersome, fuzzy, vague, or equivocal (or indeed all of these at once), but if simplicity is not desired, the benefits of such an approach become clearer. In any case, one should be wary not to disparage the importance of the SBSR: gathering all interested parties together is a noteworthy measure, especially bearing in mind the sensitivity of the question at hand.

The SBSR offers valuable insights regarding the overarching question, the role of scientific information in solving the problem of agricultural runoff: one is not to presume that mere scientific facts would suffice as justifications for governance or regulation. On the contrary, even merely offering a solid scientific base for governance actions – as is done in the work of HELCOM – may discourage some parties from working towards the aims. A more subtle approach may be beneficial; one is not asked to denounce the scientific realities but to have a more, say, holistic attitude towards the rationale of the governance. Whatever the SBSR's flaws are, this observation is rather clear.

Finally, the ambitious regulator took the demands for holistic, integrated, and adaptive water management seriously and issued the Water Framework Directive (WFD). The WFD's normative nature remained equivocal for 15 years, but the Court of Justice of the European Union (CJEU) solved the question at least partially in its Weser ruling. The Member States must now ensure that the quality of EU waters does not deteriorate, and the authorities must act accordingly also when considering the authorisation of individual undertakings, given that no derogation is granted. The assessment of derogation is founded on the scientific work guided in the WFD's meticulous annexes, scientific work that also encompasses axiological decisions. The link was partially broken in the interpretation that the CJEU opted for in the Weser ruling, although it still exists in an attenuated state. Before the Weser ruling, the most often discussed question hung over the significance of the environmental quality status classifications. The status classifications are evaluated and assessed by an extremely detailed analysis conducted according to the instructions in the WFD's annexes and in the post-regulatory decision-making called the Common Implementation Strategy (CIS). In the post-Weserian form of the WFD, the information on status classification is of relevance only to the management work: the ongoing water management must take the good status objective seriously and strive towards it. On top of that is the non-deterioration principle, which establishes the normative core of the WFD and influences all development in the EU with water impacts. Deterioration is mainly linked to two concepts – quality elements and waterbody – which are both to be defined according to the WFD but whose definitions are not as strict as the details of different statuses would be. Thus, in the contemporary WFD, the leeway granted to Member States is broader than it would have been had the CJEU made the status classifications decisive. The link between normativity and the status classifications lingers since the non-deterioration principle is partly linked to the status of the waterbody in question.

The achievements of the WFD are great: the manner in which it facilitates watershed-oriented water management based on scientific considerations and distributes the pattern through the whole EU is an accomplishment not to be understated. The endeavour that the EU legislators commenced and the CJEU resumed has been an audacious one: the controversies extending across the continent have been and are significant, as are the differences in sheer physical realities setting the prerequisites of management. In the WFD, the EU has a water management tool, the significance of which cannot be repudiated even when the details of its content are contested – or, maybe, the fierce debate over those details serves as proof of the instrument's significance. However, the story of the WFD also elucidates how decision-making capacity can trickle down to the scientists or to the post-legislative processes. The complexity of these decision-making points and their significance to the totality are established facts, and that is also why the WFD's characterisation as ambitious ought to be taken with a grain of salt. Nonetheless, the decisions made and discretion employed during scientific analysis evade judicial review in most (if not all) jurisdictions and, as such, pose a challenge to the accountability of both the legal systems studied in this volume, the national and transnational ones. The first lesson to learn is that where natural resources management is concerned, the traditional balancing act between the legislator and the judiciary is made more nuanced. If the legislator does not use the decision-making power entrusted to it, the judiciary continues by interpreting the vague pieces of legislation as it sees fit. Besides, the discretion exercised by the scientists becomes decisive. Thus the WFD and its adaptive roots promote an understanding of natural resources governance as a landscape consisting of decisions by the legislator, the executive, and the judiciary, with scientists playing multiple roles in the works of the other three and beyond.

Towards a Socio-Eco-Legal Solution?

As an outcome of the definitions above, the nature of resources management as a socio-eco-legal project becomes palpable. Due to the hydrological cycle, it is not adequate to regulate adaptive management, study adaptive regulation, or examine the most suitable options for regulation of adaptive management. In order to avoid the perils that the WFD exemplifies, all three ought to be considered in the same process: the ecological, the social, and the legal natural resources management. Complications are inevitable if the legal is attached to socio-ecological management only after the management is otherwise thought through. The WFD illustrates an option in which the legislator solved the puzzle by combining exceedingly flexible regulation with scientifically precise management practice. When the CJEU was asked to resolve the relation between legal normativity and scientific analysis, it struck a balance by making the norms stricter – understandably, since it could not have a say on the scientific side of the equation. The decision took place in a landscape significantly impacted by the CIS – which existed out of concerns that the CJEU might not interpret the instrument 'correctly.' Thus, as long as natural resources management includes separation of the scientific and the legal, unsatisfactory solutions seem unavoidable. Regardless of how bleak the situation might seem, it may still be possible to reverse it.

The theoretical foundation resulting in the yearning for a socio-eco-legal system is rather beautiful. The adaptive management paradigm cherishes the uncertainty and learning that it necessitates. In theory, learning itself is an iterative process that is strongly coupled with management practice and adopted decision-making patterns, as the example of the WFD has proved. If the adaptive management paradigm were successfully enforced, management would effortlessly react to changes in the values base encompassed by the surrounding society. The theory offers an escape from centralised governance to localised decision-making, even to the extent of becoming a form of 'pluralised democracy.' The questions that the legal has traditionally considered as its own are already present in the scientific enquiry: setting of management objectives, second-guessing whether such activity is possible at all, discussing the necessary value trade-offs, debating over the relation between participatory rights and learning (i.e. changes in management prompted by participation), and so forth. The demands that resilient socio-ecological systems pose for their managers are the learning and knowledge they entail, how and by whom the processes ought to be guided, and the definition of social learning and the relation it has with participatory rights.

Presenting these features as a list elucidates why adding regulation to the equation has been a trial. Objectifying nature – reducing it to an object to be managed – was not a productive strategy, and the cure was found in the adaptive management paradigm. Socio-ecological resources management fares equally poorly as an object to be regulated. In the worst cases, the number of questions for the legislator, administrator, or the judiciary to decide upon approaches zero. To develop such an eloquent and overarching theory, natural resources studies have needed to relinquish their desire for equilibrium, a decision that partially explains the dislike that the legal has experienced for the paradigm. With all that nonlinearity and complexity, predictability has faded, and the legal has found itself thinking about whether a system prone to disasters hides under the intuitively attractive surface. An answer to these considerations is to forgo unreasonable goals: instead of trying to knit two distinct ontologies together, the desires ought to be navigated towards a robust totality, where the resource, its governance, and the institutions involved form a joint network.

Only when the legal participates in this joint action, considering itself as a player in the field instead of the umpire, can solutions begin to appear.

If natural resources management is to be conducted in a reasonable manner, the scientific part must be taken seriously during the legal drafting process. Even if the ontologies of the science of contemporary environmental management and the law are mutually incompatible, their practical implementations are surprisingly congruent. As we have learned from the studies on adaptive socio-ecological management, the paradigm is theoretically well established and widely executed through the different sectors of natural resources management. In all its emphasis on flexibility, uncertainty, and resilience, institutionalisation results in an increase in structure and order. This is not to be taken as a normative claim: there is surely more to the adaptive management paradigm than this reading suggests. It is, however, a reading that allows the legal to understand the adaptive management paradigm. If it is accepted that cultivating adaptive management can result in a yearning for an enhanced structure, the paradigm provides grounds on which negotiations can begin. The legal side was, however, unresolved when both the transnational and national levels showed few signs of success in securing compatibility between the adaptive management paradigm and law. Descending the abstraction ladder might be advisable to allow the discourse to continue. The adaptive management paradigm is concretised at the management level, as are the rules valued by the legal. In seeking greater compatibility, the legislator ought to seek the identity of a facilitator: it ought to establish a structure where the socio-eco-legal activity could occur and in which the legal could be of equal rank as the others. This may well be an idealistic proposition for, as seen in the preceding pages, such a setting does not secure acceptable access to justice, a stipulation of any legal system's acceptability. Thus it may well be that the incompatibility remains, regardless of the best attempts to solve it. Risks of technocracy loom on one side, a risk of juristocracy on the other, and if miraculously one were to manage to avoid both, the risk of scientism endures. Sacrificing access to justice at the altar of perfecting a scientific paradigm may not, eventually, be worth it.

Thus one must go further down the ladder. At the practical level, the socio-eco-legal understanding becomes concretised when resources management procedures gain emphasis over individual authorisations. That is easier said than done, as was seen when a venture towards enhanced management was attempted with the WFD. Part of the encountered problems result from the WFD's details and could be amended without further ado. The size of a waterbody is a good example: assessment of whether a waterbody's environmental quality has deteriorated or not is coupled with the size of the area in question. These definitions are even partly in the hands of the Member States, which ought to result in interpretations sensitive to territorial needs. Some aspects are more general and can be extrapolated. If management is to gain weight over individual authorisations, the environmental quality of a given resource becomes emphasised instead of emission limits that individual polluters would shoulder. As a consequence of the shift from individual emissions towards a holistic, recipient-oriented approach, buying out existing polluters – from deteriorating the same water body – becomes a pressing issue. Replacement mechanisms are measures conducted on the resource in question, resulting in its recuperation. Being the next of kin to compensatory mechanisms, replacement mechanisms are likely to be a part of a successful and enforceable focus on management, though assuming that most practitioners would be able to buy out other ventures is an idealistic proposition.

The desire for a socio-eco-legal solution is partly explained by the poor connectivity between the different instruments targeting or influencing the agricultural runoff issue. Lack of co-ordination is a recurring theme throughout the volume. The relation between the ND and the programmes of measures according to the WFD is one side of the issue; the connection between the SBSR and the WFD is another one; and the CAP's influence on the other instruments one more still, potentially even the most decisive of them all. Whether the CAP is conceptualised as a financial income support instrument or not may be a contested question, but the reality is unchanged: the same regulator that finances agricultural production issues regulation also wishes to curb the pollution that the production causes. Whether instead of searching for a socio-eco-legal solution, one ought to be looking for a socio-eco^2-legal one is a justified question – the second 'eco' refers to the system's economic underpinnings. Noting the complexity of the CAP, socio-ecological systems, and the WFD, one is left to wonder if even the most structured and analytical approaches could solve issues of such complexity.

One must bear in mind, though, that the EU legislator's capability to deal with complex issues and competing aims has increased greatly over the past decades. In the ND, the legislator left the competing aims unprioritised. In the CAP, the complexity of the instrument's objectives is articulated, but the magnitude of the instrument makes the results difficult to analyse. Of the instruments analysed, the SBSR takes the competing, even contradicting, aims best into account, but its lack of normative weight leaves the instrument toothless. The WFD has gradually made the environmental quality more and more normative and has taken the brave stance of doing so regardless of the pollution source causing a detrimental effect on the environment. Who knows if we may one day witness an instrument comprising the wants and needs of the CAP, the ND, and the WFD in one elegant, strategic manoeuvre, answering to the calls of a more regionalised CAP and integrating the realms of the ND and the WFD for good.

Index

For Product Safety Concerns and Information please contact our EU
representative GPSR@taylorandfrancis.com
Taylor & Francis Verlag GmbH, Kaufingerstraße 24, 80331 München, Germany

www.ingramcontent.com/pod-product-compliance
Ingram Content Group UK Ltd.
Pitfield, Milton Keynes, MK11 3LW, UK
UKHW020004200926
475702UK00015B/2472
* 9 7 8 1 0 3 2 0 5 5 0 0 8 *